Library of
Davidson College

PEACOCKS AND PRIMROSES

From a drawing by D. Maclise, R.A.

PEACOCKS AND PRIMROSES
A Survey of Disraeli's Novels

by

MURIEL MASEFIELD

LONDON

GEOFFREY BLES

MCMLIII

KRAUS REPRINT CO.
Millwood, New York
1973

*Printed in Great Britain by
Butler & Tanner Ltd Frome
for Geoffrey Bles Ltd
52 Doughty Street London WC1*

First published 1953

828
B36xm

Masefield, Muriel Agnes (Bussell)
  Peacocks and primroses.

  1. Beaconsfield, Benjamin Disraeli, 1st earl of, 1804-1881.
I. Title.
[PR4087.M3 1973]   823'.8   73-12363
ISBN 0-527-62175-7

81-4453
Reprinted with the permission of the author
KRAUS REPRINT CO.
A U.S. Division of Kraus-Thomson Organization Limited

Printed in Germany

AUTHOR'S NOTE

THE author does not profess to offer anything to those already well versed in Disraeliana. This book is intended as an introduction to the novels for those who do not know them, with extracts sufficiently long to give a fair sample of Disraeli's characters and style. Some of the early novels are partly autobiographical and these are necessarily connected with his actual life, but otherwise the author has picked out especially scenes and characters which illustrate the life and manners of the period. Comparison with other contemporary novelists has been limited, so that Disraeli's pictures may be clear and unconfused, and historical commentary only used where it is helpful to verify or elucidate scenes in the novels.

The novels provide a pageant of English life from 1826 to 1880.

M. M.

CONTENTS

PART I
The Early Novels

PROLOGUE	11
Vivian Grey	22
The Young Duke	48
Contarini Fleming & Alroy	63
Henrietta Temple	82
Venetia	104

PART II
A Trilogy on Politics and Religion

Coningsby (I)	127
Coningsby (II)	148
Sybil (I)	171
Sybil (II)	186
Sybil (III)	201
Tancred (I)	213
Tancred (II)	228

PART III
The Novels of a Statesman

Lothair (I)	245
Lothair (II)	258
Endymion (I)	271
Endymion (II)	287
Falconet	301
EPILOGUE	305

PART I
THE EARLY NOVELS

CHAPTER I

PROLOGUE

IN the year 1826 a novel called *Vivian Grey* was published anonymously. The manuscript had been submitted to the publisher Colburn by a Mrs. Austen, a charming lady in whose judgment he had considerable confidence, on behalf of a protégé whose anonymity she protected by copying the entire book in her own handwriting. Colburn, realising that here was a piquant specimen of the novel of fashionable life for which Plumer Ward's *Tremaine or a Man of Refinement* had just whetted the appetite of a wide public, made shrewd use of the mystery. The book was advertised as a society novel with characters drawn from contemporary social and public life, and it was implied that the author was well qualified to indulge in his satirical portraits, but naturally did not wish to disclose his name. The publisher himself was content to take the book on trust at first—perhaps he even preferred not to know the truth which, indeed, had no prestige value, since *Vivian Grey* was the first impact upon the world at large of an unknown young man of twenty-one, saddled with debt and bearing a name which had no affinity with the English aristocracy—Benjamin Disraeli.

Vivian Grey took London by storm. Keys professing to identify the characters were passed round in society; the lovely Mrs. Norton (Sheridan's granddaughter) learned pages of it by heart, and only one reviewer, Jerdan of the *Literary Gazette*, was perspicacious enough to write that "the class of the author was a little betrayed by his frequent recurrence to topics about which the mere man of fashion knows nothing and cares less". A nemesis awaited the young Disraeli when his presumption was at last unmasked, but for the moment he basked deliciously in anonymous fame.

Vivian Grey was the first of eleven full-length novels in which we may pass in review a pageant of English life and manners from 1826 to 1880. Dukes and Marquesses, fine ladies, politicians, wirepullers, Chartists, labourers and even mill-girls crowd the stories which flowed from Disraeli's prolific pen. In the earlier books we find the traditions of Regency elegance, now a little over-blown, still a force in high society. Although Beau Brummell was now only a memory, dandies still lounged and postured at assemblies and balls, and in *Henrietta Temple* Disraeli gives us an enchanting picture of the very High Priest of the cult, Count D'Orsay, an artist in more than dress, whose gaiety and wit sparkle from the pages as freshly as they did when Disraeli himself enjoyed them at Gore House, presided over by Lady Blessington. The gilded youth of society, their manners, talk and pursuits, live for us again in these novels, and we may accompany them to the racecourse, the gaming-table, the spunging-house, the duel and on the Grand Tour of Europe. The splendid town houses and the stately country homes of the nobility, with the hierarchy of servants and that typical figure of the time, the toady, are drawn in all their real magnificence, and perhaps a little more. Disraeli loved splendour for its own sake; at this time the peacock—few of his country houses are without their peacocks—with the gorgeous plumage of its oriental ancestry, was in the ascendant in his nature, the young writer had still far to go before the English primrose could be accepted as his sign and symbol. Even now, however, his admiration was not slavish, the grandeur must be superb in its kind to please him and already the irony which was to become one of his greatest gifts acted upon his imagination as an astringent.

The young Disraeli had, in fact, a splendid society to describe; it was a period of which Mrs. Gore (a fashionable novelist) could write with some truth: "Throughout Europe it was holiday-time for people intent on promoting the greatest happiness of the smallest number." Nevertheless, beneath the surface the currents of reform and democracy, to which Disraeli himself was one day to make his contribution, were already gathering force under popular leaders of a new type. In the same year that *Vivian Grey* was published Cobbett set out on the last of the journeys described in his *Rural Rides*, in which he attacked rotten boroughs and other abuses with vitriolic gusto. Robert Owen's model factory at New Lanark was attracting more than national attention and he had already fathered the co-operative movement; it was in the magazine founded by the London Co-operative Society in this very year (1826) that he coined the significant new word "socialist". Meanwhile Francis Place, the radical tailor of Westminster, assiduously coached the factory hands brought up to town from the industrial north, whose witness enabled Joseph Hume to induce Parliament to repeal the Combination Laws, and so prepare the way for the rise of strong, legitimate trade unions. In Parliament itself reform was "in the air". The days were numbered when a Duke who regarded a Parliamentary borough as his personal property could be outraged when the electors presumed to vote against his nominee, and exclaim passionately in the House of Lords: "What! May I not do what I will with my own?"

These portents, however, barely ruffled the surface of aristocratic society when Disraeli wrote *Vivian Grey*; the gilded youths still looked down on lesser breeds from pinnacles of glory, and few would have quarrelled with the sentiment in his second novel: "Oh, to be a Duke, and to be young, it is too much!" The English "Milord" had, in fact, every excuse for regarding himself as the cream of mankind; after the defeat of Napoleon his country's prestige stood higher than that of any other in Europe, and when he travelled it was as "a proud citizen of the proudest of lands" (*Lothair*), a representative of "the wealth and authority of the richest of nations" (*Tancred*). He had behind him the august aura of Downing Street, which Disraeli could fairly describe as that "happy spot where they draw up constitutions for Syria and treaties for China with the same self-complacency and the same success!" (*Tancred*). In the charmed circle of the aristocracy values were still stable and the objects of ambition for a young man of family clear and unchallenged. High-born youths eager to prove their talents "panted for the Senate" (*Vivian Grey*); others accepted a seat in the House of Commons, representing a family borough, as part of the natural order of life, following Eton and the university or a tour of Europe. Speaking wistfully of pre-Reform Bill days, a member of a select London club could say, "I remember when there were only ten men in the House of Commons who were not either members of Brooks' or this place" (*Coningsby*). Lady Montfort (*Endymion*) was expressing a truism of her circle when she exclaimed: "Not go into Parliament? Why, what are men made for except to go into Parliament? I am indeed astounded."

Disraeli also noted with sly relish that the House of Commons, conferring immunity from arrest, could be a blessed alternative to a debtors' prison. Stapylton Toad (*Vivian Grey*) admitted that he had accepted the Chiltern Hundreds "to make room for Augustus Clay, Ernest Clay's brother, who was so involved that the only way to keep him out of the House of Correction was to get him into the House of Commons". In such circles the only perplexity was that of the younger son who was unable to command a seat in Parliament, refused the Church and could not afford the Guards.

A presage of coming change to which Disraeli gave full value in his first novel was the rise of the New Rich, when mere wealth, more widely diffused as industrial magnates made fortunes, began to encroach upon the preserves of rank. He was no sycophant of the aristocracy when he described the arrival of Mrs. Million at Château Désir, the country home of the Marquess of Carabas. Her entrance was spectacular, in crimson silk, pelisse, hat and feathers, diamond ear-rings and a rope of gold round her neck, and she was followed by a large train of toad-eaters, physicians and secretaries: "All fell back. Gartered peers and starred ambassadors, baronets with blood older than creation, and squires, to the antiquity of whose veins chaos was a novelty; all retreated, with eyes that scarcely dared to leave the ground; even Sir Plantagenet Pure, whose family had refused a peerage regularly in every century, now, for the first time in his life, seemed cowed."

Mrs. Million is not the only representative of the New Rich in the book; travelling on the Continent Vivian Grey meets the Fitzloom family:

"This family is one of those whose existence astounds the Continent much more than any of your mighty Dukes and Earls, whose fortunes, though colossal, can be conceived, and whose rank is understood. Mr. Fitzloom is a very different personage, for thirty years ago he was a journeyman cotton spinner. Some miraculous invention in machinery entitled him to a patent, which has made him one of the great proprietors of England. He has lately been returned a member for a manufacturing town, and he intends to get over the first two years of his Parliamentary career by successively monopolising the accommodation of the principal cities of France, Germany, Switzerland and Italy, and by raising the price of provisions and post-horses through a track of five thousand miles."

It was, indeed, the rise of such families as the Millions and the Fitzlooms that accounted largely for the popularity of the novel of fashionable life in the eighteen-twenties and thirties. For the most part the chief ambitions of the New Rich were to share the privileges of the aristocracy and ape their manners. They seized upon Ward's *Tremaine*, Disraeli's *Vivian Grey* and Edward Bulwer's *Pelham* as manuals of initiation, and soon silver fork fiction, as it came to be called, even superseded the tales of mystery and horror of which Mrs. Radcliffe had been the arch-priestess. Thackeray parodied silver fork fiction in a delightful Burlesque under the heading: "LORDS AND LIVERIES. By the Authoress of *Dukes and Déjeuners, Hearts and Diamonds, Marchionesses and Milliners etc.*" Few found fault with the limited personnel of such novels; Miss Edgeworth was a pioneer when she introduced scenes of Irish peasant life into her books, and so inspired Scott to look for characters amongst the lowly-born of his own country. Scott was, in fact, the only giant in the fiction of the eighteen-twenties.

Vivian Grey is, however, something more than an example of silver fork fiction in that parts of it are romanticised autobiography. Disraeli's second novel, *The Young Duke*, he himself described as half fashion and half passion, but the fashion, over-gorgeous as it is in places, is its chief interest. In *Contarini Fleming*, which followed it a year later, we can trace much of the mental and spiritual ferment of Disraeli's own youth; he called it a psychological romance and claimed that its theme was the development of the poetic character. After this he produced *The Wondrous Tale of Alroy*, the heroic story of a Jewish Prince of the Captivity in the twelfth century, which gave him a congenial chance to revel in scenes of splendour and romance, with high-flown prose to match. The next book, *Henrietta Temple*, was the fruit of a happy infatuation for a delightful mistress of his own world and was intended to be primarily a love-story, but its best features are gay and witty portraits of well-known society characters and realistic scenes at Crockford's and in a spunging-house. *Venetia* was published in the same year, owing to the fact that Disraeli was virtually a prisoner in his room at Bradenham, which he dare not leave in case he should be "nabbed" for his debts. The chief distinction of this novel is a life-like portrait of Byron as the hero, under the name of Lord Cadurcis.

After this group of early novels, written between the ages of twenty-one and thirty-three, there was a gap of seven years during which Disraeli established his position as a member of Parliament and married Mrs. Wyndham Lewis. By 1844, when he turned to writing again, Queen Victoria's court had brought a new influence to bear on morals and manners; extravagance in behaviour, dress and character were beginning to give place to dignity, modesty and sobriety. Parliament had been reformed by the Act of 1832, which gave the country a first instalment of democracy and was followed by various progressive measures, and now England had to learn that it was not everything for a country to become the workshop of the world at the expense of being unable to feed its people on its own produce. The "hungry 'forties" had begun.

Disraeli had revelled in the colourful extravagance of the pre-Victorian period. As a young man he recorded with satisfaction how one of his spectacular costumes had startled Regent Street: "The people", he wrote complacently, "quite made way for me as I passed. It was like the opening of the Red Sea, which I now perfectly believe from experience. Even well-dressed people stopped to look at me." His failure in his maiden speech in Parliament was no doubt partly due to the antagonism caused by his jet-black curls, bottle-green coat and white waistcoat covered with gold chains. Even his friend Bulwer (known later as Bulwer Lytton), himself a notable dandy, rallied him gaily on his magnificence—"Why so many gold chains, Dizzy?"—and asked him if he thought of becoming a Lord Mayor. Ten years earlier, perhaps, a man who wore rings outside his gloves might have set a fashion. Now he was suspect; the reformed House of Commons preferred young Mr. Gladstone's dark suits and serious manner. Disraeli himself commented ironically on this in his last novel (*Endymion*), in which he looked back on the eighteen-thirties with detachment: "An insular country, subject to fogs, and with a powerful middle class, requires grave statesmen."

Despite his natural affinity with a more colourful and romantic age, Disraeli did not live in the past, and he had from the first a genuine sympathy with the under-dog and a passionate faith in the individual's right to make the best of himself. At the age of twenty-eight, when he contested the seat of High Wycombe before the Reform Bill, he promised that he would "seek the amelioration of the condition of the poor", at that time an unusual bait to offer to the limited electorate (actually thirty-two voted), all of whom must of necessity be "substantial" men. He was expressing a life-long conviction when, in a famous speech at the opening of the Manchester Athenæum, he declared: "Every individual is entitled to aspire to that position which he believes his faculties qualify him to occupy."

Disraeli's seventh novel—*Coningsby or The New Generation*—represents a change of outlook. The self-interest and ambition of Vivian Grey and the introspection of Contarini Fleming give place in Harry Coningsby to a real concern for the condition of the English people, and this book gives us a picture of the Young England group, formed of idealistic young members of Parliament who adopted Disraeli as their elder brother and leader. They saw their mission as the regeneration of the monarchy, church and aristocracy in a benevolent partnership to abolish "class legislation" and serve the welfare of the whole people. They had no faith in immediate manhood suffrage, which would only lead to "a government carried on by a neglected democracy who, for three centuries, have received no education" (*Coningsby*).

Coningsby was a new phenomenon in fiction, the political novel. It was also the first of a trilogy of novels, published between 1844 and 1847, in which Disraeli set himself to diagnose the sickness of contemporary society and prescribe threefold remedies—political, social and religious. The second of these novels, *Sybil or The Two Nations*, followed *Coningsby* within a year. The best commentary on the title is a dialogue between the book's aristocratic hero, Egremont, and a young working-man who aspires to be a leader of the people:

" 'Well, society may be in its infancy,' said Egremont, slightly smiling, 'but, say what you like, our Queen reigns over the greatest nation that ever existed.'

" 'Which nation?' asked the younger stranger, 'for she reigns over two.'

"The stranger paused; Egremont was silent, but looked enquiringly.

" 'Yes,' resumed the younger stranger after a moment's interval. 'Two nations; between whom there is no intercourse and no sympathy; who are as ignorant of each other's habits, thoughts and feelings, as if they were dwellers in different zones, or inhabitants of different planets; who are formed by a different breeding, are fed by a different food, are ordered by different manners, and are not governed by the same laws.'

" 'You speak of——' said Egremont, hesitatingly.

" 'THE RICH AND THE POOR.' "

It is interesting that Mrs. Gaskell struck the same note when writing of this period (in *Mary Barton*). After saying that the working people needed a Dante to record their sufferings—"And yet even his words would fall short of the awful truth"—she states that "the most deplorable and enduring evil that arose out of these years of commercial depression was the feeling of alienation between the different classes of society". Disraeli may have given her a lead, but Mrs. Gaskell wrote from personal knowledge of poor homes in Manchester and her corroboration of his theme is valuable.

Dickens was before Disraeli in using the novel to expose social evils; while Disraeli spoke more than once in the House of Commons against the harsh pressure of the new Poor Law of 1834, Dickens pilloried it in *Oliver Twist*. Nevertheless, *Sybil* was the first complete example of a new type of book which came to be described as the condition-of-England novel, and it is a mine of social history. In particular it throws much light on the Chartist movement, which Disraeli took pains to study, staying in the north of England for the purpose. He soon realised that, although the chief articles of the Chartist faith were manhood suffrage and the secret ballot, Chartism was fundamentally a "knife and fork" agitation, a revolt against empty fireplaces and bare cupboards, and in *Sybil* he gives us some realistic and touching scenes from the life of working-people in the industrial north. Disraeli had broken new ground, but he was soon followed into this field by Mrs. Gaskell, with *Mary Barton*, and Charles Kingsley, with *Alton Locke*, who both gave their books a Chartist background.

PROLOGUE

The third novel of the trilogy—*Tancred or The New Crusade*—represents a different approach to the ills from which Europe, as well as England, was suffering. The young crusader, described by a Bishop as a visionary, posed to himself many of the same questions as the votaries of Young England, but he could not see salvation in the regeneration of national institutions or the operations of "that fatal drollery called a representative government". He came to the conclusion that the supreme need of the age was "to restore and renovate our communications with the Most High". He was irresistibly drawn to the Holy Land, where alone God had vouchsafed direct revelation to man. He would kneel at his Redeemer's tomb in vigil, as a crusading ancestor had done six centuries before, and there he would lift his voice to Heaven and ask: "What is duty, and what is faith? What ought I to DO, and what ought I to BELIEVE?" Tancred, however, had not allowed for the vagaries of the human heart, which betrayed him into uncertainty and delay; this part of the book has its full quota of Disraelian wit. The second part of Tancred's story has a vivid eastern setting, based on Disraeli's own travels.

Tancred illustrates the duality of Disraeli's own nature—the vein of oriental mysticism (or at least fantasy) and the shrewd prescience and skill of the great statesman. To many of his contemporaries the novelist seemed to belie the man of action, they deplored such lapses into extravagant fiction on the part of one who aspired to be a leader in the House of Commons. In fact, as Carlyle said, it was perhaps as well for Disraeli that many of his colleagues in the Tory party never read anything.

After this trilogy Disraeli was absorbed in a life of action and there were no more novels for twenty-three years. He was sixty-six when he published *Lothair* (1870), and his last book, *Endymion*, only appeared the year before he died, aged seventy-seven. In these books the elder statesman is no longer driven by urgent political theories or crusading against social injustice. He once said, "When I want to read a novel I write one", and in *Lothair* he seems at last to be writing to entertain himself without any ulterior motive. The main theme is the conflict between the Roman Catholic and Anglican churches for a young man's soul, but there is a characteristic diversion in which a woman of almost mystic magnetism, and of course great beauty, involves Lothair in one of Garibaldi's campaigns for the liberation of Italy. This novel, too, has its great country house and a galaxy of witty, exotic or exquisitely bored characters.

By the time *Endymion* was written Disraeli the statesman had lived to translate some of the ideas of the author of *Coningsby* and *Sybil* into Acts of Parliament. As *Sybil* had been a condition-of-England novel, so Disraeli's ministry of 1874–80 was a condition-of-England government. A Public Health Act and an Artisans' Dwellings Act provided for improvements in the care of national health and made possible the clearance of slums; a Trade Union "Charter" placed the workman on an equality with the employer in bargaining, hours of labour were limited to fifty-six a week, with a free half-day on Saturday, and various useful sanitary measures were passed. It was Disraeli, too, who, in spite of the views of *Coningsby* in 1844, gave the vote to town householders—and also originated the phrase "we must educate our masters". The young fop who had exulted in holding up pedestrians in Regent Street to stare at him had travelled far.

Disraeli had compared Gladstone's out-going ministry to a row of exhausted volcanoes; he himself in his last novel has lost his volcanic quality, but, still gently smoking, he looks back on the political and social scene of the 'thirties and 'forties with a detachment at once benign and ironic. *Vivian Grey, Contarini Fleming, Coningsby, Tancred,* and even *Alroy,* had embodied some of the agonies and ecstasies of his own youth, in *Endymion* he sees the period of his early manhood down the perspective of years with a more temperate eye.

In all Disraeli's novels the incidentals are more striking than the theme or story, and scattered about them are thinly disguised sketches of well-known people of the day. In some cases they are life-like, in others the originals have been used as little more than suggestions for characters. Through his eyes we can see and hear some famous men as they actually moved and spoke. There is this vignette of the Duke of Wellington speaking in the House of Lords, for instance:

"In the Lords, I admire the Duke. The readiness with which he has adopted the air of a debater shows the man of genius. There is a gruff, husky sort of a downright Montaignish naïveté about him, which is quaint, unusual, and tells. You plainly perceive that he is determined to be a civilian; and he is as offended if you drop a hint that he occasionally wears a uniform, as a servant on a holiday, if you mention the word *livery*" (*The Young Duke*).

There is, in fact, far too much in each of the novels, including language which is anything but simple and direct by the standards of today, although even in the most florid passages he often gives us the *mot juste*, and epigrams stand out of the verbiage with pointed finish. Scenes, characters and incidents crowd upon one another, digressions and soliloquies add to the indigestible mixture, and yet the books are full of life. G. K. Chesterton, in a Preface to a juvenile work of Jane Austen's, wrote: "Her power came, as all power comes, from the control and direction of exuberance. But there is the presence and pressure of that vitality behind her thousand trivialities; she could have been extravagant if she chose." Disraeli's exuberance is fully apparent in his early novels, and he never lost it, but it is only spasmodically brought under control, he too often chose to be extravagant.

A recent biographer (Hesketh Pearson in *Dizzy*, 1951) while disparaging Disraeli as a creative artist, reminds us that "though none of his novels is a work of genius, nearly all of them are works of a genius". Certainly the ironic wit which was so effective in the House of Commons runs through them like an electric current. Disraeli may have lacked the gift of fusing characters and story into the convincing unity that makes a really great book, but many of his faults (such as lengthy digressions) are those common to writers of his period.

CHAPTER II

Vivian Grey

VIVIAN GREY (1826) and *Contarini Fleming* (1832) taken together throw much light on the youth of Disraeli himself, his home background, his education, his dawning ideals and ambitions. Horace Grey, the father of Vivian, is certainly modelled on Isaac D'Israeli—his son deliberately dropped the apostrophe—and, like him, was a man of literary tastes with a sufficient income to enable him to indulge in a life of leisured scholarship, seldom leaving his study except in quest of rare books and fine editions. Isaac D'Israeli's miscellaneous research bore fruit in two volumes under the title *Curiosities of Literature,* and in other essays and commentaries, but he was more interested in collecting knowledge than in making use of it. He once planned a history of English Literature but did not persevere with it; the fret and bustle of striving for achievement never ruffled what his son described as "the philosophic sweetness of his disposition, the serenity of his lot". In drawing Horace Grey, Disraeli was evidently elaborating upon the touching *Memoir* which he wrote of his father, one passage of which gives the keynote of both characters:

"He was a complete literary character, a man who really passed his life in his library. Even marriage produced no change: he rose to enter the chamber where he lived alone with his books, and at night his lamp was ever lit within the same walls. Nothing, indeed, was more remarkable than the isolation of this prolonged existence. . . . He disliked business, and he never required relaxation; he was absorbed in his pursuits. In London his only amusement was to ramble among booksellers; if he entered a club, it was only to go into the library. In the country he scarcely ever left his room but to saunter in abstraction upon a terrace, muse over a chapter or coin a sentence. He had not a single passion or prejudice."

In the relations between Vivian Grey and his father there is certainly a reflection of those between Benjamin and Isaac D'Israeli. Vivian, like Disraeli himself, left school early and spent a year or so in miscellaneous reading at home, and Disraeli writes feelingly about the influence of the father's constant companionship and "severely cultivated mind" upon his immature hero. That Isaac D'Israeli could charm younger men and win their respect is proved by the affectionate veneration which Edward Bulwer (Benjamin Disraeli's senior by one year) showed for the picturesque scholar recluse, with his lustrous dark eyes and white hair flowing to his shoulders beneath a small black velvet cap. Byron, too, was an admirer of his books, and D'Israeli recorded that when they met the poet treated him with such respect—"I had almost said reverence"—that at first he thought he was "quizzing" him. It was certainly to the credit of both that with D'Israeli the poet was always "modest, gentlemanly and perfectly unaffected", even at the height of his fame.

Horace Grey, in common with D'Israeli, had "a mind unfitted for every species of business," but he is drawn as rather more a man of—or in—the world; nevertheless, we can well believe that in his exhortations to his son we catch the very tones of the latter. When Vivian carried his habit of nomadic study so far as to shock his mother's callers by bursting into her boudoir in slippers, with a lexicon under his arm, his father remonstrated reasonably: "Vivian, this will never do; you must adopt some system for your studies and some locality for your reading; have a room to yourself; set apart certain hours in the day for your books and allow no consideration on earth to influence you to violate their sacredness; and, above all, my dear boy, keep your papers in order."

When Vivian announced that he wished to study the latter Platonists, beginning with Plotinus, Horace Grey launched into a disquisition which probably had a counterpart in the talk of Isaac D'Israeli and certainly shows the freedom from passion and prejudice which Benjamin claimed for his father:

"Try to ascertain, when you are alone, what may be the chief objects of your existence in this world. I want you to take no theological dogmas for granted, nor to satisfy your doubts by ceasing to think; but, whether we are in this world in a state of probation for another, or whether we cease altogether when we cease to breathe, human feeling tells me that we have some duties to perform; to our fellow-creatures, to our friends, to ourselves. Pray tell me, my dear boy, what possible good your perusal of the latter Platonists can produce to either of these three interests? I trust my child is not one of those who look with a glazed eye on the welfare of their fellow-men, and who would dream away a useless life by idle puzzles of the brain; creatures who consider their existence as an unprofitable mystery, and yet are afraid to die. You will find Plotinus in the fourth shelf of the next room, Vivian."

The same reluctance to assert a constraining authority was shown by Horace Grey when Vivian protested against wasting his time at a University when he felt that Society called to action and now offered many openings to the adventurous and bold. His father warned him against trying to become a great man in a hurry—"one such attempt in a thousand may succeed, these are fearful odds"—and this is advice which Isaac D'Israeli may well have had occasion to give to Benjamin. The discussion was continued on a walk, of which the practical object was to see a Mazarin Bible, and in the course of it Horace Grey reached the characteristic conclusion:

"Although I would much rather that any influence which I may exercise over your mind, should be the effect of my advice as your friend than of my authority as your father; still, I really feel it my duty parentally to protest against this crude proposition of yours. However, if you choose to lose a term or two, do. Don't blame me, you know, if you afterwards repent it."

The talk ended disarmingly with the father saying: "Let us step into Clarke's and take an ice." Such a conclusion to a walk of the two Disraelis—with the contrast of flowing white locks and jet black ringlets—would have presented a fascinating picture, but perhaps it was only in imagination that Benjamin lured Isaac from his study into a pastrycook's.

The chapters in *Vivian Grey* which cover the hero's education have points of comparison with Disraeli's own. Vivian's first school was chosen by his fond mother, who was impressed by the fact that at Dr. Flummery's establishment there were sixteen young ladies, all the daughters of clergymen, merely to attend to the morals and the linen, and the only extras were pure milk, fencing and the guitar. The sixteen young ladies were a lapse into extravagance, but Miss Roper's school at Islington, to which Benjamin Disraeli was sent at a tender age, has been described as "a very high-class establishment". Twenty years later Dickens is scarcely less grandiloquent in describing Dr. Blimber's academy in *Dombey and Son*, where those young gentlemen who were condemned to a diet of bread and water received it from a liveried footman, the slice of bread on a folded napkin with a silver fork beside it.

When Vivian outgrew Dr. Flummery's his father was in favour of Eton, but Mrs. Grey could not be persuaded that a public school was anything but a place where boys are roasted alive and eventually the boy was sent to Mr. Dallas at Burnsley Vicarage in Hampshire. Mr. Dallas is described as "a clergyman, a profound Grecian and a poor man. He had edited the *Alcestis* and married his laundress; lost money by the edition and his fellowship by the match." This private school of fifty to sixty boys must, in part at least, have been drawn from Disraeli's own. In his case a public school was given up because, although Benjamin had then been baptised into the Church of England, his Jewish blood —and he was evidently a Jew—might arouse antagonism amongst his school-fellows.

Vivian went to school conspicuously well dressed, probably another autobiographical touch, and his appearance created a minor sensation—" 'A dandy, by Jove!' whispered St. Leger Smith. 'What a knowing set-out!' squeaked Johnson Secundus." Vivian met undue familiarity with disdain or insolence and the young savages felt that they had caught a Tartar, but once he had established an ascendancy over his class-mates he condescended to make himself uncommonly pleasant and interesting. Now he was admired for being "So dashing! So devilish good-tempered! So completely up to everything!" His seniors, however, were annoyed—"Cursed puppy!" whispered St. Leger Smith now, and "Thinks himself knowing!" said Johnson Secundus darkly. All, however, went well until Vivian had the notion of starting private theatricals, which had been banned by Mr. Dallas in the past. Vivian dismissed this objection airily: "Nothing is allowed in this life, but everything is done; in town there is a thing called the French Play, and that is not allowed, yet my aunt has got a private box there." The seniors were enlisted in the enterprise by flattering requests for their patronage and rehearsals were well advanced when the project was betrayed to the Headmaster by one of the ushers. These unfortunate men, who also figure in the pages of Dickens, were in this case greatly inferior in class to the pupils and had no pretensions to scholarship. Mr. Dallas employed them as a kind of police; under Vivian's leadership the boys treated them with the bare civility due to servants from gentlemen, and it was understood that anyone who voluntarily conversed with an usher was to be cut dead by the whole school. Mallet was a particularly unprepossessing specimen—"a pallid wretch with a pug-nose . . . and marked with the small-pox" —and he had suffered much, biding his time for revenge. Mr. Dallas acted at once on his information and expressed his displeasure forcibly. The ignominious collapse of the theatricals unleashed the antagonism of the older boys and Vivian was mobbed; a chorus of taunts and threats roused a demon in him and he struck St. Leger Smith in the face. A ring was formed for a fight. Vivian fought with uncanny skill and St. Leger Smith was only saved from a cruel beating by the appearance of Mr. Dallas. Here there may be some foundation in fact, as Disraeli was said to have taken secret boxing lessons in order to protect himself from indignities at the hands of bigger boys.

The next term Vivian found that St. Leger Smith and other seniors had left and the remaining boys were ready enough to placate him; but his forgiveness was not to be had on any terms, and soon the community was horrified to see that his new line was to "crony" with Mallet! Now the rule of the ushers, hitherto light and almost apologetic, became tyrannical; Mallet, in particular, interfered with the boys' doings and comfort with an ingenious insight obviously inspired by someone who knew their secrets and the workings of their minds as no usher had ever done before. The situation became so oppressive that the boys were driven to revolt; a desperate plot was formed, the door was barred when all had just assembled before morning school and the bigger boys rushed upon Vivian and Mallet with threatening shouts. Vivian, however, sprang upon his desk and, back to the wall, presented a pistol at the attackers. They fell back. Vivian threatened to fire if anyone came a step nearer to him, but urged them not to be baulked of their revenge on "yonder hound", and he stood smiling while the horrid cries of Mallet showed that the boys were "roasting" him. When Vivian felt that the wretched usher had had enough, he calmly opened the door to Mr. Dallas. It is small wonder that he was summarily expelled from the school, but Disraeli had a precedent for the extravagance of a schoolboy producing a pistol—when Byron and his friend Wildman were bent on fomenting a revolt against a new Headmaster at Harrow they carried loaded pistols about with them.

This picture of an over-weening, proud and precocious schoolboy is closely matched by that of Contarini Fleming and one complements the other. Neither Vivian nor Contarini can be taken as an exact self-portrait of Disraeli, but both had qualities in common with him, especially an early maturity of mind and feeling which in Disraeli's case was a racial characteristic. Contarini, a brooding, melancholy child, was conscious of powers and yearnings which he could not as yet understand or direct, but the plunge into the miniature world of two hundred boys revealed to him an object of ambition. Confronted by a crowd of boys, who came up to him with "curious glances of half-suppressed glee, breathless and mocking", his immediate reaction was:

"Did I tremble? Did I sink into my innermost self? Did I fly? Never. As I gazed upon them, a new principle rose up in my breast, and I perceived only beings whom I was determined to control."

With an assurance and an ingenuity of mind similar to those of Vivian Grey he soon dominated his school-fellows:

"Weeks flew away, and I was intoxicated with my new life and my new reputation. . . . Everything was viewed and done according to the new tone which I had introduced. It was decided that I was the wittiest, the most original, the most diverting of their society. A coterie of the congenial insensibly formed around me, and my example gradually ruled the choice spirits of our world. I even mingled in their games, although I disliked the exertion, and in those in which the emulation was very strong I even excelled. My ambition conquered my nature. It seemed that I was the soul of the school."

Expanding in this atmosphere Contarini formed a friendship with a boy named Musaeus and romanticised the relationship until it became a fever. Musaeus, gentle, beautiful to look at, but not Contarini's equal in birth or brain, could not fill the exalted rôle for long and, after he had visited Contarini's home and been found wanting, the friendship came to an abrupt end. Contarini returned to school gloomy and depressed. In the holidays he had found it supremely irritating to be treated as a schoolboy by his stepmother, brought to earth from lofty dreams in which he imagined himself winning fame and glory by some trivial demand for the obedience and good manners which the young owe to their elders. It was a bitter shock when he realised that "in imagination a hero, I was in reality a boy". Now school, too, palled upon him; having proved his power of dominating and fascinating his contemporaries, he no longer took any interest in doing so. The boys resented the change and focused their indignation upon Contarini's desertion of Musaeus. Musaeus himself, a boy of a simple, placid nature, had not grieved for long and even found some relief in being free from such an exacting friendship, but now the school in general took up his cause and, led by the seniors, they advanced upon Contarini as he sat in gloomy meditation on a gate and their spokesman began ominously: "We want you, Fleming!" Contarini refused to answer their questions; he would not brook being called to account, and eventually this scene also ended in a savage fight. Contarini, matched against a bigger boy, fought like one possessed, with no respect for "their silly rules of mock combat", until he had his opponent at his mercy. When the beaten boy was still brave enough to refuse to apologise Contarini lugged him away and flung him contemptuously upon a dung-heap.

It was not long before this glowering hero, whose latent genius and soaring ambition could only find an outlet in dreams, came to the conclusion that "Contarini Fleming must with all possible despatch cease to be a schoolboy". He could no longer bear the authority of minds he felt to be inferior to his own, or an education which concentrated on words rather than ideas, in which the inspired commentator was held up to admiration and true achievement represented as " a huge bunch of annotations". In Contarini's case it was not expulsion that ended his school career—he simply walked away.

These two dramas of boys who conquered their little worlds, and then turned away contemptuously from the enjoyment of popularity and power amongst mere schoolboys, suggest that Disraeli was indulging in a form of compensation for the disability he himself suffered at school because he was a Jew. At a school which he attended before his baptism he had had his first experience of being set apart from his fellows on this account; at daily prayers he and another Jewish boy stood aside, and once a week a Rabbi came to teach them Hebrew. This was all the more objectionable to Disraeli because his one Jewish companion was a boy whom he would never have chosen for a friend. It would be extreme to say that the iron entered his soul, but it was perhaps now that the first seed was sown of that *idée fixe* that he must excel at all costs, and could only do so by showing superior intellect and skill. Maurois, in his brilliant study of Disraeli, suggests that he found it difficult to enjoy the society of men—"*Il avait besoin d'être leur chef pour se sentir leur égal.*"

It is interesting to speculate on the difference it might have made to Disraeli's life and character if he, like Peel and Gladstone, had been educated at one of the greater public schools. He claimed that at his last school, under Dr. Eli Cogan (a Unitarian minister who won Isaac D'Israeli's regard in a bookseller's shop by his taste in fine editions), the drama of public school life was reproduced on a smaller scale, but there was no discipline comparable to that of a public school in those drawn in these two novels. When *Vivian Grey* was written Keate was headmaster at Eton and the birching block was in daily use; imagination boggles at the picture of Gladstone bent over it, but even he did not escape. He recorded that once when he was præposter of the Remove he was persuaded to omit from the list of boys due to be flogged the names of three who were expecting visitors from home; the headmaster missed his victims and the next morning he roared in a voice of thunder: "Gladstone, put down your own name on the list of boys to be flogged." It was much the same at Harrow, where poor Trollope owned to being a little aggrieved when the headmaster, meeting him in the street and shocked by his untidy appearance, demanded his name—"He must have known me had he seen me as he was wont to see me, for he was in the habit of flogging me constantly. Perhaps he did not recognise my face." Perhaps it was as well that Disraeli, all the more sensitive on account of his Jewish blood, was spared physical indignities on such a scale, from which Trollope emerged serenely sane. The declaration he put into the mouth of Contarini probably applied to himself as well: "At that age, whatever I may be now, I could not be driven. A soft word and I was an Abel; an appearance of force and I scowled a Cain."

In other respects Disraeli's schools had common features with the public schools; savage fights were taken for granted, the Windsor and Slough coaches sometimes stopped under the wall of the Eton playing-field so that passengers might watch them. The concentration on the classical languages, so galling to Contarini, was universal, although within two years Arnold was to begin his reforms at Rugby, which included widening the curriculum. When Disraeli next set himself to describe a boy's education eighteen years had passed and he had, no doubt, learned much of the real value of public school life from the men with whom he now habitually mixed. In *Coningsby* he gives a convincing picture of Eton, with the pageantry of *Montem*, the discussions and debates and, above all, the friendships; he had seen grey-haired men, moved by vague memories of "these mystic passages of their young emotion", mourning their vanished schooldays. The same note recurs in *Endymion*: "There is certainly a magic in the memory of schoolboy friendships; it softens the heart, and even affects the nervous system of those who have no hearts."

Harry Coningsby, the successor of Vivian and Contarini in Disraeli's schoolboy heroes, was drawn more realistically. Of course he had to be the idol of the whole school, nothing less would have been tolerable to his author, but it would have been unthinkable for him to turn away scornfully from his triumphs;

they were too glorious. There must have been some regret in Disraeli's mind for what he had missed himself as he wrote: "What power of manhood in passionate intenseness, appealing at the same time to the subject and the votary, can rival that which is exercised by the idolised chieftain of a great public school? What fame of after days equals the rapture of celebrity that thrills the youthful poet, as in tones of rare emotion he recites his triumphant verses amidst the plaudits of the flower of England? That's fame, that's power; real, unquestioned, undoubted, catholic."

A Disraeli schooled at Eton would surely have been, outwardly at least, a less flamboyant personality, and society would have been the poorer by the loss of some colourful episodes. Perhaps he might have realised his political ambitions earlier, but he would not have established such a hold upon the imagination of more than one generation of Englishmen.

Vivian Grey, like his author, did not go to a University; in Disraeli's case it was given up for the same reason as the public school. After the period of private reading at home, common to both, the careers of author and hero diverge for a time; Disraeli, at seventeen, was articled to a firm of solicitors in London, whereas Vivian was at large in society. He is described as a graceful, lively youth, with a keen wit and enough dandyism to save him from gaucheries and secure him the flattering interest of older women. Disraeli had similar social qualities and good looks, and he too scored his little triumphs at the dinner-parties given by Murray, his father's publisher and old friend. Vivian's success in society convinced him that he had a gift for managing men and women, and he was anxious to use it for his own advantage. Politics seemed the natural and congenial sphere for him, but it was impossible for a young man without influence to force his way into Parliament; he reflected that many a powerful nobleman only wanted wit to become a cabinet minister, whereas he had the wit but needed a patron who would give him a seat in return for the service of his ability. Fate played into his hands. The Marquess of Carabas came to dine with Horace Grey, with the object of securing his influence in an election for the President of the Royal Society. The Marquess was a disappointed man; before succeeding to the peerage he had, by industrious caballing, risen to be President of a Board with a seat in the Cabinet, but when he went to the Lords he was fobbed off with a lucrative sinecure, and the influence and patronage he had so much enjoyed gradually declined until he found himself treated as a political nonentity. During dinner he was involved in an argument and, unequal to proving his point, was getting very uncomfortable when Vivian, seeing his opportunity, came to his rescue. The precocious youth was astute enough not to express any opinion as his own, but by quoting eminent names unscrupulously to serve his purpose he managed to turn the tables in the Marquess's favour. He followed up his advantage by interesting the noble guest in tomahawk punch (a drink he invented on the spur of the moment) and was rewarded by an invitation to call on the Marquess with the recipe.

Vivian now embarked upon a wildly ambitious project; he would play upon the Marquess's sense of injury, persuade him that the time was ripe for a new party or group in politics, help him to found it and so establish a claim on his patronage. The campaign opened well. Vivian's skilful suggestions, proffered with a becomingly hesitant modesty, bore fruit and in due course he was invited to stay at Château Désir, where three other noblemen with grudges against the government were to be sounded as to the possibility of forming a Carabas party.

Château Désir is the first of the great country houses that Disraeli loved to picture in his novels. Vivian, already an epicure although still a nobody, took care not to arrive until the first bustle of opening up the great place for a house-party was over. In the midst of a fine park he found a vast, ornate palace in which Italian features had been imposed on Gothic architecture by a Marquess who had been ambassador at the ducal court of Venice. The adjectives gush from Disraeli's pen as exuberantly as the water spouted from the huge marble fountain in the court, presided over by "Amphitrite with her marine attendants, whose sounding shells and coral sceptres sent forth their subject element in sparkling showers".

The house-party was a little world in itself. The Marquess was the monarch of a petty court; when he received he made a grand tour of the suite of reception rooms, keeping up his influence in the county by a few appropriate words to each guest. Her Ladyship graciously bestowed what attention she could spare from her poodle and her parrot upon her guests, sending messages by a tiny page fancifully dressed in silver and green and twirling a richly-chased dirk. The guests themselves were all noble or distinguished, or confidential agents of My Lord or My Lady. One chapter is devoted to the toady, a phenomenon which was not uncommon in a society dominated by rank and wealth, in which patronage was generally accepted as the prerogative of the great and few felt it irksome or shameful to be dependent upon it. The toady came at the bottom of the scale in this system, and Disraeli gives us an inimitable picture of him in his smug self-satisfaction. There were distinctions even amongst toadies; the Common-Place Toady was merely an echo of his "feeder", whereas the Playing-up Toady adroitly pandered to his weaknesses and humoured his taste. This class of toady was ready with "a little bit of scandal for a dashing widow, or a pious little hymn for a sainted one; the secret history of a newly discovered gas for a May Fair feeder, and an interesting anecdote about a Newgate bob cap or a Penitentiary apron for a charitable one". Next came the Drawing-out Toady, who led up to his feeder's victory in an argument or a discussion; such a type is alluded to again in *The Young Duke*, where a sherry which heightens the flavour of a dish without interfering with it is described as like a toady who "keeps up a conversation he does not distract". Here Disraeli breaks off his classification with: "But we detest essay writing, so we introduce you at once to a party of these vermin."

In the sketch that follows three toadies are taking their ease together, off duty—Miss Graves, attached to the Marchioness, Miss Gusset and her supporter Dr. Sly, both in the train of Mrs. Million. Miss Gusset opens the ball:

"'Dear Miss Graves,' said Miss Gusset, 'you can't imagine how terrified I was at that horrible green parrot flying upon my head! I declare it pulled out three locks of hair.'

"'Horrible green parrot, my dear madam! Why, it was sent to my Lady by Prince Xtmnprqsklw, and never shall I forget the agitation we were in about that parrot. I thought it would never have got to the Château, for the Prince could only send his carriage with it as far as Toadcaster. Luckily my Lady's youngest brother, who was staying at Désir, happened to get drowned at the time; and so Davenport, very clever of him! sent her on in my Lord Dormer's hearse.'

" 'In the hearse! Good heavens, Miss Graves! How could you think of green parrots at such an awful moment? I should have been in fits for three days; eh! Dr. Sly?'

" 'Certainly you would, madam; your nerves are very delicate.'

" 'Well! I, for my part, never could see much use in giving up to one's feelings. It is all very well for commoners', rather rudely exclaimed the Marchioness' Toady: 'but we did not choose to expose ourselves to the servants when the old General died this year. Everything went on as usual. Her Ladyship attended Almack's; my Lord took his seat in the House; and I looked in at Lady Doubtful's, where we do not visit, but where the Marchioness wishes to be civil.'

" 'We do not visit Lady Doubtful either,' replied Miss Gusset, 'she had not a card for our *fête champêtre*. I was so sorry you were not in town. It was so delightful.'

" 'Do tell me who was there? I quite long to know all about it. I saw some account of it. Everything seemed to go off so well. Do tell me who was there?'

" 'Oh! There was plenty of Royalty at the head of the list. Really I cannot go into particulars, but everybody was there who is anybody; eh! Dr. Sly?'

" 'Certainly, madam. The pines were most admirable. There are few people for whom I entertain a higher esteem than Mr. Gunter.'

" 'The Marchioness seems very fond of her parrot, Miss Graves, but she is a sweet woman.'

" 'Oh, a dear, amiable creature! But I cannot think how she can bear the eternal screaming of that noisy bird.'

" 'Nor I, indeed. Well, thank goodness, Mrs. Million has no pets; eh! Dr. Sly?'

" 'Certainly. I am clearly of opinion that it cannot be wholesome to have so many animals about a house. Besides which, I have noticed that the Marchioness always selects the nicest morsels for that little poodle; and I am also clearly of opinion, Miss Graves, that the fit it had the other day arose from repletion.'

"'I have no doubt of it in the world. She consumes three pounds of arrowroot weekly and two pounds of the finest loaf sugar, which I have the trouble of grating every Monday morning. Mrs. Million appears to be a most amiable woman, Miss Gusset?'

"'Quite perfection; so charitable, so intellectual, such a soul! It is a pity, though, her manner is so abrupt; she really does not appear to advantage sometimes; eh! Dr. Sly?'

"The Toady's Toady bowed assent as usual.

"'Well,' rejoined Miss Graves, 'that is rather a fault of the dear Marchioness, a little want of consideration for another's feelings; but she means nothing.'

"'Oh, no! Nor Mrs. Million, dear creature! She means nothing; though, I dare say, not knowing her as well as we do, eh! Dr. Sly? you were a little surprised at the way she spoke to me at dinner?'

"'All people have their oddities, Miss Gusset. I am sure the Marchioness is not aware how she tries my patience about that little wretch Julie. I had to rub her with warm flannels for an hour and a half before the fire this morning; that is that Vivian Grey's doing.'"

This prepared the way for a cosy gossip about the guests at the Château, until the page summoned Miss Gusset away, when Miss Graves advanced from panegyric of the lady to hint that it would be better if she were more concerned to mind her own business. Finding Dr. Sly quite ready to transfer his easy allegiance to herself, she was more explicit, and they ended in a chorus of mutual admiration:

"'Ah! Miss Graves! If all ladies were like you! Oh!'

"'My dear Dr. Sly!'"

Meanwhile Vivian more than held his own in the house-party; without ever sinking to the level of a toady he was all things to most of his fellow-guests, ingratiating himself as required by precocious knowledge and tact, becoming humility and gay and impudent flirtation. The noblemen who were to be canvassed arrived. Vivian rode with Lord Courtown, drove with his lady, talked sentiment with the eldest daughter, sketched with the second and romped with the third. Lord and Lady Beaconsfield, both keen collectors, were won by easy promises of a rare medal and some notable autographs. Sir Berdmore Scrope was a tougher proposition, but fortunately he was hen-pecked and could be managed through his wife. The project of a Carabas party was at last adopted, but none of the noble sponsors felt equal to launching and leading it, even with such an able assistant as Vivian. There was only one man, they felt, who could carry it through, but Mr. Cleveland, although only thirty-three and a brilliant Parliamentary speaker, had retired from politics and, moreover, had done so because he considered that the Marquess had grossly betrayed him in the matter of a promotion. In spite of these unpromising circumstances Vivian recognised that here was *the* man for their purpose, over-rode all objections and set off on the great mission of enlisting Cleveland for the Carabas party.

Here, again, there is a parallel between Vivian's career and Disraeli's own. Disraeli had left the solicitor's office; probably he agreed with the daughter of the head of the firm—"You have too much genius for Frederick's Place, it will never do"—and also felt, like Vivian, that "to be a great lawyer I must give up my chance of being a great man". Nothing less than greatness, of course, was to be considered. He had plunged on the Stock Exchange (it was a peak period of speculation) and written pamphlets on mining companies in South America. Then he saw a grand opportunity in a tentative project of Murray's to found a new periodical which should come out oftener than his famous *Quarterly*. Disraeli would not let the idea rest and Murray was soon carried away on the flood-tide of his enthusiasm and despatched him to Scotland to exercise his persuasive powers on Lockhart, the son-in-law of Sir Walter Scott, whom they wished to secure as editor of a new daily paper. It was no easy task for "the young plenipotentiary", as his father called him now. Lockhart, good-looking, proud, a little suspicious and a little deaf, jealous of his literary reputation, was not a very approachable man, or likely to be impressed by a somewhat flamboyant young Jew, and unfortunately the letter of introduction had led him to expect Isaac D'Israeli. Disraeli wrote to his father that at first "everything looked as black as possible", but a few hours changed the situation completely—they understood each other, they were intimate. Eventually Lockhart's consent was obtained; both he and Sir Walter had felt that the editorship of a daily paper was scarcely a gentlemanly rôle, but Disraeli had explained that what was really required was "a Director of a great organisation", a phrase worthy of his hero Vivian Grey. Eventually a compromise was reached by which Lockhart was ostensibly editor of the *Quarterly* and undertook to assist in the production of the new paper by all means "consistent with his rank in life". The agreement was signed in Disraeli's presence and he returned to London triumphant.

No doubt Disraeli's own mission to Lockhart supplied many touches for Vivian's to Cleveland. Cleveland, too, was handsome, proud, inclined to be cold; he had been educated at Eton and Cambridge and Vivian at private schools; their temperaments were entirely different; Vivian was convinced of "the necessity of managing mankind by studying their tempers and humouring their weaknesses", whereas Cleveland had a lofty disdain for the tempers and foibles of his fellow-men. He was, however, now tired of four years' seclusion with his charming wife and two fine children in a "cottage orné" in Wales, where he held a judicial post; he had tried country pursuits to the point of exhaustion, his cows and his wheat could be perfected no further, a new plough had proved too ingenious to be useful, field-sports had begun to pall upon him. Vivian intended to exploit his boredom, but he was coldly received and his careful preamble interrupted by an impatient "Well, sir?" He admitted that his object was political and piqued Cleveland's curiosity by an allusion to "certain personages", who believed the time had now come for a new move in the political world, and at the same time tried to disarm his obvious contempt for the emissary's youth by a graceful apology for his inadequacy for such a great mission. Cleveland then, a little scornfully, promised him a hearing and Vivian wisely came straight to the point. Cleveland was outraged. When he had fully vented his indignation he expressed his regret that a young man of Vivian's evident talents should be the dupe and tool of that perjured peer, the Marquess of Carabas. Vivian, unabashed, launched into an adroit and moving speech in which he played alternately on the opportunity that offered—"There is that at work in England now which, taken at the tide, may lead on to fortune"—and the necessity of associating oneself with others, even fools and knaves, in politics and using them as tools. Finally he ventured to deplore the tragedy of great gifts buried in obscurity, and added, with a charming touch of boyish admiration, that his own great ambition was to found a political career under Cleveland. Cleveland, obviously shaken, made no reply, but invited Vivian to stay on at Kenrich lodge and meet his wife and family. The battle was already half won. Within three days Vivian had so skilfully played upon Cleveland's nostalgia for the old days of his Parliamentary triumphs that he swallowed his pride and undertook to direct the Carabas party.

At this point Vivian's story diverges wildly from anything in Disraeli's own experience. Cleveland duly came to Château Désir, but even Vivian's skill could not bring him and the Marquess into complete agreement in this uneasy association. Enough progress was made, however, for Cleveland, trusting in pledges given by Lord Courtown, to take a house in London, where the Carabas party was to meet again and work out a plan of campaign. The novel now degenerates into melodrama. Vivian found an evil genius in the Marquess' sister-in-law, Mrs. Felix Lorraine, who, deserted by her husband, had a mysterious hold over the Marquess, mysterious relations with Cleveland and mysterious and hysterical scenes with Vivian, in which it is difficult to see any significance, or whether they arose from love or hate. The Marquess became cold to Vivian, who set himself to get an explanation through the Marchioness, with whom he curried great favour by telling her that he had just booked an inside place on a coach for the prettiest little poodle from Paris, which waltzed like an angel and acted proverbs on its hind feet. Enchanted, and eager to oblige this wonderful young man in return, the Marchioness was easily induced to tell him in confidence that the Marquess believed he was caballing against him with Cleveland, and she added artlessly that he also now found Vivian too authoritative. Vivian received this blow with apparent nonchalance, breaking off the discussion to advise her Ladyship to change the order of the bracelets with which she was nervously fiddling and place the blue and silver one next to the maroon. He was, however, deeply disturbed, and suspected Mrs. Lorraine of influencing the Marquess against him. His suspicion was confirmed when, standing before a mirror, he saw her drop a powder into the glass of wine she was about to offer him; he emptied the glass into a bowl of goldfish and later met a footman carrying it away, with the dead fish floating on the top.

A farrago of melodramatic scenes follows, with lengthy digressions—an apostrophe to the moon covers a page and a half—and a number of letters and conversations. Some vignettes of public men are thrown in, including a lively sketch of The redoubtable Theodore Hook, editor of *John Bull*, as Stanislaus Hoax, and a glimpse of Byron as Lord Alhambra. The talk between Vivian and Cleveland, now warm friends, is not uninteresting, but the author himself ingenuously admits at the beginning of a chapter that "these conversations play the very deuce with one's story". At last matters were allowed to come to a head; Lord Courtown and Lord Beaconsfield withdrew from the Carabas party, and the final blow fell when the Marquess was relieved of his sinecure and heard that it was to be transferred to Lord Courtown. The Marquess stamped and blasphemed, and generally emptied the vials of his wrath on the head of the "monstrously clever" young man whose swindling and fawning had brought him to such a pass. Almost hounded from the house Vivian went out a broken man, although still capable of taking an unscrupulous revenge upon Mrs. Lorraine.

Vivian's despair is movingly described in terms which ring true. Disraeli had good reason to understand the agony of an ambitious young man when a cherished scheme, which had seemed well launched, crashes about his ears. He himself had had a brief period of glorious activity negotiating with printers, contributors and foreign correspondents for the new paper, *The Representative*, but shortly before its first appearance the boom of speculation ended in a collapse in the City. Disraeli was heavily involved, he could no longer hope to find the proportion of capital he had undertaken to raise for the paper, and he dropped out of the scheme. *The Representative* duly appeared, but the first numbers were poor and lifeless and after six months it came to an ignominious end, with a heavy loss to Murray. To Disraeli's personal disaster was added the galling thought that his own drive and imagination might have saved *The Representative*. Youth and inexperience would in any case have barred him from the post of editor, but perhaps he felt bitterly with Contarini Fleming that "If a person have imagination, experience seems to me of little use." He was, however, forced to recognise, as did Vivian Grey, that the cleverest youth needs the alliance, or at least the cloak, of experience for practical purposes. Disraeli, just twenty-one, oppressed by failure and saddled with debts which it took him nearly thirty years to pay in full, found relief in writing *Vivian Grey*, and thereby, no doubt, purged himself of feelings which might otherwise have festered into bitterness and despair. He allowed his hero no such relief. Vivian's failure passed swiftly to a climax of tragedy and remorse.

Facing the collapse of his high hopes, Vivian "wept as men can but once weep in this world"; the scenes of his youth passed strangely through his mind, he seemed to hear the beloved tones of his father's voice. He grieved bitterly for his friend Cleveland and his charming family, and then for his own glittering youth, gone and wasted: "All his boasted philosophy vanished; his artificial feelings fled him. Insulted nature reasserted her long spurned authority, and the once proud Vivian Grey felt too humble even to curse himself." And at this juncture, aimlessly wandering in Kensington Gardens hugging his misery, he met Cleveland's children, who greeted him eagerly as a friend. He brought his mind under control and wrote a heart-broken letter to Cleveland, explaining the part played by Mrs. Lorraine in the downfall of their hopes. Then, entering his club at night, he found himself face to face with him. Vivian held out his hand but Cleveland, who had evidently been drinking, dashed it away, exclaiming that he had no friendship for traitors. Vivian, afraid of a public scene, whispered urgently, "Cleveland! For God's sake contain yourself. I have written you a letter which explains all, but——" He was not allowed to finish, Cleveland, accusing him of duping him with his soft words, struck him in the face. There could be no sequel but a duel, and now Disraeli's style becomes direct and realistic, giving promise of the best passages of his maturity.

The duel scene cannot be dismissed as melodrama. Duelling

was in vogue all through the reign of George IV and even men in high public office were not above it. A notable duel was fought between Canning and Castlereagh in 1809, when they were respectively Foreign Secretary and Minister-at-War. Castlereagh heard that Canning had gone behind his back to the Prime Minister to ask for his removal from office and he wrote him an indignant letter of three folio sheets, concluding: "Under these circumstances I must require from you that satisfaction to which I feel myself entitled to lay claim." Canning is said to have turned the letter over distastefully, glanced at the last sentence and exclaimed, "I had rather fight him than read it, by God!" The duel took place with great secrecy on Putney Heath; Castlereagh's second was the third Marquis of Hertford, the model for Thackeray's Lord Steyne (*Vanity Fair*) and Disraeli's Lord Monmouth (*Coningsby*). Canning was wounded in the left thigh. In 1821 the editor of the *London Magazine* was killed in a duel, and in 1829 (three years after the publication of *Vivian Grey*) the great Duke of Wellington himself was involved in a duel with Lord Winchelsea, who had accused him of "introducing popery into every department of the State". They fought, with the usual secrecy, at Battersea, but they seem to have regarded the duel rather as a gesture to satisfy honour and pave the way for an apology than as a mortal combat, since the Duke deliberately fired wide at Winchelsea in the air. In 1835 Disraeli himself narrowly escaped fighting a duel. He had engaged in an exchange of insults with O'Connell, who compared him to the impenitent thief of the Crucifixion, and passions ran high, but O'Connell had already killed a man in a duel and then taken an oath that he would never fight another. His son, however, declared himself ready to defend his father's honour and Disraeli sent him a challenge. The duel was prevented by friends of the O'Connells, who informed the police, with the result that Disraeli was brought before magistrates and bound over to keep the peace.

These facts bear witness that the duel in *Vivian Grey* was true to contemporary life. Arthur Bryant, in his *Age of Elegance* (covering the period 1812–22), accounts for the prevalence of duelling by the fact that "a man's reputation as a gentleman was looked on as his most valuable possession", and consequently gentlemen were very sensitive to any aspersions on their honour and, in the current phrase, demanded satisfaction in this extreme form.

The most graphic feature of Disraeli's duel scene is his thumbnail sketch of Vivian's second, Sir John Poynings, a young baronet, a dandy and an officer in the Guards, who was much in request for these affairs of honour and an adept in the procedure. First, however, there is a characteristic address to the reader on the subject of duels in general:

"Did you ever fight a duel? No! Nor send a challenge either? Well! You are fresh indeed! 'Tis an awkward business, after all, even for the boldest. After an immense deal of negotiation, and giving your opponent every opportunity of coming to an honourable understanding, the fatal letter is at length signed, sealed and sent. You pass your mornings at your second's apartment, pacing his drawing-room with a quivering lip and uncertain step. At length he enters with an answer; and while he reads you endeavour to look easy, with a countenance merry with the most melancholy smile. You have no appetite for dinner, but you are too brave not to appear at table; and you are called out after the second glass by the arrival of your solicitor, who comes to alter your will. You pass a restless night and rise in the morning as bilious as a Bengal general. Urged by impending fate, you make a desperate effort to accommodate matters; but in the contest between your pride and your terror you at the same time prove that you are a coward and fail in the negotiation. You both fire and miss, and then the seconds interfere, and then you shake hands, everything being arranged in the most honourable manner and to the mutual satisfaction of both parties. The next day you are seen pacing Bond Street with an erect front and a flashing eye, with an air at once dandyish and heroical, a mixture at the same time of Brummell and the Duke of Wellington.

"It was a fine February morning. Sir John drove Vivian to the ground in his cabriolet.

" 'Nothing like a cab, Grey, for the business you are going on: you glide along the six miles in such style that it actually makes you quite courageous. I remember once going down, on a similar purpose, in a post and pair, and 'pon my soul, when I came to the ground my hand shook so that I could scarcely draw. But I was green then. Now, when I go in my cab, with Philidor with his sixteen-mile-an-hour paces, egad! I wing my man in a trice; and take all the parties home to Pall Mall, to celebrate the event with a grilled bone, Havannahs and Regent's punch. Ah! That is Cleveland we have just passed, going to the ground in a chariot; he is a dead man or my name is not Poynings.'

" 'Come, Sir John; no fear of Cleveland's dying,' said Vivian with a smile.

" 'What? You mean to fire in the air and all that sort of thing? Sentimental, but slip-slop.'

"The ground is measured, all is arranged. Cleveland, a splendid shot, fired first. He grazed Vivian's elbow. Vivian fired in the air. The seconds interfered. Cleveland was implacable and 'in the most irregular manner,' as Sir John declared, insisted upon another shot. To the astonishment of all he fired quite wild. Vivian shot at random and his bullet pierced Cleveland's heart. Cleveland sprang nearly two yards from the ground and then fell upon his back. In a moment Vivian was at the side of his fallen antagonist, but the dying man made no sign; he stared wildly and then closed his eyes for ever."

Vivian was utterly prostrated by the tragedy of Cleveland's death by his hand, and after a long illness he left England to seek distraction in travel. Here the novel as originally published came to an end. After its publication Disraeli himself was seriously ill, and then he, too, set off to tour the continent with his friends the Austens. The authorship of *Vivian Grey* had now leaked out and a storm of vituperation broke over both Colburn and Disraeli. The publisher was accused of shameful and shameless puffery in order to hoax the public, the author denounced for his "mean artifices" and described as an obscure person for whom nobody cared a straw, whose affectation of good breeding was ludicrous. Disraeli suffered, as a passage in *Contarini Fleming* bears witness. Contarini had written a similar book, which created a sensation on its appearance and was held up to scorn and ridicule when its author's youth and insignificance were discovered. Contarini's feelings must surely carry an echo of Disraeli's own:

"About two months after the publication of *Manstein* appeared a new number of the great critical journal of the north of Europe.

One of the works reviewed was my notorious production. I tore open the leaves with a blended feeling of desire and fear which I can yet remember. . . . With what horror, with what blank despair, with what supreme, appalling astonishment, did I find myself, for the first time in my life, a subject of the most reckless, the most malignant, and the most adroit ridicule. I was scarified, I was scalped. They scarcely condescended to notice my dreadful satire; except to remark in passing that, by the bye, I appeared to be as ill-tempered as I was imbecile. But my eloquence, and all my fancy, and all the strong expression of my secret feelings! These ushers of the court of Apollo fairly laughed me off Parnassus, and held me up to public scorn, as exhibiting a lamentable instance of mingled pretension and weakness, and the most ludicrous specimen of literary delusion that it had ever been their unhappy office to castigate and, they hoped, to cure. The criticism fell from my hand. A film floated over my vision; my knees trembled. I felt that sickness of heart that we experience in our first serious scrape. I was ridiculous. It was time to die."

The scorn heaped upon his head did not, however, crush Disraeli; *Vivian Grey* had been a best-seller, the young author needed money, and during his travels he wrote a sequel to it, which is incorporated with the first part in later editions. A great part of this is pure travelogue; scenes and characters, from a Grand Duke to a conjuror, crowd upon one another, and Vivian himself, despite two dramatic romances, loses individuality in the cosmopolitan whirl and becomes little more than a peg upon which to hang description and adventure. There is, in fact, far too much in the book; if it had been severely cut down and if Disraeli could have contented himself with the human drama of political intrigue, without dragging in the sinister Mrs. Felix Lorraine, it would have been more effective and readable. Gladstone, after reading it, tersely noted in his diary: "Finished *Vivian Grey*. The first quarter extremely clever, the rest trash." The first quarter, of course, is the only part of the book which is founded upon personal psychological experience, but to dismiss the rest as trash is too sweeping. In the latter half there are some good scenes and one outstanding character. Europe after the Congress of Vienna is well described, especially the small German courts which were then suffering from the attempt to begin the unification of Germany by combining innumerable little principalities into larger units. The Prince of Little Lilliput is an example of these "mediatised" sovereigns, and after visiting him Vivian goes on to the Grand Duchy of Reisenberg, to which Little Lilliput is now subject. There is a lively picture of this small court and its Prime Minister, Beckendorff, is a clever piece of character-drawing, probably because the author had a natural sympathy for this man who rose from being tutor to the heir to be virtual ruler of the Duchy, solely by his own genius and his skill in the management of men. Vivian reflected ruefully that he himself, with similar gifts, had dashed upon the public stage too young and, forced to rely upon older colleagues who did not even understand the purposes he meant them to serve, had inevitably failed. Beckendorff's eccentricities, his exotic aviary opening off his dining-room, his absorption in his violin, his unusual domestic routine, and the use he made of them for diplomatic purposes, are fascinatingly described. The book ends inconclusively, with Vivian abandoned when his horse had fallen dead under him in a terrible storm. The impression is that Disraeli suddenly tired of the story and dashed down the grandiloquent final paragraph in impatient distaste. It ends: "The disappointment of Manhood succeeds to the delusion of Youth: let us hope that the heritage of Old Age is not despair." In later life Disraeli was asked what really became of Vivian, and replied: "There was no inquest; it is believed that he survives."

Disraeli's own opinion of his first novel is interesting; in a preface to a reprint in 1853 he apologised for it on the ground that "books written by boys which profess to give a picture of manners and deal with human nature can only be founded on affectation". In *Contarini Fleming*, published only six years after *Vivian Grey*, he already looks back on it with superior detachment. Contarini's description of his own novel, *Manstein*, might well stand for one of Disraeli's first book:

"It was altogether a most crude performance, teeming with innumerable faults. It was entirely deficient in art. The principal character, although forcibly conceived, for it was founded on truth, was not sufficiently developed. Of course the others were much less so. The incidents were unnatural, the serious characters exaggerations, the comic ones caricatures; the wit was too often flippant, the philosophy too often forced; yet the vigour was remarkable, the licence of an uncurbed imagination not without charms, and, on the whole, there breathed a freshness which is rarely found, and which, perhaps, I may never again afford.... With all its errors, the spark of true creation animated its fiery page."

Despite this severity on the part of its author *Vivian Grey* contains epigrams which foreshadow the wit of Disraeli's maturity, and the hero, when in his flippant vein, gives promise of the exquisitely bored young men who figure in the later novels. Deploring the dullness of life in general with a lively girl Vivian exclaims:

"How those rooks bore! I hate staying with ancient families; you are always cawed to death." And: "If it were not for the General Election we really must have a war for variety's sake. Peace gets quite a bore. Everybody you dine with has a good cook, and gives you a dozen different wines, all perfect." Here Vivian is a prototype of the often quoted youth in *Sybil*—"'I rather like bad wine,' said Mr. Mountchesney, 'one gets so tired of good wine.'"

There is one chapter in *Vivian Grey* which, although artificial and of little interest in itself, shows that even so early Disraeli was alive to the distresses of the poor. In this scene Vivian visits the cottage of a labourer who has been of some service to him, finds that his poor sticks of furniture are about to be seized because he is, through no fault of his own, in arrears with his rent, and intervenes on his behalf with the estate agent, Stapylton Toad. It is almost the only instance in which Vivian is shown in a kindly light. Apparently Disraeli, in his sympathy with his hero's ambition, did not realise how shocking Vivian's self-seeking outlook and lack of personal integrity must be to readers. In the sequel he tried to atone for this by explaining that Vivian represented a "youth of great talents whose mind had been corrupted", and implying that he had always intended that he should receive due punishment, but these were second thoughts. In the first part of the book, however, one voice was raised in warning, and it was that of Horace Grey, who was so closely drawn from Isaac D'Israeli. In a letter to his son Horace Grey wrote:

"Vivian, you are a juggler; and the deception of your sleight of hand tricks depends upon instantaneous motions. When the selfish combine with the selfish bethink you how many projects are doomed to disappointment! . . . All this great society, with whom so young an adventurer has trafficked, abate nothing of their price in the slavery of their service and the sacrifice of violated feelings . . . Tell me, Vivian, what has the self-tormentor felt at the laughing treacheries that force a man down into self-contempt? . . . Let me warn you not to fall into the usual error of youth in fancying that the circle you move in is precisely the world itself. Do not imagine that there are not other beings whose benevolent principle is governed by finer sympathies, by more generous passions, and by those nobler emotions which really constitute our public and private virtues. I give you this hint, lest, in your present society, you might suppose these virtues were merely historical."

CHAPTER III

The Young Duke

DISRAELI's second publication (apart from pamphlets) was a fantasy called *Popanilla*, a political satire in which an intelligent young man, living in an island kingdom completely cut off from the world, finds a box of books washed ashore from a wreck and loses his happy, unthinking ignorance in the study of hydrostatics and political economy. He soon wearies island society by lengthy dissertations in which he tries to persuade his fellows that, if they would only follow his new precepts, they might, "instead of passing their lives in a state of unprofitable ease and useless enjoyment, reasonably expect to be the terror and astonishment of the universe, and to be able to annoy every nation of any consequence". The king soon rids himself of this pestilential bore by commissioning him to establish international and commercial relations for the island with other peoples, and ordering four of his most brawny lords to set him adrift in a boat.

Popanilla eventually reaches the great port of Hubbabub, the capital of Vraibleusia, where he creates a social sensation, is lionised and initiated into the high mysteries of currency and competition. The satire is now largely directed against the Utilitarians, for whose philosophy Disraeli had an instinctive dislike, although he had not studied it deeply. Popanilla's reading had already taught him that utility is the be-all and end-all of existence; now he sees that great principle in action and learns some astonishing facts, such as that when the annual interest on a nation's debt exceeds the whole wealth of the rest of the world that nation must be the richest in the world. The story of his further discoveries and adventures unfolds in a lively style and the book was a favourite with John Bright, although it scored no great success when it came out in 1828.

One chapter in *Popanilla* has an interesting bearing on the silver fork fiction to which Disraeli himself was a contributor. Vraibleusia, like England, had its New Rich and the true blue society was horrified by their manners—it was even whispered that when they drank wine they filled their glasses to the very brim! In order to spare both sides such embarrassments a Society for the Diffusion of Fashionable Knowledge was founded and under its auspices pamphlets were issued which, it was hoped, would provide a complete guide to behaviour without any necessity for the usual tedious process of education. The "new people" were as envious of the style of the "old class" as the old class was of their wealth, and the pamphlets were eagerly read. The first was on *Nonchalance* and inculcated that opinions and sentiments were vulgar, the true *nonchalant* would go no further than a moderate curl of the upper lip and an expressive shrug, and by such means "it was shown to be easy to ruin another's reputation and ensure your own without ever opening your mouth". Women were advised to cultivate listlessness. After this grounding in the supreme qualities of the dandy and the lady of fashion, other pamphlets followed with such titles as *On Leaving Cards, On Cravats, On Dinner Courses, On Cutting Intimate Friends, On Bores*. Under this stimulus the new people began to form ideas of their own; they even went so far as to claim that men are equal and everything is open to everybody, and therefore those who attained the necessary refinement should be accepted by fashionable society on equal terms. They failed to see any reason why, in the course of time, the whole nation should not go to Almack's—the scene of the most exclusive balls in London—on the same night. The government of Vraibleusia, with true liberal spirit and a natural wish to enlist the support of wealthy citizens, met this situation by engaging eminent writers to supply instruction in refinement in a more popular form. The publication of *Burlington, a Novel of Fashionable Life* in three volumes was a great success and needy members of the aristocracy were easily induced to follow it up with shameless revelations of society's hitherto secret codes. The result was extremely satisfactory—"When the delighted students had eaten some fifty or sixty imaginary dinners in my Lord's dining-room and whirled some fifty or sixty imaginary waltzes in my Lady's dancing-room, there was scarcely a brute left among the whole Millionaires."

Despite this lively satire on silver fork fiction, when Disraeli's second novel—*The Young Duke*—was published three years later, it opened in the approved manner of the fashionable novel. Readers must have thought they knew what to expect when they read: "George Augustus Frederick, Duke of St. James, completed his twenty-first year, an event which created almost as great a sensation among the aristocracy as the Norman Conquest." Disraeli was characteristically lavish in endowing his hero with advantages; a minority of twenty years had made the young Duke one of the wealthiest men in Europe, he owned estates in the North and West of England, a whole province in Ireland and streets and squares in London worth more than all the palaces of Vicenza and those of the Grand Canal in Venice together. In his palaces, castles, halls and lodges more fires burnt than in any other establishment in the Empire, but this "was of no consequence because the coals were his own". In addition to all this he was hereditary patron of Internal Navigation.

The modern reader with a period sense may also find much to relish in this promising start, but it is difficult for him not to suspect that, although willing to give the public what it wanted, Disraeli did so with his tongue in his cheek. Since he wrote *Vivian Grey* the vogue of the novel of fashionable life had been further stimulated by Edward Bulwer's *Pelham*, and publishers were eager for them. Bulwer was said to have written *Pelham* to please himself but his next novel to please his bookseller, and the same may well be true of Disraeli, who also needed money. *The Young Duke* was not a favourite of his but he wrote to his friend Meredith: "It is a series of scenes every one of which would make the fortune of a fashionable novel; I am confident of its success, and that it will complete the corruption of the public taste." Before its publication he wrote to his sister Sarah: "I don't care a jot about *The Young Duke*. I never staked any fame on it, it may take its chance." It is the only one of his novels (up to date) of which he made no mention in the long Preface he wrote for a new edition in 1870. *The Young Duke*, however, whether half intended as a satire or not, was taken seriously by the world at large, and Sarah Disraeli wrote ecstatically to her beloved brother that its praises were resounding, and even Jerdan had at last discovered the author's genius. Moreover, she added, some Americans who had lately come to Europe reported that it was "the text-book of the United States, from which they preach and read, and learn that important requisite, manners".

Not all opinion was so uncritical; the *Westminster Review* commended the book to "parasites, sycophants, toad-eaters and tuft-hunters" for their instruction and comfort, and Bulwer, who had read it in manuscript, had suggested that Disraeli should prune its excrescences and tone down its flippancies. Colburn, too, was a little apprehensive, but offered £500 for it, and Disraeli, now seeing his way to realise his darling project of a tour in the East, accepted it gladly and went on his travels.

The Young Duke, like *Vivian Grey*, is a crowded miscellany of story, brilliant social scenes, character-sketches, digressions (some of them autobiographical) and satirical comment. One scene, the account of a gambling session in Brighton, is as powerful as anything Disraeli wrote, some of the social vignettes are sparkling, and so is his digression on the art of various Parliamentary orators. He seems little concerned to create either affection or admiration in his readers for the hero, but is kinder to the heroine, May Dacre, who has principles—conspicuously lacking in the young Duke—and spirit, and even some individuality. The plot is better integrated than that of *Vivian Grey*, the opening situation titillates the reader's curiosity and, in spite of his egoism and his philandering, there is a superb gloss about the hero which makes him tolerable.

The opening chapters of *The Young Duke* have one quality of the good novel—they contain the germ of the dénouement. The "noble minor" was the subject of a conflict between his guardian and his uncle. The latter, Lord Fitz-Pompey, had confidently expected to be named as guardian, but the young Duke's father had chosen an old friend and neighbour, Mr. Dacre, a gentleman of ancient family with a large fortune, but a Roman Catholic. All Lord Fitz-Pompey could do was to bide his time and vent his indignation by voting against Catholic Emancipation. His opportunity came when Mr. Dacre's lovely young wife, after bearing a daughter, became "that common character, a confirmed invalid", and before long the doctors decreed that she must live in a warmer climate. The Fitz-Pompeys at once took advantage of

Mr. Dacre's absorption in his wife's health to open a campaign to capture the affections of the young Duke. Lady Fitz-Pompey called twice a week at his preparatory school with pineapples and bon-bons; the headmaster, Dr. Coronet, was delighted by this condescension and the conquest was complete when her Ladyship presented a china cup to Mrs. Coronet, and her daughter, Lady Augusta, a paper-cutter to Miss. When the time came for the young Duke to pass on to Eton Mr. Dacre had just taken his wife and daughter to live in Italy and had, perforce, to agree to his ward spending the holidays at his uncle's house. Here the boy found many attractions and every indulgence, which his uncle was careful to explain he would never have had from "old Dacre". He was taught to call his cousin Caroline his "little wife", and became, in fact, very fond of the pretty, gentle creature. Meanwhile he found the restraint of the private tutor whom Mr. Dacre had engaged to supervise him at Eton irksome, and Lord Fitz-Pompey managed, by skilful diplomacy, to replace him by a son of Dr. Coronet's, after which "the Duke of St. James got on rapidly, and also found sufficient time for his boat, his tandem and his toilet". In due course the young man decided, after an awkward scrape at Oxford, that he must travel. At the same time Mr. Dacre (now a widower) returned to England, and his attempts to keep up with his ward were frustrated by the Duke's negligence in answering letters.

After three years the Duke returned, now his own master. He had gamed a little in Paris, eaten a good deal in Vienna, studied the fine arts in Italy, paid court to distinguished ladies in various capitals and considered himself a complete man of the world. He was, in fact, sufficiently so to be chary of allowing his uncle's family to annex him, and he set up his own establishment in London, with a French cook, an Italian valet, a German jäger and a Greek page. After a calculated interval he accepted an invitation to stay at the Fitz-Pompey mansion, where he found his cousin Caroline grown into a very sweet girl, but his uncle angled in vain for his confidence, despite the "unusual conviviality and boundless affection" with which he tried to break down this reserve. It was distressing:

"Lord Fitz-Pompey, who was as consummate a judge of men

and manners as he was an indifferent speculator on affairs, and who was almost as finished a man of the world as he was an imperfect philosopher, soon perceived that considerable changes had taken place in the ideas as well as in the exterior of his nephew. . . .

". . . The Duke sipped his claret and admired his pictures. Nothing would do. An air of habitual calm, a look of kind condescension, and an inclination to a smile, which never burst into a beam, announced that the Duke of St. James was perfectly satisfied with existence, and conscious that he was himself, of that existence, the most distinguished ornament. In fact he was a sublime coxcomb, one of those rare characters whose finished manner and shrewd sense combined prevent their conceit from being contemptible."

The Fitz-Pompeys were forced to rely on the goodness of Providence and Caroline's charms for the fulfilment of their ambition to see their youngest daughter a Duchess. They were not unhopeful; her elder sisters—who were as like their irreproachable mother as a pair of diamond ear-rings are like a diamond necklace—had by now "each knocked down her Earl", triumphs which no one grudged to young ladies who were always in the best set and never flirted with the wrong man or spoke to the wrong woman. Even the Duke had to admit that he could not enter society under the auspices of a better hostess than Lady Fitz-Pompey and graciously allowed her to collect a house-party for his benefit.

Here follow some sketches of high society. There was Prince Protocoli, a great diplomatist unrivalled for the management of an opera, and his wife (suggestive of Madame Lieven), with a countenance like Cleopatra and a tiara like a constellation, famous alike for her shawls and her snuff. There was Lord Bloomerly, whose talk was "the Jockey Club filtered through White's", and another star of the diplomatic world:

"There was the Marquess of Macaroni, who was at the same time a general, an ambassador and a dandy; and who, if he had liked, could have worn twelve orders, but this day, being modest, only wore six. There, too, was the Marchioness, with a stomacher stiff with brilliants extracted from the snuff-boxes presented to her husband at a Congress. . . .

". . . The Macaroni's are most hospitable this year; and the Marquess says the only reason that they kept in before was because he was determined to see whether economy was practicable. He finds it is not; so now expense is no object."

His Grace, tall and elegant, showed an affable dignity in this society, with none of the affected indifference which suggests that nothing can compensate for the exertion of moving, which "makes the dandy, while it mars the man". The first breach in his conviction that he was the supreme ornament of society came when he was summoned to dine with the King (George IV), his godfather, and saw that the plate outshone his own. His Majesty was affability itself, uttered a *bon mot* which "blazed with all the soft brilliancy of sheet lightning", and told a brand-new anecdote of Sheridan with the skill of a practised *raconteur*. It is surprising that Disraeli should go out of his way to gild George IV (who died while he was writing the book) and even insert the strange invocation: "O, father of thy people! If thou wouldst but look a little oftener on thy younger sons their morals and their manners might be alike improved."

The Duke, determined to be superior in all fields, was shocked to find his ancestral London mansion in execrable taste:

"Nothing could exceed the horror with which he witnessed the exterior of his mansion, except the agony with which he paced through its interior." Where were the galleries, the elegant suites, the pictures, cabinets and statues to which he was now accustomed? He exclaimed indignantly, "What page would condescend to lounge in this ante-chamber? And is this gloomy vault, that you call a dining-room, to be my hall of Apollo? Order my carriage."

He sent post-haste for Sir Carte Blanche, who was regarded as the Sir Christopher Wren of the day. Hauteville House must be practically re-built; the Duke condescended to make a slight alteration in Sir Carte's design, Sir Carte admitted that it was a great improvement, and the work went forward most satisfactorily, regardless of expense.

At last there came a real and almost shattering shock to the Duke's self-complacency. All this time he had ignored his former guardian, making no attempt to see him, although he owed him a debt of gratitude for the prudence with which he had managed his estates during the minority. Under these circumstances he was abashed to find that a girl of striking beauty, to whom he burned to be introduced, was May Dacre, and that her father, far from being the curmudgeonly "old Dacre" of his imagination, was a man of forty-five only, extremely distinguished and master of any society he chose. From this point the central interest of the story is the re-education of the Duke of St. James at the hands of May Dacre, which has a touch of the quality of Elizabeth Bennet's spirited treatment of the haughty Mr. Darcy. There are, however, many subsidiary themes, incidents and entanglements—amorous, social and financial—before the reluctant lady is won at long last by the Duke's secret dash to London by night, in a common stage coach, in order to deliver an eloquent speech in the House of Lords in favour of Catholic Emancipation.

All Disraeli's novels are more worth reading for the incidentals than for the story, and in *The Young Duke* we may pass in review many aspects of social life, including gambling, racing (with a notable St. Leger with ninety starters, and a clever digression on the nature of jockeys), fêtes and balls, the appurtenances of a dandy's toilet-table, the occupations of young ladies in country houses and the novel excitement of a great bazaar. It is difficult to choose extracts to illustrate the character and style of the book, but Disraeli's ironic vein can be seen in an account of a debate in the House of Lords, when there was nothing particular to be debated:

"Lord Ex-Chamberlain thought the nation going on wrong, and he made a speech full of currency and constitution. Baron Deprivyseal seconded him with great effect, brief but bitter, satirical and sore. The Earl of Quarterday answered these, full of confidence in the nation and in himself. When the debate was getting heavy Lord Snap jumped up to give them something light. The Lords do not encourage wit, and so are obliged to put up with pertness. But Viscount Memoir was very statesmanlike, and spouted a sort of universal history. Then there was Lord Ego, who vindicated his character, when nobody knew he had one, and explained his motives, because his auditors could not understand his acts. Then there was a maiden speech, so inaudible that it was doubted whether, after all, the young orator did really lose his virginity. In the end up started the Premier, who, having nothing to say, was manly and candid and liberal; gave credit to his adversaries and took credit to himself, and then the motion was withdrawn.

"While all this was going on, some made a note, some made a bet, some consulted a book, some their ease, some yawned, a few slept. Yet . . . even the most indifferent looked as if he would come forward if the occasion should demand him, and the most imbecile as if he could serve his country if it required him. When a man raises his eyes from his bench and sees his ancestor in the tapestry, he begins to understand the pride of blood."

More seriously Disraeli compares the styles of notable speakers he himself has heard in the House of Commons, giving the palm to Sir Francis Burdett as the most commanding. Canning he describes as a "consummate rhetorician", but with "a dash of commonplace in all he said. . . . To the last he never got clear of 'Good God, sir' and all the other hackneyed ejaculations of his youthful debating club." He ends this digression with an assertion which, at twenty-three, suggests that he himself had a spice of the "sublime coxcomb" in him:

"One thing is quite clear—that a man may speak very well in the House of Commons and fail very completely in the House of Lords. There are two distinct styles requisite. I intend, in the course of my career, if I have time, to give a specimen of both. In the Lower House *Don Juan* may perhaps be our model; in the Upper House, *Paradise Lost*."

The social background of *The Young Duke* is extravagantly magnificent; no doubt ducal life was very splendid, but Disraeli had not as yet seen it from inside, as Isaac D'Israeli said, "What does Ben know of Dukes?" He improved upon what he did know much as he describes the landscape gardener improving upon nature: "They wandered in the wilderness, where the invention of consummate art presented them with the ideal of nature." When the Duke of St. James entertained on a grand scale a rivulet of rosewater, with gold and silver fish disporting in it, ran down the centre of every table, the bouquets were changed every half hour and soft music induced a mood which was "a union of delicacy and voluptuousness." When the guests rose from the table they found a Dutch Fair set up on the lawn:

"Numerous were the booths, innumerable were the contents. The first artists had arranged the picture and the costumes; the first artists had made the trinkets and the toys. And what a very agreeable fair, where all might suit their fancy without the permission of that sulky tyrant, a purse! Annesley offered a bouquet of precious stones to Charlotte Bloomerly and it was accepted, and the Duke of St. James showered a sack of whimsical breloques among a scrambling crowd of laughing beauties."

When the delights of the Fair were exhausted the guests were led to the riverside to lay bets on four painted and gilded galleys which were to race one another. The evening ended with a ball and illuminations. This Arabian Nights' entertainment was drawn after Disraeli's own heart, but he could have found models almost as lavish; at an actual *fête champêtre* in 1828 extensive paths were watered with eau-de-cologne, and at Lady Londonderry's rustic fête tea was served in cups of solid gold.

At one of the Duke's establishments the banqueting hall was fitted up as an Eastern tent, with scarlet wall-hangings looped with ropes of gold; richly gilt lions bore lances which supported coloured lights and a cresset lamp fed by an aromatic oil distilled an exquisite scent. His Grace's toilet matched his sumptuous surroundings. His dressing-table was covered with richly cut bottles, china vases, implements of gold and ivory and rosewood brushes; when he aimed at elegant simplicity his only ornament was an eye-glass on a hair chain set with diamonds—"This was the only weight the Duke of St. James ever carried, it was a bore but it was indispensable." Having satisfied himself at the pier glass that his dress was irreproachable he then deliberately assumed "the look, the air that befit the occasion; cordial but dignified; sublime but sweet". He descended like a deity from Olympus to a banquet of illustrious mortals.

Yet in the midst of this display a touch of Disraeli's wit brings a breath of reality into the artificial scene; there is a recognisable quality about "a tall fair girl who looked sentimental but was only silly", and genuine reflections slip in, such as his comparison of Society to a great pumice-stone which smooths down the edges of thoughts and manners. In Arundel Dacre, a cousin of May, a type is drawn from life. This aloof young gentleman who enjoyed the reputation of family, talents and fashion, seldom spoke to anyone and consequently "his attentions elevated their object". Even Lady Fitz-Pompey was pleased when he condescended to talk to her in public.

In *The Young Duke* Disraeli forecast the passing of the exquisitely groomed and nonchalant dandy in his description of Lord Marylebone, a new star who rose to challenge the Duke's supremacy in the world of fashion. His Lordship was even the Duke's superior in wealth, for whereas the Duke had only benefited by a twenty years' minority Lord Marylebone was a posthumous child. Short, thick, swarthy, he rattled up Bond Street in a red drag and changed the fashions: "Beards, and great-coats even rougher, bull-dogs instead of poodles, clubs instead of canes, cigars instead of perfumes, were the order of the day. There was no end to boat-racing; Crockford's sneered at White's; and there was even talk of reviving the ring." Society was enchanted—"So unaffected! No super-refinement, no false delicacy." The Duke of St. James found that his tailor and hatter would only supply the coat, hat or cane that Lord Marylebone wore or bore. It was the beginning of the end of the dandy's empire.

This novel is distinguished by one scene of real dramatic power. It occurs after the Duke has played havoc with his fortune and received a disquieting letter from his banker. As he had nothing to do at the moment he decided that he might as well amuse himself by looking into his affairs, but this proved such a disagreeable pastime that he broke it off to run down to Brighton for a change of scene, and here it occurred to him that he might do worse than try to retrieve his fortunes at the gaming-table; the risk of a few more thousands was negligible. He found "rattling the bones" a strange amusement and soon began to suffer from the annoyances of a gaming circle, including the intrusions of men he would once have scorned to notice. Lord Bagshot, who formerly would no more have thought of calling on the Duke of St. James than at the Pavilion, now lounged in upon him and had the impertinence to praise His Grace's rooms. The first few flutters were followed up by a really serious party for *écarté* at the house of Baron de

Berghem. After a plain dinner at which little wine was drunk the company settled down to play in earnest, with the Baron's confidential servant, Tom Cogit, in attendance. Midnight passed, but there had been no decisive result of the pitched battle, although the Duke had already lost heavily. Tom Cogit served supper in the room and they set to again:

"Every half hour they had a new pack of cards, and threw the used one on the floor. All this time Tom Cogit did nothing but snuff the candles, stir the fire, bring them a new pack, and occasionally make a tumbler for them. At eight o'clock the Duke's situation was worsened. The run was greatly against him, and perhaps his losses were doubled. He pulled up again in the next hour or two; but nevertheless at ten o'clock owed everyone something. No one offered to give over; and everyone, perhaps, felt that his object was not yet obtained. They made their toilets and went downstairs to breakfast. In the meantime the shutters were opened, the room aired, and in less than an hour they were at it again.

"They played till dinner-time without intermission; and though the Duke made some desperate efforts, and some successful ones, his losses were, nevertheless, trebled. Yet he ate an excellent dinner and was not at all depressed. . . . At first he had limited himself to ten thousand; after breakfast it was to have been twenty thousand; then thirty thousand was the ultimatum; and now he dismissed all thoughts of limit from his mind, and was determined to risk or gain everything. At midnight he had lost forty-eight thousand pounds. Affairs now began to be serious. His supper was not so hearty. . . .

". . . On they played and the Duke lost more. . . . Another morning came and there they sat, ankle-deep in cards. No attempt at breakfast now, no affectation of making a toilet or airing the room. The atmosphere was hot, to be sure, but it well became such a Hell. There they sat, in total, in positive forgetfulness of everything but the hot game they were hunting down. There was not a man in the room, except Tom Cogit, who could have told you the name of the town in which they were living. There they sat, almost breathless, watching every turn with the fell look in their cannibal eyes which showed their total inability to sympathise with their fellow-beings. All forms of society had been long forgotten. There was no snuff-box handed about now, for courtesy, admiration or a pinch; no affectation of occasionally making a remark upon any other topic but the all-engrossing one. Lord Castlefort rested with his arms on the table; a false tooth had got unhinged. His Lordship, who, at any other time, would have been most annoyed, coolly put it in his pocket. His cheeks had fallen, and he looked twenty years older. Lord Dice had torn off his cravat, and his hair hung down over his callous, bloodless cheeks straight as silk. Temple Grace looked as if he were blighted by lightning; and his deep blue eyes gleamed like a hyena's. The Baron was least changed. Tom Cogit, who smelt that the crisis was at hand, was as quiet as a bribed rat.

"On they played till six o'clock in the evening, and then they agreed to desist till after dinner. Lord Dice threw himself on a sofa. Lord Castlefort breathed with difficulty. The rest walked about. While they were resting on their oars the young Duke roughly made up his accounts. He found he was minus about one hundred thousand pounds.

"Immense as this loss was, he was more struck, more appalled, let us say, at the strangeness of the surrounding scene than even by his own ruin. As he looked upon his fellow gamesters, he seemed, for the first time in his life, to gaze upon some of those hideous demons of whom he had read. He looked in the mirror at himself. A blight seemed to have fallen over his beauty, and his presence seemed accursed. He had pursued a dissipated, even more than a dissipated career. . . . Haggard had sometimes even been the lustre of his youth. But when had been marked upon his brow this harrowing care? . . . What! Was it possible! It could not be that in time he was to be like those awful, those unearthly, those unhallowed beings that were around him. He felt as if he had fallen from his state, as if he had dishonoured his ancestry, as if he had betrayed his trust. . . . He thought of May Dacre, he thought of everything that was pure, and holy, and beautiful, and luminous, and calm. . . . His losses seemed nothing; his Dukedom would be too slight a ransom for freedom from these ghouls, and for the breath of the sweet air."

The Duke refused to play again. The others begged him to take his revenge, but he sat down and wrote out three cheques for the sums he owed to each. When Lord Castlefort once more suggested that he should pay them when they met again he replied: "I think it very improbable that we shall meet again, my Lord. I wished to know what gaming was. I had heard a great deal about it. It is not so very disgusting, but I am a young man, and cannot play tricks with my complexion."

This scene must have had close counterparts in real life. All through George IV's reign games of chance were still regarded as part and parcel of the life of the man of fashion; Beau Brummel and Count D'Orsay both ruined themselves at the gaming table. Various clubs fostered the cult, and in 1828, three years before *The Young Duke* came out, William Crockford, the son of a fishmonger, opened an establishment *de luxe*, of which the diarist Creevey wrote: "Crockford's new concern is magnificent and perfect in taste and beauty. For a suite of rooms it is the greatest lion in England, and is said by those who know the palace at Versailles to be even more magnificent than that!" Here enormous sums were lost and won; Lord Rivers, known as the Wellington of gamesters, lost £23,000 in one night. The yearly cost of the dice alone was £2,000. By the time he retired in 1840 Crockford was a millionaire. Of this event Disraeli wrote to his sister: "Last night Crockford sent in a letter announcing his retirement. 'Tis a thunderbolt and nothing else is talked of. . . . Some members are twelve years in arrear of subscription. One man owed £700 to the coffee-room; all must now be booked up. The consternation is general." Crockford had notable rivals in White's and Brook's, and in addition there were numbers of minor gaming establishments which had ingenious methods of evading the various laws intended to bring them under control.

In a book which is largely a lively *jeu d'esprit* it is surprising to find long autobiographical passages of reflection. These are in the fashionable Byronic tradition; Disraeli was ill, he had been disappointed, his feelings must be sublimated into lofty despair. Once more the note of wasted genius is struck, and that still more heart-rending one of genius doubting itself. He tells us that he writes amidst the ruins of ancient Rome with an aching head and a quivering hand. Fled were the deeds, the fame and aspiration he had dreamed of as a boy:

"I find the world just slipping through my fingers, and cannot grasp the jewel ere it falls. . . . My life has been a blunder and a blank, and all ends by my adding one slight ghost to the shadowy realm of fatal precocity." In another passage, which opens, "I am one, though young, yet old enough to know Ambition is a demon", he cites the anguish of "unrecognised Caesar, with his wasting youth. . . . The obscure Napoleon starving in the streets of Paris", and he asks what success can ever compensate for these withering pangs? St. Helena was not so bitter, for "visions of past glory might illumine even that dark imprisonment, but to be conscious that his supernatural energies might die away without creating their miracles—can the wheel or the rack rival the torture of such a suspicion?" And then comes the even darker thought: "To doubt the truth of the creed in which you have been nurtured is not so terrific as to doubt respecting the intellectual vigour on which you have staked your happiness." Not all the sentiments are so gloomy; in a lighter vein Disraeli admits his own puppyism, conceit, affectation and egotism but, nevertheless, thinks that he writes a pretty style. There is also an address to his father, written on the crest of emotion, but in his most ornate style:

"Oh, my father! . . . Our friendship is a hallowed joy, it is my pride, let it be thy solace. O'er the waters that cannot part our souls, I breathe good wishes. Peace brood o'er thy lettered bowers, and Love smile in the cheerful hall, that I shall not forget upon the swift Symplegades, or where warm Syria, with its palmy shore, recalls our holy ancestry."

The Young Duke was an ebullition of youth, with youth's extravagance, and it sprang from Disraeli's restless wit (and his need of money) rather than from his heart, but much of it has the effervescent, sparkling quality of an imagination that outran life.

CHAPTER IV

Contarini Fleming and *Alroy*

DISRAELI gave to his third novel, *Contarini Fleming* (1832), the subtitle of *A Psychological Romance*, changed at Murray's suggestion to *A Psychological Autobiography*, and it reflects the turn of his own mind when, after the shock he had suffered in the world of action, he was inclined to exalt the literary character. He recorded in a diary that *Vivian Grey*, *Alroy* and *Contarini Fleming* represented the secret history of his own feelings, the first his active and real ambition, the second his ideal ambition, the third the development of his poetic character, and that after these he would write no more about himself. Actually, he himself only wrote one serious poem—*The Revolutionary Epick* (1834)—and he is not altogether faithful to his intention of making Contarini an exponent of the poetic character in formation; action had too great an attraction for this hero, as it had for Disraeli himself. For a great part of the book the original motive is almost lost: Contarini, in fact, falls between two stools and fails to illustrate consistently either the poetic temperament or that of the man of action. Describing the young poet's recovery after an attempt at suicide, Monypenny (Disraeli's biographer) comments sardonically: "For anything he ever seems to accomplish he might just as well succeed in his purpose of self-destruction." Nevertheless, *Contarini Fleming* is an important key to Disraeli's own psychological development, and it arose white hot from the mental ferment of his own youth, recorded, as he claims through Contarini, "while my memory is still faithful, and while the dewy freshness of youthful fancy still lingers on my mind". Whatever Disraeli intended, the outstanding theme of the early chapters is not so much the development of a poet as the consciousness of great powers burning for a sphere of action and fretted by the weakness and uncertainty of youth. The poet's primary urge is to create or describe beauty for its own sake, but Contarini had little use for unacknowledged genius; while still a schoolboy he reached the conviction that life must be intolerable unless he were the greatest of men, and when he realised how many years must pass before he could fulfil his ambition he gnashed his teeth (for which there was Byronic precedent) in silent rage. His was not, however, merely ambition for ambition's sake, but rather a desperate longing to bring to fruition the powers he felt in himself; in the few dark hours when his faith in his own genius failed him his despair was abysmal: "They know not, they cannot tell, the cold, dull world; they cannot even remotely conceive the agony of doubt and despair which is the doom of youthful genius. To sigh for fame in obscurity is like sighing in a dungeon for light; yet the votary and the captive share an equal hope. But, to feel the strong necessity of fame, and to be conscious that without intellectual excellence life must be insupportable, to feel all this with no simultaneous faith in your own power, these are moments of despondency for which no immortality can compensate."

This *cri du coeur* no doubt applied to Disraeli himself in his darker moments; we have seen the same idea invading even the gay nonsense of *The Young Duke*, and when, in brighter mood, he felt gloriously assured, like Contarini, that "there is that in me which may yet mould the life and fortunes of my race", he still had to face a haunting anxiety as to whether he could ever command opportunity. When he wrote *Contarini Fleming* his ability was still, as it were, held on a leash, with no sure direction. That he did give an impression of great ability is proved by Edward Bulwer's account of a dinner-party to which he invited Disraeli in the year that *Contarini Fleming* was published. Amongst the company of young men one was to be an ambassador, another a Cabinet minister, another Lord Chief Justice, and Bulwer himself was a best-selling novelist and a future Secretary of State. Bulwer described Disraeli's dress on this occasion—green velvet trousers, a canary waistcoat, silver shoe buckles, lace at his wrists and his hair in ringlets—and added: "If on leaving the table we had been severally taken aside and asked which was the cleverest of the party we should have been obliged to say, 'The man in the green velvet trousers.'"

Contarini was more fortunate than his author in that his background was in favour of his finding the opportunity he needed to realise his ambitions. He was of noble birth and his father, Baron Fleming, was a man of great wealth and held high political office. Contarini was the only child of the Baron's first wife, an Italian of the noble Contarini family, who had died in giving birth to her son in Venice. His father had married again and the dark, temperamental and predominantly Italian boy had two fair, phlegmatic, Nordic stepbrothers, but the Baron had a real affection for his first-born, although he was too busy to show it often, and was ambitious for his career. Contarini both worshipped and feared him. His school-days have already been sufficiently described; there were other influences in his boyhood and adolescence; he adored a beautiful young woman, he transferred his adoration to the Magdalen for a short period of religious fervour, he found a monitor in a distinguished and philosophic painter of humble family. When he ran away from school he was at last driven to present himself, tattered and dirty from his adventures, at the Foreign Office, where his father now presided. Disraeli's picture of his reception is graphic.

Having induced a doubtful porter to show him into a large, well-furnished room fitted up with desks, Contarini found two young men fencing, another copying music and trying notes on a guitar, a fourth posturing before a pier-glass and a fifth reading a newspaper, the only pretence at political employment. He was ignored for some time, but at last the reader told him peevishly that he must go upstairs if he wanted to see Baron Fleming. Here he was seized upon by two pompous messengers, who tried to hustle this ragamuffin away from the sacred precincts, but he ran to the nearest door, that of the Under Secretary's office, and kicked it violently. The Under Secretary's private secretary came out indignantly, but the boy announced firmly, "I am Baron Contarini Fleming", and eventually he was admitted to his father's room:

"I entered the lofty room. My father was writing, he did not look up as I came in. I stood at his table a second; he raised his eyes, stared at my odd appearance, and then, pointing to a chair, he said, 'How do you do, Contarini? I have been expecting you for some days.' Then he resumed his writing."

The slow minutes passed and Contarini's courage sank to a low ebb:

"At length he rang his bell; one of my friends, the messengers, entered. My father sent for Mr. Strelamb, and before Mr. Strelamb, who was his private secretary, appeared, he had finished his letter, and given it to the other messenger. Then Mr. Strelamb came in and seated himself opposite to my father, and took many notes with an attention and quickness which appeared to me quite marvellous; and then my father, looking at the clock, said he had an appointment with the Prussian ambassador, at his palace: but, while Mr. Strelamb was getting some papers in order for him, he sent for the Under Secretary, and gave him so many directions that I thought the Under Secretary must have the most wonderful memory in the world. At length my father left the room, saying as he quitted it, 'Rest you here, Contarini.'"

Left alone Contarini reflected that this was indeed a great man, and he was proud to be his son. When at last the interview between father and son takes place it is described with a real appreciation of character and psychology, and even a touch of tenderness. The boy was nervous, but anxious to justify himself intelligently: the practised diplomat treated him with courtesy and spoke to him as if he were a rational and responsible being rather than a truant schoolboy in disgrace. Once the Baron was stung from his suavity, when Contarini said boldly that it was a waste of time for him to stay at a school where he could only learn words, when he wished to study ideas. He was abashed by the sharp reply: "Some silly book, Contarini, has filled your head with these ridiculous notions about the respective importance of words and ideas. Few ideas are correct ones, and what are correct no one can ascertain, but with words we govern men." As the conversation developed, however, Contarini, flattered by the great man's giving so much time and attention to his youthful problems, began to dramatise the scene in his own mind and consciously enjoyed acting his part, as no doubt Disraeli often did throughout his life, not least in his interviews with Queen Victoria. Yet the distress of the lonely child broke down Contarini's pose—or exaggerated it—and the father showed a genuine though studiously restrained concern as he checked the emotional outburst of this far from Nordic son.

Contarini continued his education at home; this included taking part in the social life of his father's house and the great diplomat gave him much advice in the vein of Chesterfield or Polonius:

"Do not talk too much at present; do not *try* to talk. But whenever you speak, speak with self-possession. Speak in a subdued tone, and always look at the person whom you are addressing. Before one can engage in general conversation with any effect, there is a certain acquaintance with trifling but amusing subjects which must first be attained. You will soon pick up sufficient by listening and observing. Never argue. In society nothing must be discussed; give only results. If any person differ from you, bow and turn the conversation ... Talk to women, talk to women as much as you can. This is the best school. This is the way to gain fluency, because you need not care what you say, and had better not be sensible. They, too, will rally you on many points, and as they are women you will not be offended. Nothing is of so much importance and of so much use to a young man entering life as to be well criticised by women."

In the course of time Contarini went to a University, where at first he felt "the ennobling pride of learning" and formed schemes of great researches in which imagination might complement erudition, and he sampled the ecstasy and throes of composition in a prize-winning essay. It was, however, from his father that he received the most pregnant advice as to his reading. Believing as firmly as Horace Grey that the young should not be too directly persuaded for their good, the Baron casually suggested that it might be interesting "to turn over Voltaire". Contarini was enchanted: "I drew out *Zadig*. Never shall I forget the effect this work produced on me. What I had long been seeking offered itself. This strange mixture of brilliant fantasy and poignant truth, this unrivalled blending of ideal creation and worldly wisdom, it all seemed to speak to my two natures. I wandered a poet in the streets of Babylon, or on the banks of the Tigris. A philosopher and a statesman, I moralised over the condition of man and the nature of government. The style enchanted me. I delivered myself up to the full abandonment of its wild and brilliant grace. I devoured them all, volume after volume. Morning, and night, and noon, a volume was ever my companion."

This passage and much that follows is convincing evidence that

Disraeli himself fell under the same spell, and its influence can be clearly seen in his novels, in which fantasy is so often combined with practical worldly sense and wit; *Popanilla* and *Ixion in Heaven* are of the same kind as *Candide*.

Contarini now had a severe reaction from "disgusting pedantry" and found a new interest in forming a "secret union for the amelioration of society". Here is an early sign of Disraeli's own awakening interest in social reform, which was not a common preoccupation of well-to-do youth in 1832. Absorbed in this society Contarini neglected his work and was warned that he was in danger of being sent down from the University, whereupon the young ameliorators decided to fly from the world and set up an ideal society "founded upon the eternal principles of truth and justice". Contarini passionately exhorted them: "Let us fly from the feudal system. Nobles and wealthy, let us cast our titles to the winds, and our dross to the earth which produced it. Let us pride ourselves only on the gifts of nature, and exist only on her beneficence."

The realistic account of this experiment in a ruined castle in the heart of a deep forest has its humours; in time the band of idealists were forced into a life of gentlemanly brigandage to support themselves, and their high-flown scheme ended in an ignominious flight before police and soldiers. The next phase of Contarini's career is more plausible. After he had failed to find a publisher for a romantic tragedy he was ripe for the suggestions of his astute father, who urged that if he would but control his imagination he might yet realise his ambition to be a great man and influence others. His father suggested that the chance of his becoming a Homer, though not impossible, was remote, and that man's natural sympathy is with action—"A man of great energies aspires that they should be felt in his life-time, that his existence should be rendered more intensely vital by the constant consciousness of his multiplied and multiplying power. Is posthumous fame a substitute for all this?" He added the advice: "Mix in society and I will answer that you lose your poetic feeling; for in you, as in the great majority, it is not a creative faculty originating in a peculiar organisation, but simply the consequence of a nervous susceptibility that is common to all."

The upshot of this was that Contarini was to serve an apprenticeship to politics as his father's private secretary. It was a Machiavellian education, in fact there is a hint of the authoritarianism of the next century in the father's attitude to life; confident in his own power and proud of his dexterity in managing men and affairs, he required his subordinates "not to think but to act, not to examine but to obey; and, animating their brute force with his own intelligence, he found the success which he believed could never be attained by the rational conduct of an enlightened people".

Gallantry was one of the weapons in the Baron's armoury, and as he humoured the gay or serious nonsense of women—"gracefully waving his handkerchief in his delicate and jewelled hand"—he seemed merely a consummate Lord Chamberlain, but his eye belied this superficial impression. In his office Contarini was introduced to an astonishing scene of intrigue:

"I found that in some of his colleagues I was only to perceive secret enemies, and in others but necessary tools and tolerated encumbrances. I delighted in the danger, the management, the negotiation, the suspense, the difficult gratification of his high ambition."

Contarini was an apt pupil; he adopted self-interest as the spring of all action, believed that no man was to be trusted and no woman genuinely loved; within two years he had become a skilful politician. In society he was assured, arrogant and bitter, but easy and not ungraceful. The following year a new Prime Minister had to be chosen and Contarini realised that his suave, imperturbable father was devoured by ambition and that his life would be as gall and wormwood to him if he was baulked of this prize, as he well might be by the jealousy of brother nobles. Contarini threw himself into a campaign after his own heart, writing pamphlets full of skilful innuendo and disparaging a rival by ingenious ridicule. Meanwhile he marvelled to see the smiling indifference of his father's public appearances compared with "the agonies of ambition it was my doom alone to witness". The seals of the Foreign Office were dangled before a dangerous enemy, Count De Bragnaes, although he was a political dolt; the Baron "required only tools, and felt himself capable of fulfilling the duties of the whole ministry". These machinations succeeded, and Contarini was appointed Under Secretary of the Foreign Office, where he soon had De Bragnaes under his control, suggesting opinions to him in such a way that he imagined they were his own.

At this period Contarini met, for the third time in his life, the beautiful Countess Christiana Norberg, the idol of his boyhood, and this brought about a revulsion of feeling. He saw his naked ambition for the ugly thing that it was, and wept as he remembered his youthful fervour for beauty and the "deep sympathy for all creation" which was once his. He had a dream and saw in a vision himself as the poet he had it in him to be, but even now his was not a pure devotion to art for art's sake, fame still had its old appeal—"I beheld, seated upon a glorious throne on a proud Acropolis, one to whom a surrounding and enthusiastic people offered a laurel crown." He set himself to write, but not, after all, poetry; within seven days he produced *Mannstein*, a novel about a young man with a nobly poetic temperament whose nature was thwarted by his education and environment. The political scene, and living characters, were sketched with malignant satire and the book set all society speculating as to the author.

Meanwhile Contarini scored a great diplomatic triumph at a Conference of European statesmen, whose policy threatened the position of the monarchy in his own country. He describes his mood of "happy audacity" on the great day, he gloried in a mixture of recklessness and self-confidence, he "spoke epigrams". The political manoeuvring and mounting suspense during the Conference are vividly brought out; Contarini bided his time and only produced his brilliantly conclusive arguments when the older diplomats had had their say. His intervention saved the King from a humiliating loss of independence and power. The statesmen filed out of the hall, Baron Fleming left with the King, Contarini paced up and down in a ferment of excitement. The passage which follows is picked out by Monypenny as an example of Disraeli's serious style at its best:

"I was alone. I was excited. I felt the triumph of success. I felt that I had done a great action. I felt all my energies. I walked up and down the hall in a frenzy of ambition, and I thirsted for action. There seemed to me no achievement of which I was not capable, and of which I was not ambitious. In imagination I shook thrones and founded empires. I felt myself a being born to breathe in an atmosphere of revolution.

"My father came not. Time wore away and the day died. It was one of those stern, sublime sunsets, which is almost the only appearance in the north in which nature enchanted me. I stood at the window, gazing on the burnished masses that for a moment were suspended in their fleeting and capricious beauty on the far horizon. I turned aside and looked at the rich trees suffused with the crimson light, and ever and anon irradiated by the dying shoots of a golden ray. The deer were stealing home to their bowers, and I watched them till their glancing forms gradually lost their lustre in the declining twilight. The glory had now departed, and all grew dim. A solitary star alone was shining in the grey sky, a bright and solitary star.

"And as I gazed upon the sunset, and the star, and the dim beauties of the coming eve, my mind grew calm, and all the bravery of my late reverie passed away. And I felt indeed a disgust for all the worldliness on which I had been late pondering. And there arose in my mind a desire to create things beautiful as that golden sun and that glittering star.

"I heard my name. The hall was now darkened. In the distance stood my father. I joined him. He placed his arm affectionately in mine, and said to me, 'My son, you will be Prime Minister of . . . . ; perhaps something greater.' "

In the very hour of Contarini's triumph the secret of the authorship of *Mannstein* was discovered, with the results already described—"I was ridiculous, it was time to die." Contarini determined to re-educate himself and develop his poetic power, and as a first step he wanted to travel and learn more about the world. His father, too, thought that, all things considered, he had better leave the country for a time, and secured for him the appointment of Secretary of Legation in London. Contarini set out attended by his father's highly trusted *chasseur*, Lausanne, and reached Paris, but there he was moved to throw off all his former connections (except the invaluable Lausanne) and future prospects and go to Venice, the place of his birth and for long the ideal Mecca of his dreams.

The story now becomes a mixture of unrealistic romance, fantasy, guide-book passages and reflections by the way. Venice had an almost mystic attraction for Disraeli, who had persuaded himself (with little or no foundation) that his own ancestors, threatened by the Inquisition in Spain, had sought refuge in the Venetian Republic. This feeling is transferred to Contarini, reinforced in his case by dreams and portents. Eventually Contarini eloped with the lovely Alcesté, the last of the Contarini family, and betrothed to another. After a period of idyllic bliss on the island of Candia, Alcesté died in childbirth and her son was stillborn. Contarini, saved from suicide by the ever efficient Lausanne, travelled again, came to feel that he could not live without an object and turned once more to fame and poetic creation—placing fame first. In a state of exaltation he realised that his own sorrows were but petty "to one who could exercise an illimitable power over the passions of his kind". Surely he could find comfort in "the love of nations and the admiration of ages"? After a frenzy of writing, however, he had a nervous breakdown of the same kind as Disraeli's own, and was brought back to active life by the painter Winter.

Winter, who flits through the story with philosophy to suit the occasion, is a type to which Disraeli recurs; Sidonia, the Jewish superman in *Coningsby*, is the supreme example, but a quarter of a century later minor variations of the detached philosopher, Mr. Phoebus and the Syrian called Paraclete, crop up in *Lothair*. While Contarini was still at school Winter had given him some talismanic rules of life copied from an obelisk in ruined Thebes. Now, when he found him sunk in apathy and waiting for death, he applied a tonic briskness, and here almost the only touch of Disraelian irony in this book occurs. Winter would not believe that Contarini was dying:

" 'There is no one of my acquaintance who has less chance of dying.' "

" 'How so?' I remarked, rather quickly. For when a man really believes he is dying he does not like to lose the interest such a situation produces. 'If you knew all——' "

Winter suggested that he was merely suffering from natural exhaustion; if there can be anything more exhausting than love it is sorrow, or than sorrow it is writing poetry. Contarini revived in a short time, travelled to Spain, Turkey, Greece, Syria, Arabia, Egypt, Palestine and returned to Italy. Here he met Winter again in the Forum at Rome and received more bracing advice:

"I tell you what, my friend, the period has arrived in your life when you must renounce meditation. Action is now your part. Meditation is culture. It is well to think until a man has discovered his genius, and developed his faculties, but then let him put his intelligence in motion. Act, act, act; act without ceasing, and you will no longer talk of the vanity of life."

Shortly afterwards Contarini's father died; he had always made him a princely allowance, now he left him a fortune. Contarini bought a palace and estate near Naples, collected specimens of fine art and determined to spend his life in studying and creating beauty. Yet he still cherished a hope that he might play a part in history, perhaps in the regeneration of Italy. On this note the book ends: "Yet if I am to be remembered, let me be remembered as one who, in a sad night of gloomy ignorance and savage bigotry was prescient of bright philosophy, as one who deeply sympathised with his fellow-men, and felt a proud conviction of their perfectibility; as one who devoted himself to the amelioration of his kind, by the destruction of error and the propagation of truth."

In the latter part of the book there are some interesting reflections on literary composition and Disraeli's own methods. Contarini, who in this case may be taken as Disraeli, could only write in the morning, when all he had planned the evening before flowed easily from his pen; he believed that meditation should be long and slow but execution quick. He revolved one projected piece of work in his mind for several months before he began to write it: "It was never out of my consciousness. I fell asleep musing over it: in the morning my thoughts clustered immediately upon it, like bees on a bed of unexhausted flowers. In my rides, during my meals, in my conversation on common topics, I was indeed, the whole time, musing over this creation."

In a more matter-of-fact vein Trollope claimed a similar method; when readers were shocked by his confession that he sat down to write so many words in a given time he pointed out that he had been evolving scenes and characters as he travelled many miles on the business of the Post Office.

This book contains interesting descriptions of scenes and places, with Disraeli's commentary drawn from his own journeys. Florence Contarini found disappointing as a city, its palaces gloomy and the Arno muddy, yet there was nowhere he would rather live. He came to the conclusion that its spell was in the character of its art, the fact that its painters, sculptors, writers and astronomers—whose works or memorials rose on every side—were not only great men but the greatest, men who invented arts, formed language and discovered, not merely planets, but "the whole celestial machinery". There are similar reflections in many cities; from Spain to Constantinople, and in the deserts of Arabia, Contarini is the mouthpiece of his author, upon whom the glamour of his own travels still rested. In describing nature Disraeli was inevitably a writer of his period; to-day authors try to find some idiosyncratic angle, or at least original similes, in picturing landscapes and views, but in the nineteenth century they were content to give faithful detail, such as that in the paintings of Millais, and liked to clothe them in rhetorical passages which had some body and dignity. Disraeli himself thought that *Contarini Fleming* represented the perfection of English prose! Without going so far as this, it can be granted that the book contains some fine passages of period writing, and it is freer from affectations and carelessness of style than some of his later novels.

There is little material for the student of English life and manners in this novel, but in the *chasseur*, Lausanne, there is an example of the perfection of service which matched the cult of magnificence. Lausanne, whom Baron Fleming commended to Contarini as the best servant in the world for travelling, was almost a magician in his own line; when Contarini decided to cross a continent at an hour's notice all was ready and the journey ran smoothly down to the smallest detail; when he wanted to elope with Alcesté a priest, a ship and an island paradise were produced for him in a trice, like rabbits out of a conjuror's hat. Lausanne's genius was admitted to be exceptional, but today it is difficult to conceive the service which the wealthy and noble then took for granted. It is, for instance, a shock to read as a casual detail in Tolstoy's *War and Peace* how, when Nadia chose to read in bed to a late hour, her maid sat up in the next room waiting to come at a call to blow out the candle when her young mistress was ready to sleep.

Contarini Fleming was not an immediate success as *Vivian Grey* had been. Disraeli felt at first that it was almost still-born, and that none of his critics had any idea of the nature or purposes of the book, and this was the more disappointing because, to him, it represented deep thought and feeling. Both these may be found in it, but probably the author himself did not realise how far he had strayed from his declared purpose of showing the development of the poetic character. The general reader missed the wit and sparkle of *Vivian Grey* and *The Young Duke* and found that the many reflective passages palled upon him, but it was highly praised by some whose praise was a distinction, notably Beckford and Heine.

* * *

Contarini Fleming was followed within a year by the *Wondrous Tale of Alroy* (1833), the heroic romance of a Jewish Prince of the Captivity in the twelfth century. Disraeli had been attracted by the story soon after finishing *Vivian Grey* and had even begun to write it, but he then laid it aside until, when he visited Jerusalem in 1831, it once more took possession of his mind. No doubt he was deeply moved by his first sight of Jerusalem and his imagination took fire as he thought of Israel's past glory, the distinctive character of the race from which he sprang and the enduring poetic literature of its faith. He may well have dreamed of a possible revival of racial glory and power, even indulged in visions of himself as the inspiring hero of such an epic drama; this, at least, seems the most plausible explanation of his claim that *Alroy* represented his ideal ambition for himself.

The young Prince whom he took as his hero had at first a shadowy authority over his race under the actual government of their Mohamedan conquerors, at a time when the rule of the alien Caliph was weakened by divisions amongst his own peoples. David Alroy was able to take advantage of this and for a short time he led a fervid Jewish army to victory, even entering Bagdad as a conqueror, but history does not bear out the first idealistic impression of the Prince which Disraeli gives his readers, although he does not shirk the end of Alroy's high endeavour in the arms of the Caliph's beautiful daughter, only redeemed by his death as a martyr. Disraeli was not so much concerned with exact history as with a romantic and miraculous drama only partly founded on fact.

In the opening chapter the familiar theme of *Vivian Grey* and *Contarini Fleming* appears once more in a different setting. The Prince of the Captivity, conscious of great mental and spiritual powers within himself, frets against his helpless subordination to the brute force of the conquerors of his race:

"Oh my heart is full of care, and my soul is dark with sorrow. What am I? What is all this? A cloud hangs heavy o'er my life. God of my fathers, let it burst!

"I know not what I feel, but what I feel is madness. Thus to be is not to live, if life be what I sometimes dream, and dare not think it might be. To breathe, to feed, to sleep, to wake and breathe again, again to feel existence without hope; if this be life, why then these brooding thoughts which whisper death were better.... Hark! The trumpets that sound our dishonour. Oh, that they sounded to battle! ... God of my fathers! For indeed I dare not style thee God of their wretched sons; yet, by the memory of Sinai, let me tell thee that some of the antique blood yet beats within these pulses, and there is yet one who fain would commune with thee face to face, commune and conquer."

Again the tragedy of ambitious genius apparently doomed to be forever ineffectual is stressed:

"Ah! Worst of woes to dream of glory in despair. No, no; I live and die a most ignoble thing; beauty and love, and fame and mighty deeds, the smile of women and the gaze of men, and the ennobling consciousness of worth, and all the fiery course of the creative passions, these are not for me, and I, Alroy, the descendant of a sacred line of kings, and with a soul that pants for empire, I stand here extending my vain arm for my lost sceptre, a most dishonoured slave."

In this last book of the trilogy in which Disraeli admitted that he embodied three aspects of his own ambition he probably completed the purge of the dreams and emotions which had haunted him since adolescence, and found some compensation for the enforced disabilities of the race to which he was always proud to belong by blood if not by religious observance.

The factual story—Alroy's brief career of victory, the delirious enchantment of his love for Schirene, the Caliph's daughter, his downfall when his mind turned to mere worldly conquest, his redeeming death after he had refused to deny his faith—is interwoven with miracle and mystery. He was instructed in cabalistic lore by the High Priest Jabaster, with whom he took refuge in a cave, and Disraeli takes pains to prove the correctness of these mysteries in one of the eighty-two Notes which he appended to the book. A miraculous journey brought the Prince to "an illimitable hall", on each side of which a line of kings sat upon golden thrones, and he was greeted in solemn chorus with: "All hail, Alroy! Hail to thee, brother king! Thy crown awaits thee!" Upon a loftier throne, approached by fifty steps of ivory, each guarded by a golden lion, was a figure with the majesty of a God, and from him—the mighty Solomon himself—Alroy received the sceptre which was to be the symbol of his royalty. Miracle and prophecy continue to play their part in the story, and the whole book is permeated with oriental feeling and imagery. Disraeli also luxuriates in the opportunity of describing exotic splendour, as in the scene when Alroy, still an unknown youth in Bagdad, under the protection of the Caliph's physician, is taken on a visit to the palace. First there is a mighty gate made of one vast block of green and red jasper and guarded by two fearsome jewelled serpents:

"The physician of the Caliph, taking his dagger from his girdle, struck the head of one of the serpents thrice. The massy portal opened with a whirl and a roar, and before them stood an Abyssinian giant, holding in a leash a roaring lion.... The jasper portal introduced the companions to a long and lofty chamber, lighted by high windows of stained glass, hung with tapestry of silk and silver, covered with prodigious carpets surrounded by immense couches. And thus through similar chambers they proceeded, in some of which were signs of recent habitation, until they arrived at another quadrangle nearly filled by a most singular fountain which rose from a basin of gold encrusted with pearls, and which was surrounded by figures of every rare quadruped in the most costly materials. Here was a golden tiger, with flaming eyes of ruby and flowing stripes of opal.... A cameleopard raised its slender neck of silver from the centre of a group of every inhabitant of the forest; and brilliant bands of monkeys, glittering with precious stones, rested in every variety of fantastic posture on the margin of the basin. The fountain itself was a tree of gold and silver spreading into innumerable branches, covered with every variety of curious birds, their plumage appropriately imitated by the corresponding tints of precious stones, and which warbled in beautiful melody as they poured forth from their bills the musical and refreshing element."

Such passages are common. When the Caliph went hunting he was preceded by four hundred men, each leading a white bloodhound with a collar of gold and rubies; the Nubian eunuchs in attendance were dressed in scarlet and carried ivory battle-axes. Before the victorious Alroy entered Bagdad a procession of citizens met him, bearing gifts. There were negroes with ivory, ostrich feathers and caskets of gold dust, Persians and Indians with vases of atar-gul, panniers of pearls of Ormuz and shawls of Cashmere; an Arab in a blue burnouz, surrounded by children each holding alternately a white or a fawn gazelle, led a tawny giraffe by a cord of crimson silk. When Alroy drank coffee in the palace of the defeated Caliph a eunuch presented it in a cup of transparent pink porcelain studded with pearls.

Disraeli evidently had misgivings as to whether his readers would swallow so much magnificence, as he quotes authority for detail in his series of Notes. A passage from Gibbon describes a fountain very like Alroy's; white bloodhounds are said to have been part of the hunting train of Mahoud the Gaznevide; a great Turk by whom Disraeli himself was entertained, drank coffee from just such a cup. In fact the Notes are a treasury of information, throw much light on Disraeli's own travels and are more interesting than the book itself.

In parts of *Alroy* Disraeli experimented in what he described as "occasional bursts of lyric melody", which he felt to be suitable "illustrative music" to the drama. These passages of rhythmic prose are not successful, they are too artificial and add to the general effect of unreality, although Disraeli claimed that the common reader seemed to like the poetry and the excitement. The critics were not impressed, although "golden opinions" reached the author from individuals. Mrs. Jameson said that reading it was like riding an Arab, and the traveller, Slade, found it "the most thoroughly oriental book he had ever read". It is, however, difficult to feel moved in any way by such a typical rhythmic exercise as this:

"It is the tender twilight hour, when maidens in their lonely bower sigh softer than the eve! The languid rose her head upraises, and listens to the nightingale, while his wild and thrilling praises from his trembling bosom gush: the languid rose her head upraises, and listens with a blush. . . .

". . . The daughter of the Caliph comes forth to breathe the air, her lute her only company. She sits her down by a fountain's side, and gazes on the waterfall. Her cheek reclines upon her arm, like fruit upon a graceful bough . . . She starts; a warm voluptuous lip presses her soft and idle hand. It is her own gazelle. With his large and lustrous eyes, more eloquent than many a tongue, the fond attendant mutely asks the cause of all her thoughtfulness." Then the rhythmic prose lapses into absurdity.

" 'Ah, bright gazelle! Ah, bright gazelle!' the Princess cried, the Princess cried; 'thy lips are softer than the swan, thy lips are softer than the swan; but his breathed passion when they pressed, my bright gazelle! My bright gazelle!' "

One pleasing feature of *Alroy* is the devotion between the Prince and his sister Miriam. Only when he was with her was his mind truly at rest: "They walked in silence, the brother and the sister, before the purity of whose surpassing love even ambition vanished." It was Miriam who, secretly visiting Alroy in the dungeon where he waited to be led out to a cruel death, comforted and fortified him before the last ordeal. Alroy told her that he believed that God had forgiven him for his fall from his first high purpose, and Miriam replied:

" 'I cannot doubt it, David. You have done great things for Israel; no one in these latter days has risen like you. If you have fallen, you were young, and strangely tempted.' "

" 'Yet Israel! Israel! Did I not feel a worthier leader will yet arise, my heart would crack. I have betrayed my country!'

" 'Oh no, no, no! You have shown what we can do and shall do. Your memory alone is an inspiration. A great career, although baulked of its end, is still a landmark of human energy. Failure, when sublime, is not without its purpose. Great deeds are great legacies, and work with wondrous usury. By what Man has done, we learn what Man can do; and gauge the power and the prospects of our race.'

" 'Alas! There is no one to guard my name. 'Twill be reviled; or worse, 'twill be forgotten.'

" 'Never! The memory of great actions never dies. The sun of glory, though awhile obscured, will shine at last. And so, sweet brother, perchance some poet, in some distant age, within whose veins our sacred blood may flow, his fancy fired with the national theme, may strike his harp to Alroy's wild career, and consecrate a name too long forgotten!'

" 'May love make thee a prophetess!' exclaimed Alroy, as he bent down his head and embraced her."

And then she took her farewell:

"O Alroy, farewell! Let me kiss you again, once more. Let me kneel and bless you. Brother, beloved brother, great and glorious brother, I am worthy of you: I will not weep. I am prouder in this dread moment of your love than all your foes can be of their hard triumph!"

Amidst all the artificialities of the story Miriam stands out a real woman and the tenderness of brother and sister for one another suggests that between Disraeli and his sister Sarah, to whom this book is dedicated. Family affection Disraeli understood well; one of the most moving letters he wrote was that to Sarah, when his travelling-companion, Meredith, to whom Sarah was engaged, died of smallpox at Cairo. With imaginative insight for a young man he realised that she would see life stretching before her as a terrible void and he offered her his own need of her love, as the best means of making her feel that she had still something to live for. The letter is written in the high-flown style then thought appropriate to emotion, but it rings true:

"Oh! My sister, in this hour of overwhelming affliction my

thoughts are only for you. Alas! My beloved, if you are lost to me, where am I to fly for refuge? I have no wife, I have no betrothed; nor since I have been better acquainted with my own mind and temper have I sought them. Live then, my heart's treasure, for one who has ever loved you with a surpassing love, and who would cheerfully have yielded his own existence to have saved you the bitterness of this letter. Yes, my beloved, be my genius, my solace, my companion, my joy. We will never part, and, if I cannot be to you all our lost friend was, at least we will feel that life can never be a blank while gilded by the perfect love of a sister and a brother."

Alroy marks the end of a stage in Disraeli's writing; after it the effervescence and ferment of youth give place to a more mature and certain outlook upon life and there are fewer of the introspective digressions in which he seemed to be forming his own opinions as he wrote, sometimes at the reader's expense. There are still some extravagances to come, but the phase of the peacock is almost past.

CHAPTER V

Henrietta Temple

HENRIETTA TEMPLE: *A Love-Story* (1837) was written when Disraeli was himself in love, and Henrietta was the name of his mistress. Presumably he was paying tribute to her (and surely also to his sister) in one of his digressions:

"Few great men have flourished, who, were they candid, would not acknowledge the vast advantages they have experienced in the earlier years of their career from the spirit and sympathy of woman. It is woman whose prescient admiration strings the lyre of the desponding poet, whose genius is afterwards to be recognised by his race.... How many an official portfolio would never have been carried, had it not been for her sanguine spirit and assiduous love! How many a depressed and despairing advocate has clutched the Great Seal, and taken his precedence before princes, borne onward by the breeze of her inspiring hope, and illumined by the sunshine of her prophetic smile! A female friend, amiable, clever and devoted, is a possession more valuable than parks and palaces; and, without such a muse, few men can succeed in life, none be content."

Disraeli's representation of an ideal love is a strange mixture of turgid extravagance and human touches which every lover can match from his own experience. Tennyson went so far as to say that all "the silly sooth" of love is to be found in this book. Certainly the general descriptions of first love and of the condition of a man in love are convincing. The latter ends: "A man in love wanders in the world as a somnambulist, with eyes that seem open to those that watch him, yet in fact view nothing but their own inward fancies."

The modern reader will probably find *Henrietta Temple* overweighted with sentimental reflections, especially in the earlier chapters, and occasionally even ridiculous, but there is some good characterisation. Henrietta is far more than a puppet and the secondary heroine, Katherine Grandison, develops a real personality in the course of her trials. It is, however, the background characters that, as so often in Disraeli's novels, give distinction to the book. Hitherto his subsidiary characters have been lightly sketched types—the toady, Mrs. Million, the diplomat, the dandy —but by now he had established himself in London society and he could draw from life. Lady Bellair, the great hostess, Bond Sharpe, the wealthy proprietor of a Hell (gaming-house), Count Mirabel, the prince of dandies, the bailiff, and even the waiter at the spunging-house, were drawn from life.

There is considerable drama in the love-story of Ferdinand Armine and Henrietta Temple, but it develops slowly. Ferdinand was the only child of parents who were living in seclusion in part of an old house standing in a beautiful park near the picturesque ruins of a half-built family castle. Sir Ratcliffe Armine was the victim of the splendid extravagance of his father, whose romantic and spectacular career fills the first chapter of the book. Sir Ratcliffe himself had served in the army but "his was not one of those minds born to command and to create, and his temper was too proud to serve and to solicit", and by the time the story opens he has made a love match with the charming Constance Grandison and settled down on his mortgaged estate to eke out his comparatively small income as best he might. Soon all the hopes and pride of the couple were centred on their only child, Ferdinand, who was strikingly like his dashing grandfather but, despite his high spirits, was amenable to the loving discipline of his parents and never gave them a moment's anxiety. The Armines were an old Roman Catholic family and Ferdinand's education was carried out at home by a beloved priest who had also been his father's tutor, and who settled in a suite of rooms in an old tower in the park. This character, Adrian Glastonbury, is charmingly drawn. He was a scholar, an antiquarian and a botanist, gentle, serene and wise; he had contemplated entering a monastery, but his devotion to the Armine family came first and he could not fail them in their need.

The time came when it was necessary for Ferdinand to go out into a larger world and Glastonbury, through an old friendship with a Duke, obtained the offer of a commission in the army for him, for which he insisted on paying the considerable price himself. Before joining his regiment in Malta Ferdinand visited his maternal grandfather, Lord Grandison, who, relieved that he had not been asked to provide for him, made a great favourite of this handsome grandson. Not long afterwards Lord Grandison's only son died, and it seemed certain that the Armine family would inherit a great part of the old man's wealth. Ferdinand, in fact, was easily persuaded by sanguine friends that he, the favourite grandson, was bound to be the chief heir. It was a period when many young men lived on "expectations" and the rumour of Ferdinand's obtained him easy credit, which made it difficult for him to resist the temptations lavishly offered him. Disraeli describes his first emancipation feelingly:

"Charming hour when you first order your own servants and ride your own horses, instead of your father's! It is delightful even to kick about your own furniture; and there is something manly and magnanimous in paying your own taxes. Young, lively, kind, accomplished, good-looking and well-bred, Ferdinand Armine had in him all the elements of popularity; and the novelty of popularity quite intoxicated a youth who had passed his life in a rural seclusion, where he had been appreciated but not huzzaed."

In time Ferdinand launched out further and further; he bought a yacht, rented a villa and had the finest racing-stable in Malta except the Governor's. Sometimes a grim misgiving entered his mind, and here Disraeli indulges in a solemn warning against debt, which has all the poignancy of personal experience. And yet—what is to be said for a youth governed by prudence and economy? He sees his hero's dilemma as he must have seen his own:

"But when we are young we must enjoy ourselves. True; and there are few things more gloomy than the recollection of a youth that has not been enjoyed. What prosperity of manhood, what splendour of old age can compensate for it? Wealth is power; and in youth, of all seasons of life, we require power, because we can enjoy everything that we can command. What, then, is to be done?"

Nemesis overtook Ferdinand Armine. Lord Grandison died and left his whole fortune to his granddaughter, the only child of his son. There was now but one course open to Ferdinand, according to the ideas of the period; if he were not to bring his beloved parents' grey hairs in sorrow to the grave he must marry Katherine Grandison. He hastened home, found his cousin "mild, elegant and pretty", but knew within twenty-four hours that he could not fall in love with her. He resolved to do the next best thing by making her fall in love with him, and he had an easy success; Katherine soon adored him and felt that there could be no one in the world so handsome, so good and so clever. They were engaged, but decorum required a year's mourning for Lord Grandison before the marriage, and Ferdinand was glad of the respite; he never faltered in his resolution to save his parents from heartbreak, settle his debts and restore the family fortunes by this sacrifice, but there were moments when he wished that he had no family to consider.

In this mood, at a time when he happened to be alone at Armine, he met a beautiful girl in the park. The passage describing Henrietta Temple and Ferdinand's feelings as he watched her is an example of Disraeli's most flowery and artificial prose, and yet even in this there are flashes of insight:

"Her countenance was raised and motionless. It seemed to him that it was more radiant than the sunshine. He gazed with rapture on the dazzling brilliancy of her complexion, the delicate regularity of her features, and the large violet-tinted eyes, fringed with the longest and the darkest lashes he had ever beheld. From her position her hat had fallen back, revealing her lofty and pellucid brow, and the dark and lustrous locks that were braided over her temples. The whole countenance combined that brilliant health and that classic beauty which we associate with the idea of some nymph tripping over the dew-bespangled meads of Ida, or glancing amid the hallowed groves of Greece. Although the lady could scarcely have seen eighteen summers, her stature was above the common height; but language cannot describe the startling symmetry of her superb figure.

"There is no love but love at first sight. . . . All other is the illegitimate result of observation, of reflection, of compromise, of comparison, of expediency. The passions that endure flash like the lightning: they scorch the soul, but it is warmed for ever. Miserable man whose love rises by degrees upon the frigid morning of his mind!"

There follows an almost hysterical panegyric upon love—"magnificent, sublime, divine sentiment"—and the lover, to whom all else becomes indifferent: "He is a mariner, who, in the sea of life, keeps his gaze fixedly on a single star: and if that does not shine, he lets go the rudder, and glories when his barque descends into the bottomless gulf."

Ferdinand was now, and instantaneously, in the grip of this mighty passion:

"Pale and trembling, he withdrew a few paces from the overwhelming spectacle, and leant against a tree in a chaos of emotion. What had he seen? What ravishing vision had risen upon his sight? What wild, what delicious, what maddening impulse now pervaded his frame? A storm seemed raging in his soul, a mighty wind dispelling in its course the sullen clouds and vapours of long years. Silent he was indeed, for he was speechless; though the big drop that quivered on his brow and the slight foam that played upon his lip proved the difficult triumph of passion over expression. But, as the wind clears the heaven, passion eventually tranquillises the soul. The tumult of his mind gradually subsided ... and a feeling of bright serenity succeeded, a sense of beauty and of joy, and of hovering circumambient happiness."

After perpetrating this high-flown opening Disraeli settles in earnest to describe the troubled course of this sudden love. There was nobility in Henrietta. When their love overpowered them both she was deeply troubled because Ferdinand pressed her to keep it a secret from her dearly loved father until he had seen his parents, now staying at Bath with Katherine Grandison, and discussed ways and means with them. At last she unwillingly consented, but more than once Ferdinand knelt before her with "streaming eyes", she wept passionately herself, she fainted in his arms, and when they parted he "pressed to his bosom her noble and throbbing form". This excessive sensibility was not so ridiculous then as it seems today, women and even men in love were apparently prone to weep; when Gladstone and Lord Lyttelton proposed to the two Glynne sisters Gladstone alone kept his composure and soothed my Lord while the girls fled to shed delicious tears together.

Ferdinand left for Bath, intending to confess all to Katherine, come what might, but there he found an agent of one of his creditors dogging his footsteps and he was forced to go into society with his cousin as her fiancé to allay suspicion and stave off arrest. All this was reported to the Temples by an old friend who came from Bath to stay with them, and Henrietta felt that it was a confirmation of her vague suspicion that her wonderful lover had not been candid with her. She was utterly prostrated and her father carried her off to Italy, taking care to leave no clues by which Ferdinand might trace them. After Henrietta had had a severe nervous breakdown and Ferdinand had almost died of brain fever, fresh complications arose. Through the good offices of old Glastonbury Katherine magnanimously released Ferdinand from his engagement, although his parents were not to be told as yet, but meanwhile Henrietta had succumbed to the wooing of Lord Montfort, who had set himself to mend her broken heart with exceptional charm and delicacy, which the reader too finds very winning, more so than Ferdinand's impassioned outbursts. Before the sorry tangle was unravelled to everyone's satisfaction the various actors in the story were thrown together in London society, and this is the best part of the book, memorable for the life-like portrait of old Lady Cork as Lady Bellair, a sketch of Crockford (of the famous club) as Bond Sharpe and, above all, D'Orsay as Count Alcibiades de Mirabel.

Old Lady Cork ranked with Lady Holland amongst the first hostesses in London and Disraeli was a favourite with her. She had a taste for the bizarre, her page was dressed in a fantastic green livery with a plume of black feathers in his cap, and her macaw was celebrated in *Memoirs of a Macaw of a Lady of Quality*. In one of his letters to his sister Sarah Disraeli gives a dialogue between Lady Cork and Lord Carrington, founded upon a conversation reported to him by Lady Sykes, who was present. Lady Cork declared that she doted upon the Disraelis (father and son) and when Lord Carrington objected that the young man was an extraordinary sort of person she retorted tartly, "I should think that *you* could not taste him", adding that he was the best *ton* in London, and there was not a party that went down without him, but he would not dine with Lord Carrington if he were to ask him—"He does not care for people because they are lords; he must have fashion, or beauty, or wit, or something; and you are a very good sort of person, but you are nothing more."

As Disraeli brings out in his sketch of her in *Henrietta Temple*, Lady Cork was a link between two centuries: in the eighteenth she sat to Sir Joshua Reynolds, argued with Dr. Johnson and encouraged Charles Fox in his early ambitions; in the nineteenth she entertained the Prince Regent, Canning, Castlereagh, Lord John Russell, Peel, Byron and Scott. Madame d'Arblay (Fanny Burney) describes her when she was still Miss Monckton, a famous blue-stocking hostess:

"Miss Monckton, who is here with her mother, the Dowager Lady Galway, has sent various messages of her earnest desire to be acquainted with Mrs. Thrale and your humble servant to command. Dr. Johnson she already knew, for she is one of those who stand foremost in collecting all extraordinary or curious people to her London conversaziones, which, like those of Mrs. Vesey, mix the rank and the literature and exclude all else beside."

This passage is cited by those who hold that Dickens drew his famous lion-hunting hostess Mrs. Leo Hunter, from Lady Cork. Madame d'Arblay pictures her in the year 1782: "Miss Monckton is between thirty and forty, very short, very fat, but handsome; splendidly and fantastically dressed, rouged not unbecomingly, yet evidently and fantastically desirous of gaining notice and admiration. She has an easy levity in her air, manner, voice and discourse, that speak all within to be comfortable; and her rage of seeing anything curious may be satisfied, if she pleases, in a mirror."

In *The Diary and Letters of Madame d'Arblay* we may still eavesdrop upon the conversation of Miss Monckton with Dr. Johnson, Sir Joshua Reynolds and Burke, but the most pleasing sample of her skirmishes with Dr. Johnson is provided by Boswell:

"She insisted that some of Sterne's writings were very pathetic; Johnson bluntly denied it. 'I am sure,' said she, 'they have affected me.' 'Why,' said Johnson, smiling and rolling himself about, 'that is because, dearest, you are a dunce.' When she some time afterwards mentioned this to him, he said, with equal truth and politeness, 'Madam, if I had thought so, I certainly should not have said it.'"

In 1786 Miss Monckton became the second wife of the Earl of Cork and Orrery, whom she survived by forty-two years. In her nineties she was still a famous London hostess, diminutive but autocratic, her eccentricities excused and endeared by her great age.

Lady Cork was already a very old lady when Disraeli knew her, and in describing her as Lady Bellair in *Henrietta Temple* he wrote that if she was not actually immortal, yet her friends felt that "it was at least her strange destiny not so much vulgarly to die, as to grow old like the heroine of a fairy-tale, each year smaller and smaller—'Fine by degrees, and beautifully less'—until her Ladyship might at length subside into airy nothingness, and so rather vanish than expire."

There is a delightful description of her—as Lady Bellair—arriving to stay with the Temples—it was she who brought the devastating news that Ferdinand Armine was about to marry the great heiress Katherine Grandison. Lady Bellair was on her way to visit her grandson in Northumberland and had condescended to notice a rich parvenue, Mrs. Montgomery Floyd, with the object of allowing this lady the honour of placing her carriage at her disposal for the journey. Mrs. Montgomery Floyd stepped out first, a gorgeous figure in a maroon pelisse, an emerald bonnet with a golden ribbon and a richly embroidered bag worthy of holding the Great Seal itself. A green parrot in a sparkling cage was handed out next, and then came my Lady herself:

"And then came forth the prettiest, liveliest, smallest, best-dressed and, stranger than all, oldest little lady in the world. Lady Bellair was of child-like stature, and quite erect, though ninety years of age; the tasteful simplicity of her costume, her little plain white silk bonnet, her grey silk dress, her apron, her grey mittens and her Cinderella shoes, all admirably contrasted with the vast and flaunting splendour of her companion, not less than her Ladyship's small yet exquisitely proportioned form, her highly finished extremities, and her keen sarcastic grey eye."

A servant lifted her up bodily and placed her on the steps; the Temples, knowing that she disliked being watched in the tricky ritual of getting out of the carriage, were not at the door and she burst out testily:

" 'Here! Where's the butler? I don't want you, stupid (addressing her own servant), but the butler of the house, Mister's butler; what is his name, Mr. Twoshoes' butler? I cannot remember names. Oh! You are there, are you? I don't want you. How is your master? How is your charming lady? Why don't you answer? Why do you stare so? Miss Temple! No, not Miss Temple! The lady, my lady, my charming friend, Mrs. Floyd! To be sure so; why did you not say so before? But she has got two names. Why don't you say both names? My dear,' continued Lady Bellair, addressing her travelling companion, 'I don't know your name. Tell all these good people your name, your two names! I like people with two names. Tell them, my dear, tell them; tell them your name, Mrs. Thingabob, or whatever it is, Mrs. Thingabob Twoshoes.' "

Lady Bellair was soon match-making for Henrietta, it must be someone who can "taste" her, and she concluded: "Well, my dear, it shall be Lord Fitzwarrene, then. I shall give a series of parties this year and ask Lord Fitzwarrene to every one. Not that it is very easy to get him, my child. There is nobody so difficult as Lord Fitzwarrene. That is quite right. Men should always be difficult. I cannot bear men who come and dine with you when you want them."

Later on in the story Lady Bellair recognised her Bath favourite, Ferdinand Armine, in a London street and stopped her carriage:

" 'You wicked man,' said her little ladyship, in a great rage. 'Oh! How I hate you! I could cut you up into minced meat; that I could. Here have I been giving parties every night, all for you, too. And you have been in town and never called on me. Tell me your name. How is your wife? Oh, you are not married. You should marry; I hate a *cidevant jeune homme*. However, you can wait a little. Here, James, Thomas, Peter, what is your name, open the door and let him in. There, get in, get in; I have a great deal to say to you.' And Ferdinand found that it was absolutely necessary to comply."

The autocratic old lady scattered good advice lavishly. To Henrietta it was: "Pretty women, my sweet child, should never be alone. Not that I was pretty, but I was always with pretty women, and at last the men began to think that I was pretty too."

To Ferdinand she offered: "I hear you are great friends with Count Thingabob; the Count whose grandfather I danced with seventy years ago. That is right; always have distinguished friends. Never have fools for friends; they are no use."

Count Mirabel now enters the story. Disraeli had become intimate with Alfred D'Orsay and actually stayed with him in 1837 in his cottage *orné* near Gore House, and to him this novel, of which he is a chief ornament, was dedicated. Dandyism had always had a fascination for Disraeli, he indulged in it himself, and in D'Orsay it was carried to a fine art. Lesser specimens of the breed may be merely contemptible, especially in an increasingly democratic world, but real art cannot be altogether despicable and D'Orsay was the perfect illustration of such adjectives as elegant, exquisite and sublime. He was intelligent and witty, he was also an artist in the true sense of the word, able to catch the subtleties of personality in his delicate portraits of his contemporaries, which included one of the young Disraeli. His *joie-de-vivre* is like a warm current exuding from the pages of *Henrietta Temple* and his light-hearted raillery sparkles like champagne. Disraeli was more concerned with these than with his dress, the Carlyles did fuller justice to his appearance. Carlyle called him the Phœbus Apollo of dandyism—"a tall fellow of six foot three, built like a tower, with floods of dark auburn hair, with a beauty, with an adornment unsurpassable on this planet". Jane Carlyle filled in the details: "A sky-blue satin cravat, yards of gold chain, white French gloves, light drab great-coat lined with velvet of the same colour, invisible inexpressibles, skin-coloured and fitting like a glove." She added that he came whirling to Cheyne Row in a chariot resplendent in sky-blue and silver, which "struck all Chelsea into mute amazement".

Gronow, another actual observer, said that D'Orsay driving in his tilbury looked like some gorgeous dragon-fly skimming through the air. Jane Carlyle was even more impressed when he came to call on her five years later, because he had had the subtlety of taste to tone down his humming-bird colours to a sober richness more suited to a maturer age. This time he was all in black and brown, enhanced by one breast-pin consisting of a magnificent pear-shaped pearl set in a cup of diamonds. His hostess wrote with discerning appreciation: "Well! That man understood his trade; if it be but that of a dandy, nobody can deny that he is a perfect master of it. A bungler would have made no allowance for five more years at his time of life."

D'Orsay was the *grande finale* of dandyism. The cult had almost outlived the conditions that bred it; the privileged aristocracy which, at its best, achieved the fine flower of personality preserved for us in the portraits of Reynolds and Gainsborough, was now being slowly forced from its exclusive upper air down to common earth. In Disraeli's and Thackeray's novels we have embalmed some of the last of the exquisites, the eccentrics and the autocrats who still carried on the eighteenth-century traditions of the days before the cry of liberty, equality and fraternity first shook the old civilisation; now their charmed circle had been breached. Lord Monmouth in *Coningsby*, leaving England after the Reform Bill, said to his grandson: "Goodbye, my dear Harry, I am going abroad again. I cannot remain in this radical-ridden country. Remember, though I am away, Monmouth House is your home—at least as long as it belongs to me. I understand my tailor has turned Liberal and is going to stand for one of the metropolitan districts; a friend of Lord Durham; perhaps I shall find him in it when I return."

By the eighteen-thirties dandyism was a cultured rather than a natural efflorescence, young men who aspired to excel in it conformed to a code. The hero of Bulwer's *Pelham* composed some maxims for their guidance which throw an interesting light on the art of dress. Amongst them are these:

"Never in your dress altogether desert that taste which is general. The world considers eccentricity in great things genius, in small things folly."

"Keep the mind free from all violent affections at the hour of the toilet. A philosophic serenity is perfectly necessary to success. A man must be a profound calculator to be a consummate dresser."

"One must not dress the same whether one goes to a minister or a mistress, an avaricious uncle or an ostentatious cousin. There is no diplomacy more subtle than that of dress."

"Dress so that it may never be said of you 'What a well-dressed man!'—but 'What a gentleman-like man!'"

Disraeli had already shown such rules in practice in the person of Annesley in *The Young Duke*, in whom he drew a type well: "Charles Annesley could hardly be called a dandy or a beau. There was nothing in his dress, though some mysterious arrangement in his costume, some rare simplicity, some curious happiness, always made it distinguished. . . . His little house in Mayfair, his horses, his moderate stud at Melton, were all unique, and everything connected with him was unparalleled for its elegance, its invention, its refinement. But his manner was his magic. His natural and subdued nonchalance, so different from the assumed non-emotion of a mere dandy; his coldness of heart, which was hereditary, not acquired; his cautious courage, his unadulterated self-love, had permitted him to mingle much with mankind without being too deeply involved in the play of their passions. . . . All feared, many admired, none hated him. He was too powerful not to dread, too dexterous not to admire, too superior to hate."

D'Orsay in *Henrietta Temple* is a more human and warm-hearted study because it was drawn from the man himself; Disraeli was no longer limited to types. This extraordinary being, born in Paris in 1801, was the son of a general in Napoleon's imperial army, whose father had bought the title of Count D'Orsay; but his grandmother was the supreme influence in Alfred D'Orsay's early life. This remarkable woman, the illegitimate daughter of the Duke of Wurtemberg and an Italian dancer, married a wealthy Englishman, Quintin Craufurd, who was involved in the plot for the escape of Louis XVI and Marie Antoinette which ended disastrously at Varennes. After Waterloo the Craufurds were again established in Paris and Madame was ambitious and lavish in launching her grandchildren upon society. Alfred D'Orsay was for a time an officer in the Garde Royale—equipped with a sumptuous dressing-case, gold plate and gold-mounted harness for his horses—and his sister, at seventeen, married the Duc de Guiches. In 1822 Lord and Lady Blessington came to Paris, and then began the long association between Lady Blessington and D'Orsay the nature of which is still a mystery, in spite of various conjectures. D'Orsay became an indispensable member of the Blessington circle, described as the Blessington Circus by a contemporary who watched the long procession of laden carriages set out from Paris to convey the magnificent ménage to Italy.

At Naples young D'Orsay lived with the Blessingtons in a palace overlooking the bay. It was resplendent with rare marbles and doors of oriental alabaster, and the five reception salons, the billiard-room, the suites of bed- and dressing-rooms, and even the private chapel and sacristy, were sumptuously furnished. Rich rose-coloured carpets set the tone of warm luxury, and, as in all Lady Blessington's houses, the rooms were full of rare and precious *objets d'art*. A year later when his only son died, Lord Blessington made a codicil to his will providing that, on marriage to one of his daughters (then eleven and twelve), Count Alfred D'Orsay should inherit the Blessington estates and fortune, subject to an annuity for the Countess. The elder daughter was illegitimate, the younger the child of a former wife. After Lord Blessington's death the younger girl, Harriet Gardiner, aged only fifteen, was duly married to D'Orsay in Naples, but Lady Blessington is said to have insisted that the marriage should not be consummated for four years. D'Orsay took little interest in his pale, unresponsive and somewhat sulky bride, and he scarcely noticed when she grew into an attractive young woman with a will of her own. Other men were not so impervious to Harriet's charms and eventually she left her husband, probably to the relief of both, but neither D'Orsay nor Lady Blessington could escape some social censure for their part in this unpleasing story.

In 1830 Lady Blessington transplanted her ménage to London, where she presided over an establishment which was a triumph of gorgeous artistry at Seamore Place, and afterwards at Gore House, and received most men of fashion and fame, although their ladies cold-shouldered her. Disraeli was a frequent visitor and some of the splendid interiors in his novels may well have been modelled on Lady Blessington's salons, for which D'Orsay designed the tasteful décor to set off the many precious treasures, such as the two superb vases in royal-blue Sèvres, mounted in ormulu and bearing five-branch lily candelabra, which had belonged to Marie Antoinette, and the gold étui of Madame de Sevigné, set with agates and brilliants. Disraeli stayed at Gore House while he was writing *Venetia* and called Lady Blessington his heroine's godmother. Here he could peacock it to his heart's content in the perfect setting, and he has been described as lounging elegantly in one of the salons with the last rays of the sun reflected from the gold flowers of his fine waistcoat, gold chains round his neck and in his hand a white cane with a black cord and tassel. Money troubles beset both Lady Blessington and D'Orsay, but she turned to writing novels and also edited some of the popular albums and *de luxe* annuals which were to be found in every drawing-room, while he relied upon his luck and skill at the gaming-table.

D'Orsay was now at the zenith of his reign in the world of fashion. His biographer, Michael Sadleir, writes of him in these years (1832–41): "His horsemanship was a virtuosity, his clothes an intoxication; his sangfroid at the gaming-table, his wit and unfailing good temper in the dining-room, smoking-room or paddock were irresistible. Never has a man established a more complete mastery over the minds of gilded youth than did D'Orsay in his nine years of social despotism." It is sad to record that at last his creditors overtook him. He dared not leave Gore House except by night. Once an ingenious sheriff's officer entered the house dressed as a pastrycook's boy, carrying a tray of tarts, and burst into the Count's room to arrest him. D'Orsay asked for time to dress suitably, prolonged his toilet until sunset and then suavely pointed out that after this hour the writ was no longer valid. He was, however, forced to fly to France. He rented a studio in Paris and made a bust of Lamartine, while hoping that Napoleon III would give him an appointment. When at last he was given the newly-created post of Director of Fine Arts the recognition came too late; his mind and powers were failing, he could not grasp the opportunity which, had it come earlier, might have made him a man of distinction in the world of art. He died within a year of the appointment, aged fifty-one. He and Lady Blessington lie together under the stone pyramid of the mausoleum he designed for her.

Ferdinand Armine first met Count Mirabel at a dinner given by Mr. Bond Sharpe (drawn from Crockford) at which Ferdinand had condescended to show himself in return for a loan from his host. Mirabel came in with his shadow, Mr. Bevil, who was more successful in aping his model's dress than his manners:

"The Count Mirabel could talk at all times, and at all times well; Mr. Bevil never opened his mouth. Practised in the world the Count Mirabel was nevertheless the child of impulse, though a native grace and an intuitive knowledge of mankind made every word pleasing and every act appropriate. Mr. Bevil was all art, and he had not the talent to conceal it. The Count Mirabel was gay, careless, generous; Mr. Bevil was solemn, calculating and rather a screw. . . . His essence of high breeding was never to be astonished, and he never permitted himself to smile, except in the society of intimate friends."

Presently the Count asked Ferdinand if he was glad to be back in England and he replied that he hardly knew. "Then, by all means, rejoice," said the Count, "for if you are in doubt it is surely better to decide upon being pleased?" Lord Catchimwhocan growled that he thought England the most infernal country there ever was, and Mirabel took him up with great animation, cited various delights of life in England and concluded: "Of what, then, have you to complain?" Catchimwhocan replied "Oh! The damned climate." "On the contrary," said Mirabel, "it is the only good climate there is. In England you can go out every day, and at all hours; and then, to those who love variety, like myself, you are not sure of seeing the same sky every morning you rise, which, for my part, I think the greatest of all existing sources of ennui."

Ferdinand broke in, smiling, with "You reconcile me to my country, Count," and Mirabel replied: "Ah! You are a sensible man; but that dear Catch is always repeating nonsense which he hears from somebody else. To-morrow," he added in a low voice. "he will be for the climate."

The Count, who defied time and could not understand ill-health, from which he had never suffered, even for five minutes, and who settled everything disagreeable by dismissing it as a *bêtise*, elaborated his philosophy with gusto:

"The sun shines on all, every man can go to sleep: if you cannot ride a fine horse it is something to look upon one; if you have not a fine dinner, there is some amusement in a crust of bread and Gruyère. Feel slightly, think little, never plan, never brood. Take the world as you find it; enjoy everything. *Vive la bagatelle!*"

As he also defined his "few wants" as including a fine house, carriages, horses, a complete wardrobe, the best opera-box, the first cook and pocket-money, this carried little conviction. Another of the company remarked bitterly: "You are a lucky fellow, Mirabel. I have had horses, houses, carriages, opera-boxes and cooks, and I have had a great estate; but pocket-money I never could get. Pocket-money was the thing which always cost me the most to buy of all."

Ferdinand found it impossible to hug his misery in the company of his new friend, who burst in upon him radiantly—"the best-dressed man in London, fresh and gay as a bird, with not a care on his sparkling visage and his eye bright with bonhomie". When they drove down to Richmond together the Count enjoyed it as if he had never been there before. No doubt Disraeli had had the memorable experience of driving with D'Orsay, who handled the reins in faultless white gloves, scented with eau-de-cologne or eau-de-jasmin, in the most perfect cabriolet in town and behind a superb horse, while the small "tiger" alternately perched precariously on the footboard at the back and swung out in the air hanging on a strap. At Richmond there was a chance meeting with the Temples and Lord Montfort, who were inclined to be prejudiced against the famous dandy, but the Count, whose tact was the finest in the world, soon enchanted them, in fact they found that "his secret spell, after all, was perhaps that he was always natural".

Disraeli is at pains to show Mirabel as the confidant and friend of many young men in distress, priding himself on his ingenuity in dealing with their scrapes, but in the case of D'Orsay (and remembering Harriet) this seems to have been part of his careful build-up of his own character rather than genuine good-nature. Yet when Bond Sharpe has shown Ferdinand his magnificent gaming-house Disraeli makes the millionaire proprietor say to him with bitterness that although there is not a man in the room who is not his slave not one of them "if I were to break tomorrow, would walk down St. James'-street to serve me. Yes! There is one; there is the Count. He has a great and generous soul." Certainly Ferdinand had good reason to bless Mirabel's interest in his affairs. The Count soon set himself to work upon Henrietta's feelings by confiding to her his fear that his unhappy friend will one day commit suicide to put an end to the misery of unrequited love. Having begged a flower from her to cheer the poor wretch, he burst into Ferdinand's room, on his way to a dinner-party, as graceful as a Versailles Apollo:

"*Cher ami!* I cannot stop one minute. . . . I have done your business capitally. Here is a pretty flower! Who do you think gave it me? She did, pardy. . . . But I romanced at a fine rate for it. It is the only way with women. She thinks we have known each other since the Deluge. Do not betray me. But, my dear fellow, I cannot stop now. Only, mind, all is changed. Instead of being gay, and seeking her society, and amusing her, as we talked of last night, mind, suicide is the system. Tomorrow I will tell you all. . . . In the meantime enjoy your flower; and rest assured, that it is your own fault if you do not fling the good Montfort in a very fine ditch."

When Ferdinand was arrested at last and carried off to a spunging-house Mirabel was his first visitor and came in radiating high spirits:

"Armine, *mon ami! Mon cher!* Is this your friendship? To be in this cursed hole and not send for me! *C'est une mauvaise plaisanterie* to pretend that we are friends! How are you, good fellow, fine fellow, excellent Armine?" Then, having dismissed the waiter, "'My dear fellow,' continued the Count, twirling the prettiest cane in the world, 'this is a *bêtise* of you to be here and not send for me. Who has put you here?'"

Even the Count was a little staggered when he heard the amount of Ferdinand's debts, but still he was sure he could raise the money somehow, and when Ferdinand refused to let him canvass his friends, he exclaimed:

"But you cannot stop here. *Quel drôle appartement!* Before Charley Doricourt was in Parliament he was always in these sort of houses, but I got him out somehow or other; I managed it. Once I bought of the fellow five hundred dozen of champagne."

Mirabel insisted on dining with his friend, and the waiter, seeing that these were "two regular nobs", at once ordered green-pea soup, turbot, beefsteak, roast duck, boiled chicken and champagne in ice. After this even Ferdinand's spirits rose; Mirabel promised to dine with him every day until he could get him out, and meanwhile he offered to bring him a novel by Paul de Kock. When Ferdinand admitted that he had not read this author Mirabel was delighted:

"What a fortunate man to be arrested! Now you can read Paul de Kock! By Jove, you are the most lucky fellow I know. You see, you thought yourself very miserable in being arrested. 'Tis the finest thing in the world, for now you will read *Mon Voisin Raymond*. There are always two sides to a case."

Ferdinand, however, was unable to keep his thoughts from Henrietta, and presently he asked Mirabel when he supposed she would be married. The Count replied gaily: "When you please." Ferdinand begged him not to mock him and Mirabel was indignant:

" 'By Jove, I am quite serious!' he exclaimed. 'I am as certain that you will marry her as I am that we are in this damned spunging-house.'

" 'Nonsense!'

" 'The very finest sense in the world. If you will not marry her, I will myself, for I am resolved that good Montfort shall not. It shall never be said that I interfered without a result. Why, if she were to marry Montfort now, it would ruin my character. To marry Montfort after all my trouble: dining with that good Temple, and opening the mind of that little Grandison, and talking fine things to that good duchess; it would be failure.'

" 'What an odd fellow you are, Mirabell!'

" 'Of course! Would you have me like other people and not odd? We will drink *la belle Henriette!* Fill up! You will be my friend when you are married, eh? Mon Armine, excellent garçon! How we shall laugh some day; and then this dinner will be the best dinner we ever had!' "

At eleven o'clock, when all the rooms were locked up, Mirabel departed, humming *Vive la bagatelle*, went on to Crockford's, broke the bank three times and sent a note to Ferdinand to say that his debts should be paid before mid-day. Ferdinand, however, did not need Mirabel's generosity as Katherine Grandison, informed by Glastonbury, paid the debts, and at the same time announced her engagement to Lord Montfort, whom Henrietta had released. There was a fine dinner-party at the Temples' house in honour of both couples, and, as Henrietta had now become an even greater heiress than Katherine, Ferdinand's troubles were over. At the dinner Lady Bellair and Count Mirabel sat next to each other and she told him that she had danced a minuet with his grandfather at Versailles seventy years ago. He replied that this was well recollected in the family and the old lady congratulated him on a good lie. She continued:

" 'You must come and dine with me,' said Lady Bellair to Count Mirabel, 'because you talk well across a table. I want a man who talks well across a table. So few can do it without bellowing. I think you do it very well.'

" 'Naturally,' replied the Count. 'If I did not do it well, I should not do it at all.' "

Speaking of an old friend Lady Bellair explained:

" 'He was a great talker, but then he was the tyrant of conversation. Now, men were made to listen as well as to talk.'

" 'Without doubt,' said the Count; 'for Nature has given us two ears, but only one mouth.' "

One dialogue in this book is a good example of Disraeli's characterisation and style when he is content to be simple and direct, and evidently drawing from life. It occurs in the spunging-house. Ferdinand, being obviously a "swell", was naturally taken by the bailiff who arrested him to one of those boarding-houses in which imprisonment was gilded for those gentlemen whose friends were likely to pay not only their debts but the considerable expenses of board-residence. We have seen that this was provided on a lavish scale, including choice wines.

Ferdinand found himself in a room with barred windows and old-fashioned furniture and no means of occupation except a Hebrew Bible and a Racing Calendar. Soon he could bear the inactive solitude and silence no longer and he rang the bell. A waiter appeared and Ferdinand burst out:

" 'This place is intolerable to me,' said Armine. 'I really am quite sick of it. What can I do?'

"The waiter looked a little perplexed.

" 'I should like to go to gaol at once,' said Ferdinand.

" 'Lord, sir!' said the little waiter.

" 'Yes, I cannot bear this,' he continued: 'I shall go mad.'

" 'Don't you think your friends will call soon, sir!'

" 'I have no friends,' said Ferdinand. 'I hope nobody will call.'

" 'No friends!' said the little waiter, who began to think Ferdinand was not such a nob as he had imagined. 'Why, if you have no friends, sir, it would be best to go to the Fleet, I think.'

" 'By Jove, I think it would be better.'

" 'Master thinks your friends will call, I am sure.'

" 'Nobody knows I am here,' said Ferdinand.

" 'Oh!' said the little waiter, 'you want to let them know, do you, sir?'

" 'Anything sooner; I wish to conceal my disgrace.'

" 'O sir! You are not used to it; I daresay you never were nabbed before?'

" 'Certainly not.'

" 'There it is; if you will be patient, you will see everything go well.'

" 'Never, my good fellow; nothing can go well.'

" 'O sir! You are not used to it. A regular nob like you, nabbed for the first time, and for such a long figure, sir, sure not to be diddled. Never knowed such a thing yet. Friends sure to stump down, sir.'

" 'The greater the claim, the more difficulty in satisfying it, I should think,' said Ferdinand.

" 'Lord, no sir! You are not used to it. It is only poor devils nabbed for their fifties and hundreds that are ever done up. A nob was never nabbed for the sum you are, sir, and ever went to the wall. Trust my experience. I never knowed such a thing.'

"Ferdinand could scarcely refrain from a smile. Even the conversation of the little waiter was a relief to him.

" 'You see, sir,' continued that worthy, 'Morris and Levison would never have given you such a deuce of a tick unless they knowed your resources. Trust Morris and Levison for that. You done up, sir! A nob like you, that Morris and Levison have trusted for such a tick! Lord, sir! You don't know nothing about it. I could afford to give them fifteen shillings in the pound for their debt myself, and a good day's business too. Friends will stump down, sir, trust me.'

"'Well, it is some satisfaction for me to know that they will not, and that Morris and Levison will not get a farthing.'

"'Well, sir,' said the incredulous little functionary, 'when I find Morris and Levison lose two or three thousand pounds by a nob who is nabbed for the first time, I will pay the money myself, that is all I know.'"

It is interesting to compare Disraeli's spunging-house with the one described by Thackeray in *Vanity Fair* which is said to represent the same establishment. When Rawdon Crawley was arrested in the street for a long-standing debt he found himself in the hands of Mr. Moss, assistant officer to the Sheriff of Middlesex and himself the proprietor of a spunging-house, in which Colonel Crawley had already been a lodger more than once. Mr. Moss ushered him in with almost fatherly concern, suggesting a glass of something warm after his drive and promising him his old room, which had been kept aired for him by the best of company. In fact, the last occupant, Captain Famish of the Fiftieth Dragoons, had had a party of tip-top swells to visit him every night and punished Mr. Moss's champagne cruelly. The proud and genial proprietor then named some of the present residents, including various military and other gentlemen who knew a good glass of wine, and a Doctor of Divinity. He concluded: "And Mrs. Moss has a tably-dy-hoty at half-past five, and a little cards or music afterwards, when we shall be most happy to see you." Upon this he left Colonel Crawley to his reflections in a bedroom of tawdry and somewhat dirty splendour, in which the only sinister signs of his situation were the bars in the windows. Mr. Moss even provided a fine silver dressing-case for the use of gentlemen who were brought in with nothing but the clothes in which they had been arrested.

Dickens, too, provides his quota of spunging-houses. Mr. Pickwick was carried off to an establishment with barred windows, of which the door-posts were inscribed "Namby, Officer to the Sheriffs of London", but he did not stay there long. The scenes in the coffee-room, with its sanded floor and reek of stale tobacco smoke, distressed him. After a few hours in a private sitting-room he decided he would prefer the Fleet prison to this shabby-genteel boarding-house. Dickens's description of Mr. Solomon

Jacobs' establishment in Cursitor Street is more detailed (*Sketches by Boz*). When Mr. Gabriel Parsons called upon his friend Mr. Watkins Tottle there he was shown into a common-room which was partitioned off into boxes. The floor was unswept, the ceiling blackened by the flare of an oil-lamp, cigar ends were scattered about everywhere, and empty glasses and porter-pots bore witness to the frequency with which Mr. Solomon Jacobs' "guests" sought to drown their sorrows. In one of the boxes two men were playing cribbage, on a board which had been hacked out on the wooden table with a penknife and a two-pronged fork. In another a stout man was eating some dinner which his wife had brought to him in a basket. At the back of the room a young wife was weeping as she talked to her husband. The stout man's wife looked at the couple pityingly and remarked: "Poor creeturs! Ah! When they've seen as much trouble as I and my old man here, they'll be as comfortable under it as we are."

Mr. Watkins Tottle soon rescued his friend from this company, leading him to the front drawing-room, where "rich debtors did the luxurious at the rate of a couple of guineas a day".

It was not until 1869 that the Debtors' Act abolished imprisonment for debt. In one of his election campaigns Disraeli was openly accused of seeking a seat in Parliament in order to avoid arrest for his debts.

CHAPTER VI

Venetia

DISRAELI wrote *Venetia* (1837) in a few months when he was in urgent need of money, in fact he was obliged to stay in seclusion at his father's house in order to avoid arrest for pressing debts. In these circumstances it occurred to him to make use of his special knowledge of Byron as the foundation of a saleable novel. Byron had died in 1824 but the Byronic cult did not die with him. Despite the influence of D'Orsay there were still young men who preferred the open-necked shirt to the elegant cravat and affected a manner that was moody and aloof, like Lord Cadurcis in *Venetia* when, standing apart, haughty and melancholy, he "impressed everyone with an idea that some superior being had, as a punishment, been obliged to visit their humble globe". Disraeli gives an amusing illustration of this type as Apollo, in his sketch *Ixion in Heaven*:

" 'All about Greece interests me,' said Apollo, who, although handsome, was a somewhat melancholy, lack-a-daisical personage, with his shirt collar thrown open, and his long curls theatrically arranged. 'All about Greece interests me. I always consider Greece my peculiar property. My best poems were written at Delphi. I travelled in Greece when I was young. I envy mankind.'

" 'Indeed!' said Ixion.

" 'Yes: they at least can look forward to a termination of the ennui of existence, but for us Celestials there is no prospect. Say what they like, immortality is a bore.'

" 'You eat nothing, Apollo,' said Ceres.

" 'Nor drink,' said Neptune.

" 'To eat, to drink, what is it but to live; and what is life but death, if death be that which all men deem it, a thing insufferable, and to be shunned. I refresh myself only with soda water and biscuits. Ganymede, bring some.'

"Now, although the *cuisine* of Olympus was considered perfect, the forlorn poet had unfortunately fixed upon the only two articles which were not comprised in its cellar or larder. In Heaven there was neither soda water nor biscuits. A great confusion consequently ensued; but at length the bard, whose love of fame was only equalled by his horror of getting fat, consoled himself with a swan stuffed with truffles, and a bottle of strong Tenedos wine.

" 'What do you think of Homer?' enquired Minerva of Apollo. 'Is he not delightful?'

" 'If you think so.'

" 'Nay, I am desirous of your opinion.'

" 'Then you should not have given me yours, for your taste is too fine for me to dare to differ with it.'

" 'I have suspected for some time that you are rather a heretic.'

" 'Why, the truth is,' replied Apollo, playing with his rings, 'I do not think much of Homer. Homer was not esteemed in his own age, and our contemporaries are generally our best judges. The fact is, there are very few people who are qualified to decide upon matters of taste. . . . But what is poetry, and what is criticism, and what is life? Air. And what is air? Do you know? I don't. All is mystery and all is gloom, and ever and anon from out the clouds a star breaks forth, and glitters, and that star is poetry.' "

There is a touch from real life here; Byron asked for hard biscuits and soda-water when dining with Rogers, whose cook was one of the most famous in London; the establishment could not produce them and he had to fall back upon potatoes mashed in vinegar.

Disraeli himself was not above an occasional Byronic gesture of cool affectation. In Malta, when he was watching a rackets match and the ball fell at his feet, he picked it up distastefully and handed it to a stiff young rifleman sitting beside him for return to the court, remarking that he had really never thrown a ball in his life. The military messes soon buzzed with this story and Disraeli wrote complacently to his father: 'Affectation succeeds better here than wit.''

There is no record of any actual meeting between Byron and Disraeli but the poet had always been regarded with admiration, and even affection, in Isaac D'Israeli's house, and his son had some curious links with him. In Switzerland he sought out

Byron's boatman, Maurice, on the Lake of Geneva and went out with him in a rowing-boat several times. In the same year his friend Clay, who joined him in his travels, found Tita, Byron's Greek valet, living from hand to mouth in Malta and took him into his own service. This hero had first been Byron's gondolier in Venice, but Shelley recorded that he once valeted him and that he was the most good-natured looking fellow he ever saw, despite his prodigious black beard and the fact that he had stabbed two or three people. Disraeli wrote of him from Malta: "Byron died in his arms, and his moustachios touch the earth. Withal as mild as a lamb, though he has two daggers always about his person." Tita had achieved his own little niche in fame through a couple of lines in *Don Juan*:

> "Battista, though (a name call'd shortly Tita)
> Was lost by getting at some acqua vita"

The two young men took Tita to the Levant with them, after which Disraeli brought him back to Bradenham, where employment was found for him and he married the housekeeper. On Isaac D'Israeli's death Disraeli obtained a place for him as a messenger at the Board of Control, and in 1875 he wrote personally to Queen Victoria to recommend Tita's widow for a pension. No doubt Tita was a piece of living romance after Disraeli's own heart, but how far he drew on his reminiscences for *Venetia* is unknown.

When Disraeli was writing the book it was only twelve years since Byron's death and he felt that he would have a freer hand if he transferred his fictional Byron wholly to the eighteenth century, and he similarly transplanted Shelley, who appears in the novel as Marminon Herbert. In both cases the actual facts of their lives are changed, in Shelley's to a startling extent, as in this story his republican principles lead him to offer his services to the American colonists in the War of Independence and he is introduced as a distinguished and victorious general! Disraeli also gives him a wife who seems to be partly modelled on Lady Byron; Lady Annabel Herbert in *Venetia* is intelligent, highly educated, by disposition religious and inclined to conventional views and behaviour, a woman of strong character. All this fits Lady Byron, who was called Annabelle, but Disraeli does not endow his Lady

Annabel with her namesake's gift for mathematics, which led Byron to write of her as the Princess of Parallelograms. Disraeli, in fact, used his models more for character building than for the events of his story; some of Byron's circumstances are transferred to Lord Cadurcis, but the latter is spared Byron's club-foot and, although this weakens his motive for asserting his superiority on every possible occasion, the reader appreciates the delicate restraint on the author's part. Despite the confusion of facts, once the plot of the novel has been accepted as almost pure fiction its drama can be enjoyed in its own right.

The story opens at Cherbury, a country house belonging to Marmion Herbert, where Lady Annabel Herbert and her lovely little daughter Venetia were living in extreme seclusion. There is an idyllic quality about Cherbury, with its ivy-grown walls, turreted gables, clusters of tall chimneys, chapel and clocktower, set in a park surrounded by a crescent of fine woods. Deer browsed in the park, peacocks strutted on the terrace, pigeons sunned themselves on the roof, and a fountain hedged with honeysuckle plashed gently in front of the house. Here the accomplished and still beautiful young mother devoted herself entirely to the education of her daughter, and for recreation they walked in the park, attended by Lady Annabel's faithful maid and a groom leading Miss Herbert's donkey. Their only visitor was Dr. Masham, an old friend whom Marmion Herbert had appointed vicar of the parish in which Cherbury, although far from the church, was included. Dr. Masham has points in common with Dr. Grant in *Mansfield Park*; he does not boast a Moor Park apricot, but his red-brick house, shaded by great elms, is covered by a famous vine, his garden is stocked with fine fruit trees and his strawberries and cream are memorable; he also has a bowling green and a grotto. He is not quite so much interested in his food as Dr. Grant, but he can both eat and give a good dinner, the latter of the substantial type, with his housekeeper, Goody Blount, presiding from behind his chair, in lace cap and ruffles. The Doctor's library, however, was his chief pride, as he was a scholar of repute and had been a fellow of his Oxford college.

Cherbury and Marringhurst Vicarage were Venetia's whole world, and in this setting Disraeli pictures the child with delicacy and tenderness, and more true to life than he achieved in his boyhood sketches of Vivian Grey and Contarini Fleming. There was one cloud in Venetia's otherwise sunny sky, she did not know if she had a father, and she realised very early that this was a delicate subject. Then one day she saw an opening to ask a question. Lady Annabel had heard that a neighbouring Abbey, long deserted and somewhat ruinous, was to be inhabited again, by a Mrs. Cadurcis and her son, little Lord Cadurcis, who had lately succeeded to the title but not to a corresponding income. Mrs. Cadurcis was a widow and Lady Annabel commented on this to Dr. Masham, who was eating his Sunday dinner with her:

" 'Poor woman,' said Lady Annabel, 'I hope her child is her consolation.'

"Venetia had not spoken during this conversation, but she had listened to it very attentively. At length she said, 'Mamma, is not a widow a wife that has lost her husband?'

" 'You are right, my dear,' said Lady Annabel rather gravely.

"Venetia mused a moment and then replied, 'Pray, Mamma, are you a widow?'

" 'My dear little girl,' said Dr. Masham, 'go and give that beautiful peacock a pretty piece of cake.' "

Upon this the Doctor and Lady Annabel rose from the table. Venetia soon had something else to think about, when Mrs. Cadurcis and her son arrived at the Abbey and her mother's sympathy induced her to waive her strict rule of no visiting and no visitors in this case. It was not long before Lady Annabel realised that the relations between Mrs. Cadurcis and her son were very different from those between Venetia and herself. Here Disraeli was working on fact. Mrs. Byron was born a Gordon of Gight, an unruly family once described as "a dangerous breed of well-born brigands", and she was liable to fits of rage in which she threw anything that came to hand at her son and chased him round the house. Her small means limited her society and, although her thrift deserved credit, this was not a virtue to appeal to a high-spirited boy, for whom she was no match in intelligence, and whose sensitive pride was outraged by her lapses into vulgarity. In the scenes between mother and son in *Venetia* Disraeli's imagination served him well. There is a notable one when the pair made their first call at Cherbury. Lady Annabel noted with interest that Mrs. Cadurcis was a short, stout woman with a rubicund face, and that her dress was a mixture of the shabby and the tawdry. The boy, then about eleven years old, was pale and slender, with long curling black hair and large black eyes, his manner was shy and even a little sullen. After his mother had fussily exhorted him to make his bow he sat silent on the edge of his chair, the picture of dogged indifference. Mrs. Cadurcis always had her eye on him and nagged him about this or that, but he only curled his lip. Presently she spoke of the prospect of a lonely winter at the Abbey:

" 'My spirits are always dreadfully low. I only hope Plantagenet will behave well. If he goes into his tantrums at the Abbey, and particularly in winter, I hardly know what will become of me.'

" 'I am sure Lord Cadurcis will do everything to make the Abbey comfortable to you. Besides, it is but a short walk from Cherbury, and you must come often to see us.'

" 'Oh! Plantagenet can be good if he likes, I can assure you, Lady Annabel, and behave as properly as any little boy I know. Plantagenet, my dear, speak. Have not I always told you, when you pay a visit, that you should open your mouth now and then? I don't like chattering children,' added Mrs. Cadurcis, 'but I like them to answer when they are spoken to.'

" 'Nobody has spoken to me,' said Lord Cadurcis in a sullen tone.

" 'Plantagenet, my love!' said his mother in a solemn tone.

" 'Well, mother, what do you want?'

" 'Plantagenet, my love, you know you promised to be good.'

" 'Well, what have I done?'

" 'Lord Cadurcis,' said Lady Annabel, interfering, 'do you like to look at pictures?'

" 'Thank you,' replied the little Lord, in a more courteous tone, 'I like to be left alone.'

" 'Did you ever know such an odd child?' said Mrs. Cadurcis, 'and yet, Lady Annabel, you must not judge him by what you see. I do assure you he can behave, when he likes, as pretty as possible.'

" 'Pretty!' muttered the little Lord between his teeth.

Before long Mrs. Cadurcis found fault with the way the boy

was sitting—"'Plantagenet, my dear, I do insist on your behaving yourself. Sit like a man.'

"'I am not a man,' said Lord Cadurcis very quietly, 'I wish I were.'

"'Plantagenet!' said the mother, 'have I not always told you that you are never to answer me? It is not proper for children to answer! . . . Plantagenet, do you hear me?' exclaimed Mrs. Cadurcis, with a face reddening to scarlet, and almost menacing a move from her seat.

"'Yes, everybody hears you, Mrs. Cadurcis,' said the little Lord."

This was insult to injury and Mrs. Cadurcis did not take long to work herself up to violence and hysterics, with her son defending himself from her onslaught with Lady Annabel's worktable. Upon this scene Venetia entered; Lord Cadurcis was captivated by her fair hair and radiant face and the gentle way she spoke to him, and the children made friends while Lady Annabel attended to Mrs. Cadurcis.

After this Cadurcis spent more and more of his time at Cherbury, where he showed himself amenable and charming, and shared Venetia's lessons with her mother and Dr. Masham. Venetia confided to him the mystery of a wing of the house which was always kept locked, and he told her that once, when he was staying at Cherbury and could not sleep, he had gone out into the corridor and seen Lady Annabel go into the closed rooms with a candle.

At home Cadurcis' chief solace in winter was his own little room, where he could read in solitude. One day he found that his mother had forbidden the servants to light a fire there; he marched downstairs and announced that he intended to ask his guardian to send him to Eton at once. Mrs. Cadurcis said he should go to Eton when she thought proper, and another argument was opened:

"'I wish you would think it proper now, then, Ma'am.'

"'I won't be dictated to,' said Mrs. Cadurcis fiercely.

"'I was not dictating,' replied her son calmly.

"'You would if you could,' said his mother.

"'Time enough to find fault with me when I do, Ma'am.'

" 'There is enough to find fault with at all times, sir.'

" 'On which side, Mrs. Cadurcis?' enquired Plantagenet with a sneer.

" 'Don't aggravate me, Lord Cadurcis,' said his mother.

" 'How am I aggravating you, Ma'am?'

" 'I won't be answered,' said the mother.

" 'I prefer silence myself,' said the son."

The interchange went on until Mrs. Cadurcis, in an hysterical rage, rushed at the boy, and after some dodging about the room he delivered an ultimatum:

"Mother, I am in no humour for frolics. I moved out of your way that you might not strike me, because I have made up my mind that if you ever strike me again I will live with you no longer. Now I have given you warning; do what you please; I shall sit down in this chair and not move. If you strike me you know the consequences."

No sooner had he seated himself than Mrs. Cadurcis rushed at him and boxed his ears. Cadurcis went out of the room, quiet and expressionless, saddled his pony and rode away.

The story develops melodramatically. Cadurcis was befriended by some gipsies, and before he had been traced by Dr. Masham his mother had died from a heart attack brought on by rage and anxiety, and only the tender care of Lady Annabel and Venetia saved the boy's reason. In due course he was sent to Eton and in time he dropped correspondence with his Cherbury friends, who did not see him again until he was eighteen.

Meanwhile Venetia was haunted more and more by the mystery about her father, but an attempt to open the subject with her mother led to an estrangement of twenty-four hours which almost broke the girl's heart. At last, when her mother was away calling on Dr. Masham, she took a key she had seen in Lady Annabel's jewel-case, opened the forbidden door and passed into the closed rooms. Venetia found a large room richly furnished, and evidently as a bridal chamber, as there was a bed of which the hangings and curtains were of white satin, with a wreath of withered white roses below the canopy. On one wall was a picture covered with a curtain of green velvet. Trembling, she drew it back, and the harsh sound of the brass rings sliding on the rod in the deathly silence terrified her for a moment. Then she looked up and saw the full-length portrait of a man—"A man in the very spring of sunny youth, and of radiant beauty." The description which follows might be that of Shelley in his youth. The word "father" rose to Venetia's lips, and yet she could not speak it. Here Disraeli destroys the real drama of the moment by one of his typical grandiloquent passages:

"She looked around her with an eye glittering with unnatural fire, as if to supplicate some invisible and hovering spirit to her rescue, or that some floating and angelic chorus might warble the thrilling word whose expression seemed absolutely necessary to her existence. Her cheek is flushed, her eye wild and tremulous, the broad blue veins of her immaculate brow quivering and distended; her waving hair falls back over her forehead, and rustles like a wood before the storm. She seems a priestess in the convulsive throes of inspiration, and about to breathe the oracle."

Venetia mastered herself sufficiently to find a vellum-bound volume containing manuscript poems by Marmion Herbert, and amongst them was one with the title *On the Night our Daughter was Born*, which she learned by heart before she left the sacred room. It was, of course, a foregone conclusion that such an experience must end in brain-fever, the first of four almost fatal illnesses which the poor girl suffered in the course of her story. Venetia was nursed back to life by her devoted mother, and after her long illness she shrank from confessing her discovery. She did not know that she had betrayed herself in delirium, and that her mother had slashed the portrait, torn up the volume of poems, double locked the door and thrown the key down a well, frantically determined that her child should never again come under the fatal spell of Marmion Herbert's beauty.

The story is long and intricate, and the next notable scenes are those in which Cadurcis is shown in London society. He had revisited Cherbury and fallen in love with Venetia, and even cherished the hope—at eighteen—of settling down with her at the Abbey to a life of love in rural solitude, but Venetia was still obsessed by the idea of her father and she gently refused the love of her dear "brother" Plantagenet. Cadurcis then again passed out of her life for several years, during which he discovered his genius and became a famous poet and the idol of society.

This phase in the life of Cadurcis produces some of the liveliest scenes in the book. He was almost annexed by Lady Monteagle, a young woman but a great Whig hostess, who is drawn from Lady Caroline Lamb, the wife of the future Lord Melbourne, who in later life initiated Queen Victoria into her duties. Lady Caroline Lamb, adorable, capricious, unconventional and mentally unstable, fell a victim to Byron's melancholy beauty at first sight, as the well-known entries in her diary bear witness. After their first meeting she wrote: "Mad, bad and dangerous to know", and then, "That beautiful pale face is my fate." At the height of her infatuation she constantly sent him letters and presents by her fantastically dressed little page or dressed as a page herself to deliver them; she stood waiting in the rain to watch him come away from a ball, and once disguised herself as a carter, pretending to come from his beloved Newstead Abbey, in order to get admitted to his rooms. No wonder that Byron wrote wearily that the Turks, who lock up their women, are happier—"Give a woman a looking-glass and a few sugar-plums and she will be satisfied."

Disraeli first introduces Cadurcis in London as a subject of conversation between Lord and Lady Monteagle, in which their characters are admirably contrasted. Lady Monteagle told her husband that she was reading an advance copy of Cadurcis' latest poem, and he replied:

" 'Is it good?'

" 'Good! What crude questions you do always ask, Henry!' exclaimed Lady Monteagle. 'Good! Of course it is good. It is something better than good.'

" 'But I mean, is it as good as his other things? Will it make as much noise as his last thing?'

" 'Thing! Now, Henry, you know that if there be anything I dislike in the world, it is calling a poem a thing.'

" 'Well, my dear, you know I am no judge of poetry. But if you are pleased, I am quite content.' "

Cadurcis is shown at a dinner-party at Monteagle House, where two of his fellow-guests discuss him:

" 'Watch Cadurcis,' said Mr. Horace Pole to a fine lady. 'Does not he look sublime?'

" 'Show me him,' said the lady eagerly. 'I have never seen him yet; I am actually dying to know him. You know we have just come to town.'

" 'And have caught the raging epidemic, I see,' said Mr. Pole with a sneer. 'However, there is the marvellous young gentleman! Alone in a crowd, as he says in his last poem. Very interesting!'

" 'Wonderful creature!' exclaimed the dame.

" 'Charming!' said Mr. Pole. 'If you ask Lady Monteagle, she will introduce him to you, and then, perhaps, you will be fortunate enough to be handed to dinner by him.'

" 'Oh! How I should like it!'

" 'You must take care, however, not to eat; he cannot endure a woman who eats.'

" 'I never do,' said the lady simply, 'at least at dinner.'

" 'Ah! Then you will quite suit him; I daresay he will write a sonnet to you, and call you Thyrza.'

" 'I wish I could get him to write some lines in my book,' said the lady; 'Charles Fox has written some; he was staying with us in the autumn, and he has written an ode on my little dog.'

" 'How amiable!' said Mr. Pole, 'I daresay they are as good as his elegy on Mrs. Crewe's cat. But you must not talk of cats and dogs to Cadurcis. He is too exalted to commemorate any animal less sublime than a tiger or a barb.' "

The lady was fortunate in finding herself seated opposite to the hero of the hour at table, and he was actually in a genial mood, because he had just found that Dr. Masham, now a Bishop, was amongst the guests, and his heart was softened by childhood memories. The lady resolved to eat next to nothing, but Cadurcis gaily rallied her on her lack of appetite, helped himself to every dish and urged her to fortify herself for a party to Ranelagh after the dinner. Emboldened, she ventured to speak of her album and flatteringly explained how honoured, how happy she would be if—

" 'Oh, I shall be most happy,' said Lord Cadurcis, 'I really esteem your request quite an honour: you know I am only a literary amateur, and cannot pretend to vie with your real author.... The blues have quite excommunicated me. Never mind, I leave them to Miss Hannah More: but you are quite a different sort of person. What shall I write?'

" 'I must leave the subject to you,' said his gratified friend.

" 'Well, then,' said his Lordship, 'I daresay you have got a lap-dog or a broken fan; I don't think I could soar above them. I think that is about my tether.' "

Unfortunately for the lady a conversation with Dr. Masham after dinner, in which the good Bishop firmly but kindly discouraged his young friend's sudden eagerness to try his fate again with Venetia, depressed Lord Cadurcis, and when the ladies, heartened by the account of his affability at table, clustered round him they found him now sullen, sarcastic and even morose. This was no moment to proffer albums, and as for the proposed party to Ranelagh, his Lordship now declared that if he had to choose a punishment for his bitterest enemy it would be "the barbarous infliction of a promenade in that temple of ennui".

Cadurcis and Venetia soon met—a strange turn of fortune had brought her and her mother into London society—and he returned to his rooms to write a poem for her. Here there is a pleasing little touch which shows that Disraeli's imagination was not only concerned with the world of fame and fashion: he interpolates that Lord Cadurcis' coachman, accustomed to wait, often until five o'clock in the morning, outside Monteagle House, could scarcely believe his good fortune in being spared the usual trial of his patience.

Venetia was very much moved by the poem, particularly because it paid a tribute to her father (whom she now knew to be living and famous), to whose revolutionary views Cadurcis had become a convert. Lady Annabel, however, was now implacably prejudiced against Cadurcis; his poems—and not least their egotism—had shocked her, and she was convinced that if she married him Venetia would only suffer a disillusionment like her own. Accordingly she worked upon her daughter's feelings with practised skill until she exacted a promise from her that she would never marry without her mother's consent. Cadurcis, discouraged once again by Venetia, returned to his rooms in a black mood and the following characteristic scene occurred:

"He was soon at home, gave his horse to a servant, for he had left his groom behind, rushed into his library, tore up a letter of Lady Monteagle's with a demoniac glance, and rang his bell with such force that it broke. His valet, not unused to such ebullitions, immediately appeared.

" 'Has anything happened, Spalding?' said his lordship.

" 'Nothing particular, my Lord. Her Ladyship sent every day and called herself twice, but I told her Ladyship that you was in Yorkshire.'

" 'That was right. I saw a letter from her. When did it come?'

" 'It has been here several days, my Lord.'

" 'Mind, I am at home to nobody; I am not in town.'

"The valet bowed and disappeared. Cadurcis threw himself into an easy chair, stretched his legs, sighed, and then swore; then, suddenly starting up, he seized a mass of letters that were lying on the table and hurled them to the other end of the apartment, dashed several books to the ground, kicked down several chairs that were in his way, and began pacing the room with his usual troubled step; and so he continued until the shades of twilight entered his apartment. Then he pulled down the other bell-rope, and Mr. Spalding again appeared.

" 'Order posthorses for to-morrow,' said his Lordship.

" 'Where to, my Lord?'

" 'I don't know; order the horses.'

"Mr. Spalding again bowed and disappeared.

"In a few minutes he heard a great stamping and confusion in his master's apartment, and presently the door opened and his master's voice was heard calling him repeatedly in a very irritable tone.

" 'Why are there no bells in this cursed room?' enquired Lord Cadurcis.

" 'The ropes are broken, my Lord.'

" 'Why are they broken?'

" 'I can't say, my Lord.'

" 'I cannot leave this house for a day but I find everything in confusion. Bring me some Burgundy.' "

This is not the exaggeration it might seem; Byron, who inherited a demoniac temper from both sides of his family, did indulge in such exhibitions; on one occasion he flung a clock on to the floor and then ground it to pieces with a poker.

At this juncture Disraeli introduces Lady Caroline Lamb's visit to Byron disguised as a farm lad. Hearing that a youth from the Abbey was begging to see him, Cadurcis had an impulse of kindness, he would not like to go abroad, as he intended to do now, and leave anybody in trouble at the Abbey. The lad was shown in and Cadurcis spoke to him kindly:

" 'Well, my good fellow,' said Cadurcis, 'what do you want? Are you in any trouble?'

"The boy hesitated.

" 'Speak out, my good fellow; do not be alarmed. If I can serve you, or anyone at the Abbey, I will do it.'

"Here Mr. Spalding entered with the lights. The lad held a cotton handkerchief to his face; he appeared to be weeping; all that was seen of his head were his locks of red hair. He seemed a country lad, dressed in a long green coat with silver buttons, and he twirled in his disengaged hand a peasant's white hat.

" 'That will do, Spalding,' said Lord Cadurcis. 'Leave the room. Now, my good fellow, my time is precious; but speak out and do not be afraid.'

" 'Cadurcis!' said the lad in a sweet and trembling voice.

" 'Gertrude, by God!' exclaimed Lord Cadurcis, starting. 'What infernal masquerade is this?'

" 'Is it a greater disguise than I have to bear every hour of my life?' exclaimed Lady Monteagle, advancing. 'Have I not to bear a smiling face with a breaking heart?'

" 'By Jove! A scene!' exclaimed Cadurcis in a piteous tone.

" 'A scene!' exclaimed Lady Monteagle, bursting into a flood of indignant tears. 'Is this the way the expression of my feelings is ever to be stigmatised? Barbarous man!'

"Cadurcis stood with his back to the fireplace, with his lips compressed, and his hands under his coat-tails. He was resolved that nothing should induce him to utter a word. He looked the picture of dogged indifference.

" 'I know where you have been,' continued Lady Monteagle. 'You have been to Richmond; you have been with Miss Herbert.

Yes, I know all! I am a victim, but I will not be a dupe. Yorkshire indeed! Paltry coward!'

"Cadurcis hummed an air.

" 'And this is Lord Cadurcis!' continued the lady. 'The sublime, ethereal Lord Cadurcis, condescending to the last refuge of the meanest, most commonplace mind, a vulgar, wretched lie! You may delude the world, but I know you. And I will let everybody know you. I will tear away the veil of charlatanism with which you have enveloped yourself. The world shall at length discover the nature of the idol they have worshipped. All your meanness, all your falsehood, all your selfishness, all your baseness, shall be revealed. I may be spurned, but at any rate I will be revenged!'

"Lord Cadurcis yawned.

" 'Insulting, pitiful wretch!' continued the lady. 'And you think that I wish to hear you speak! You think the sound of that deceitful voice has any charm for me! You are mistaken, sir! . . . I am here to speak myself; to express to you the contempt, the detestation, the aversion, the scorn, the hatred which I entertain for you!'

"Lord Cadurcis whistled.

"The lady paused; she had effected the professed purport of her visit; she ought now to have retired, and Cadurcis would most willingly have opened the door for her, and bowed her out of his apartment. But her conduct did not exactly accord with her speech. She intimated no intention of moving. Her courteous friend retained his position, and adhered to his policy of silence. There was a dead pause, and then Lady Monteagle, throwing herself into a chair, went into hysterics.

"Lord Cadurcis, following her example, also seated himself, took up a book and began to read.

"The hysterics became fainter and fainter; they experienced all those gradations of convulsive noise with which Lord Cadurcis was so well acquainted; at length they subsided into sobs and sighs. Finally there was again silence, now only disturbed by the sound of a page turned by Lord Cadurcis.

"Suddenly the lady sprang from her seat, and firmly grasping the arm of Cadurcis, threw herself on her knees at his side.

" 'Cadurcis!' she exclaimed in a tender tone, 'do you love me?'

"'My dear Gertrude,' said Lord Cadurcis, coolly, but rather regretting he had quitted his original and less assailable posture, 'you know I like quiet women.'

"'Cadurcis, forgive me!' murmured the lady. 'Pity me! Think only how miserable I am!'

"'Your misery is of your own making,' said Lord Cadurcis. 'What occasion is there for any of these extraordinary proceedings? I have told you a thousand times that I cannot endure scenes. Female society is a relaxation to me; you convert it into torture. I like to sail upon a summer sea; and you always will insist upon a white squall.'

"'But you have deserted me!'

"'I never desert anyone,' replied Cadurcis calmly, raising her from her supplicating attitude and leading her to a seat. 'The last time we met you banished me your presence, and told me never to speak to you again. Well, I obeyed your orders, as I always do.'

"'But I did not mean what I said,' said Lady Monteagle.

"'How should I know that?' said Lord Cadurcis.

"'Your heart ought to have assured you,' said the lady.

"'The tongue is a less deceptive organ than the heart,' replied her companion.

"'Cadurcis,' said the lady, looking at her strange disguise, 'what do you advise me to do?'

"'To go home; and if you like I will order my vis-a-vis for you directly', and he rose from his seat to give the order.

"'Ah! You are sighing to get rid of me!' said the lady, in a reproachful but still subdued tone.

"'Why, the fact is, Gertrude, I prefer calling on you, to your calling on me. When I am fitted for your society, I seek it; and, when you are good-tempered, always with pleasure; when I am not in the mood for it, I stay here. And when I am at home, I wish to see no one. I have business now, and not very agreeable business. I am disturbed by many causes, and you could not have taken a step which could have given me greater annoyance than the strange one you have adopted this evening.'

"'I am sorry for it now,' said the lady, weeping. 'When shall I see you again?'

" 'I will call upon you to-morrow, and pray receive me with smiles.' "

Cadurcis could now afford to be kinder; he offered Lady Monteagle some refreshment, rallied "Mr. Gertrude" on her wig and handed her to his carriage.

Disraeli is not only concerned with the spectacular aspect of Byron; in analysing the character of Cadurcis he brings out other traits. His determination to dominate his circle is like that of Vivian Grey and Contarini Fleming; when the child Venetia says piteously, "O, Plantagenet, I hope they will be kind to you at Eton!" the boy replies, "I will make them." The real Byron, on whom Disraeli's schoolboy heroes may have been partly modelled, did not care to be second to anyone; when his friend Wildman planned the revolt against a new headmaster at Harrow he asked Byron to lead it, as the only way of ensuring his support. To return to Cadurcis, when he left Eton he quickly adapted himself to the society of his august Guardian's circle and made the impression he aimed at: "Naturally impatient of control, he endeavoured by his precocious manhood to secure the respect and independence which would scarcely have been paid or permitted to his years. From an early period he never permitted himself to be treated as a boy."

Other characteristics of Byron which are brought out in Cadurcis are sensibility, a latent vein of tenderness and a capacity for gaiety when in a happy mood. His moods are accounted for by the fact that he "ever magnified both misery and delight with all the creative power of a brooding imagination".

After the London scenes in *Venetia* Disraeli transplanted all his characters, including Marmion Herbert, to Italy. Cadurcis left England in disgust after he had had to fight a duel with Lord Monteagle (here there is no foundation in fact) and wounded him severely. A slanderous version of his affair with Lady Monteagle was generally accepted and public opinion turned violently against him. In Italy Cadurcis and Venetia were brought together again and, after various dramatic episodes, Marmion Herbert was reconciled to his wife.

The portrait of Shelley, as Marmion Herbert, is both less true to fact and less living than that of Byron as Cadurcis, although it has considerable charm. Actually Shelley was three years younger than Byron but in this novel he is represented as already in middle age, while Cadurcis is still a young man. Worn alike by his revolutionary philosophy and his life of great action in the American War of Independence, Marmion Herbert was now chastened in spirit, and he confessed to Cadurcis: "Mine were but crude dreams. I wished to see man noble and happy; but if he will persist in being vile and miserable, I must even be content. I can struggle for him no more." Yet when Cadurcis agreed too readily that men have always been fools and slaves, and fools and slaves they will always be, the tired idealist was up in arms at once, declaring that he still had faith in a great and glorious future for mankind, although he did not now expect to live to see it. Herbert, in fact, was now ready to surrender to the soft enchantment of domestication, which in his youth he had been unable to endure, and again he made Cadurcis his confidant: "Once I sacrificed my happiness to my philosophy, and now I have sacrificed my philosophy to my happiness." He did not obtrude his heretical views on his wife and she was upheld by a secret hope that in time, under the influence of herself and their child, he might come to feel the grace of God and be a worshipping Christian. In this happy interlude Herbert, with his richly cultured mind, poured forth "a flood of fine fancies and deep intelligence", to the delight of his wife and daughter. Disraeli does not shrink from reproducing these flights of eloquence and from such a flood it is impossible to isolate passages of reasonable length, but Herbert's reflections on life, death and literature have considerable interest, and Cadurcis contributes a spice of humour to the dialogue. When the two poets were discussing infinite possibility Herbert exclaimed:

"Why should we be surprised that the nature of man should change? Is not change the law of nature? My skin changes every year, my hair never belongs to me a month, the nail on my hand is only a passing possession. I doubt whether a man at fifty is the same material being that he was at twenty-five.'

" 'I wonder,' said Lord Cadurcis, 'if a creditor brought an action against you at fifty for goods delivered at five-and-twenty, one could set up the want of identity as a plea in bar. It would be a consolation to an elderly gentleman.' "

In the happy atmosphere now established Venetia bloomed and expanded, and despite her excessive sensibility she showed something of the charm which Cadurcis found in her—"You always put me in mind of a violet, so fresh, sweet and delicate." His proposal of marriage was characteristic; after claiming that he had at heart been constant to her as boy, youth and man, he threatened her with dire consequences if she should refuse his love again: "But reject me, reject me, and I devote all my energies to the infernal gods; I will pour my lava over all the earth until all that remains of my fatal and exhausted nature is a black and barren cone surrounded by bitter desolation."

Venetia did not reject him this time but their love-story ended in a tragedy. Herbert and Cadurcis were drowned together when Herbert's yacht capsized in the Gulf of Spezia. Venetia, once more prostrated by a prolonged illness, returned to Cherbury with her mother, and here consolation was provided for her in the person of George Cadurcis, who had long been a faithful friend and was now the heir of his cousin, the late Lord Cadurcis. So Venetia became Lady Cadurcis after all, a neat *dénoûement*, but a strain on the reader's credulity.

Venetia suffers from having been written in a hurry, with creditors clamouring for payment and Disraeli's facile pen running on with no discriminating checks; some passages are even ridiculous, and there is all too little of his characteristic irony. One digression, about the British public in one of "its periodical fits of morality", is borrowed from Macaulay; parts of Herbert's share in the various dialogues are, quite excusably, taken from Shelley's *Discourse on the Manners of the Ancients*; there is a long quotation from *Don Quixote*. It was then quite a bold undertaking to adopt Shelley as a co-hero in a novel and show him as an idealist of the highest order. There is no doubt that Disraeli had caught something of that elusive spirit. He had met Trelawny, a friend of both Byron and Shelley, who had had the sad distinction of assisting at the burning of Shelley's body on the shore of Tuscany and may have talked to him about the poet's life and character.

There is romance, if somewhat artificial, and drama in the story of Venetia, and the opening chapters give us a picture of quiet beauty in Cherbury, and also a charming study of a childhood, such as was all too rare in the fiction of the period, and a surprising achievement for Disraeli, a bachelor of thirty-three.

After *Venetia* Disraeli wrote no more novels for seven years; when he turned to fiction again it was with a mind fully matured and with far more experience of the world at his command.

PART II
A TRILOGY ON POLITICS AND RELIGION

CHAPTER VII

Coningsby (I)

AFTER the general election of 1841, when the Conservatives at last won a decisive majority over the Whig government which had been responsible for the Reform Bill, Disraeli was passed over by Peel in forming his Ministry. He had made his mark as a brilliant speaker and been included in Peel's "shadow cabinet" while the party was in opposition, and his exclusion from office now seemed to him a public humiliation. He needed all his patience and perseverance to surmount this check to his political ambitions, but he was already used to fighting against odds, whether due to his race and lack of hereditary status or, as in some cases, of his own creation. At the very outset of his Parliamentary career he had had to live down the fiasco of his maiden speech, to which there is a poignant reference in *Coningsby:* "Music, artillery, the roar of cannon, and the blare of trumpets, may urge a man on to a forlorn hope; ambition, one's constituents, the hell of a previous failure, may prevail on one to do a more desperate thing—speak in the House of Commons." Now, after four years in Parliament, his disappointment was severe and wrung the heart of his devoted wife so cruelly that she herself wrote an agonised note to Peel on her husband's behalf, but without his knowledge. It was of no avail, and to those who study the debates of the preceding year dispassionately Peel's attitude is not surprising. Disraeli, always prone to take an independent line, had embarrassed his leader as often as he had supported him, and Peel liked to exercise an autocratic control over his party; wayward brilliance must have its lesson. So Disraeli, at thirty-seven, had still to wait for an opportunity that matched his ambition, but his life was to prove his own dictum that "patience is genius".

Disraeli had already been attracted to a little group of young men who had recently carried their Eton and Cambridge friendship into the House of Commons. Their leaders were the brilliant and erratic George Smythe, son of Lord Strangford, and the charming and idealistic Lord John Manners, son of the Duke of Rutland, youths to whom Eton, Cambridge and Parliament were a natural sequence, and who were Conservative by birth and breeding. Their most notable associate in the House was Alexander Baillie Cochrane, a young Scottish laird whom Disraeli described as "fiery and generous". Full of faith and fervour, eager to operate on what they considered a sick society, these young idealists were soon disgusted by Peel's caution and practical opportunism and correspondingly attracted by Disraeli's occasional fulminations against what he, too, believed to be an uninspired policy without any basic principle behind it. Disraeli, always sympathetic to promising youth (and this was gilded youth, too), and himself not too old to win their confidence, soon became the mentor of the group, and George Smythe gaily suggested that they might well call themselves the Diz-Union. Actually they became known as Young England, but it is not clear whether the name was originally used disparagingly or deliberately adopted by the group.

In the autumn of 1843 Disraeli and Smythe were both the guests of Henry Hope, a sympathiser, at Deepdene, and he suggested that Disraeli should embody the ideals of Young England in some literary form. This was the origin of *Coningsby*, the first of a trilogy of novels in which he dealt with the ferment of the period which opened with the Reform Bill from the political, social and religious points of view. Thus his unwelcome freedom from the cares of office bore fruit in three books which caused a furore in their own day and are still read for their lively political satire and as valuable commentaries on the political and social conditions of the period.

The trilogy—*Coningsby*, *Sybil* and *Tancred*—naturally shows an advance in maturity since the publication of *Henrietta Temple* and *Venetia* seven years earlier. Ambition is still a ruling passion in Harry Coningsby, but it is not so naked and unashamed as in Vivian Grey and Contarini Fleming, although he falls far short of the modesty of Endymion Ferrars (Disraeli's last hero), who actually blushed when betrayed into the confession that he would like to have power. We are on familiar ground when Coningsby's motive in life is described as "that noble ambition, the highest and the best... which will not let a man be content unless his intellectual power is recognised by his race, and desires that it should contribute to their welfare". He even out-soared Vivian Grey in the sublimity of his aim—"He was one of those who was not content with excelling in his own circle, if he thought there was one superior to it. Absolute not relative distinction, was his noble aim." Nevertheless, after admitting to a chosen friend that he preferred fame to life, Coningsby added that the consciousness of heroic deeds is even more to be desired than the most widespread celebrity, and he proved himself capable of sacrificing his ambition to principle and loyalty.

The transports of love are treated more realistically in these novels. When Ferdinand Armine first saw Henrietta Temple beads of perspiration gathered on his brow and a light foam on his lips. Egremont, the hero of *Sybil*, was subjected to a far more spectacular first sight of the heroine. Visiting the ruins of an ancient abbey (supposed to be Fountains) at sunset, he was gazing through an arch at the twilight star when he was startled by a voice of "almost supernatural sweetness" chanting an evening hymn. Presently an extremely beautiful young woman appeared for a moment framed in the starlit arch, but she passed swiftly out of sight, apparently without even seeing him. Ferdinand, no doubt, would have been completely unmanned, but Egremont neither sweated nor foamed, and had no prophetic inkling that he had met his fate, although the vision lingered in his mind with "a strange and sweet perplexity". True, he had already passed through the furnace of first love, but even then Disraeli spared him the fevered raptures Ferdinand endured, and the affair was dismissed with tonic common sense: "Happily 'tis the season of youth for which the first lessons of experience are destined; and, bitter and intolerable as is the first blight of our fresh feelings, the sanguine impulse of early life bears us along. Our first scrape usually leads to our first travel. Disappointment requires change of air; desperation change of scene. Egremont quitted his country never to return to it again and returned to it after a year and a half's absence a much wiser man."

We miss here the extravagance of Disraeli's youth, and with it some of the gusto which gave riotous vitality to *Vivian Grey* and *The Young Duke*. The heroes of the trilogy are more realistic than those of the earlier books, but Coningsby is somewhat colourless and almost a prig, and Egremont little more than an illustration of the regenerated aristocrat. Tancred in his first phase is a charming young visionary whose human nature betrays him, but his individuality develops little in the gorgeous and tumultuous scenes of his Eastern adventure. On the other hand, the minor characters are better than ever. Disraeli himself said that the comic characters in *Vivian Grey* were caricatures, now he draws them with a surer touch. The toadies of *Vivian Grey*, for instance, have a successor in Captain Grouse of *Sybil*, whose nature and position are admirably developed. Acting as a kind of aide-de-camp to the Earl of Marney, he "killed birds and carved them; played billiards with him and lost; had, indeed, every accomplishment that could please woman or ease man; could sing, dance, draw, make artificial flies, break horses, exercise a supervision over stewards and bailiffs, and make everybody comfortable by taking everything on his own shoulders".

When Lord Marney was in a mood for argument Captain Grouse allowed himself to be overpowered, but not too soon, as "he was well aware that his noble friend's passion for controversy was equal to his love of conquest". He showed similar tact when playing chess with the earl. He was never at a loss. In the awkward period in the drawing-room before dinner was announced he occupied himself in teaching Lady Marney's spaniel to beg with a zeal which almost amounted to enthusiasm. When he indulged himself in a day off-duty, in order to play for Marney in a cricket-match, Lord Marney regarded his absence from dinner as "a cursed bore" which Grouse should not have inflicted upon him.

Coningsby opens with a promising scene which enlists the reader's interest for the young hero, but the political motive is soon introduced and the agitation for the Reform Bill of 1832 is a constant background to the first part of the story. In setting the stage for this political drama Disraeli gives a masterly analysis of the state of the country in the period after the twenty years of intermittent war with France had come to an end at Waterloo: "Now commenced that condition of England question, of which our generation hears so much. During five-and-twenty years every influence that can develop the energies and resources of a nation had been acting with concentrated stimulation on the British Isles. National peril and national glory; the perpetual menace of invasion, the continual triumph of conquest; the most extensive foreign commerce that was ever conducted by a single nation; an illimitable currency; an internal trade supported by swarming millions, whom manufactures and inclosure bills called into existence; above all, the supreme control obtained by man over mechanical power; these are some of the causes of that rapid advance in material civilisation in England, to which the annals of the world can afford no parallel. But there was no proportionate advance in our moral civilisation. In the hurry-skurry of money-making, men-making and machine-making, we had altogether outgrown, not the spirit, but the organisation of our institutions.

"The peace came; the stimulating influences suddenly ceased; the people, in a novel and painful position, found themselves without guides. They went to the Ministry; they asked to be guided; they asked to be governed; trade required a currency; the unfranchised subject solicited his equal privilege; suffering labour clamoured for its rights; a new race demanded education. What did the Ministry do?"

The answer to that question, with Disraeli's commentary and the alternative solutions he had to offer, form the social-political backbone of *Coningsby* and *Sybil*. Many passages are tedious to the reader of today who is not a student of the inner history of politics, but all can appreciate the shrewd character-sketches of such leading statesmen as Peel and the Duke of Wellington, and the tension of the Reform Bill drama lives again in Disraeli's pages. To appreciate this it is necessary to bear in mind the outline of the story. In 1831 Lord Grey and Lord John Russell, the leaders of the Whig party, proposed that "rotten" and "pocket" boroughs should be abolished and seats given to large, hitherto unrepresented towns, such as Manchester and Birmingham. At the same time the franchise was to be extended to those who paid a rent of £50 in the country and £10 in the towns. The Bill only passed its second reading in the House of Commons by one vote. This was the occasion of which Macaulay wrote: "It was like seeing Cæsar stabbed in the Senate House, or seeing Oliver taking the mace from the table; a sight to be seen only once and never to be forgotten. . . .

You might have heard a pin drop as Duncannon read the numbers. Then again the shouts broke out and many of us shed tears. I could scarcely refrain. And the jaw of Peel fell; and the face of Twiss was as the face of a damned soul; and Herries looked like Judas taking his necktie off for the last operation. We shook hands, clapped each other on the back, and went out laughing, crying and huzzaing into the lobby." The Bill was, however, defeated in committee. Parliament was then dissolved, and a general election brought the Whigs back with increased strength. The Bill now passed triumphantly through its three readings in the Commons, but was thrown out by the Lords. Lord Grey resigned and the King asked the Duke of Wellington to form a Tory government. By now feeling ran high in the country; the Iron Duke was pulled from his horse in the street and the windows of his house were smashed. Birmingham was placarded: "No taxes paid here until the Reform Bill is passed"; in Nottingham the castle was burned down, and in Bristol the Mansion House, the prison and the bishop's palace. Eventually the King asked Lord Grey to return to office, but he refused to do so without a promise that, if necessary, His Majesty would create enough new peers to pass the Bill through the House of Lords. When the King hesitated London broke out into a rash of placards proclaiming; "More Lords or none!" The promise was given and the Bill was again passed through the Commons and sent up to the Lords. It was not, however, necessary to create new peers, as the Duke of Wellington and many of his Tory colleagues undertook to abstain from voting. The Reform Bill became law in 1832.

Disraeli passes in brief review the years between Waterloo and the Reform Bill, and even if some of his facts are of less interest now than they were to his own generation, the writing is often brilliant. It was, for instance, an impish inspiration to call Lord Liverpool, a Prime Minister who presided over a Cabinet of abler but ill-assorted men, the Arch-Mediocrity. Disraeli dismisses him trenchantly: "He was peremptory in little questions, and great ones he left open." He admits that various "ameliorating" Acts were passed by Liverpool's government, but, in Disraeli's opinion, this Cabinet of brilliant elements (Canning, Peel, Huskisson) might have effected settlements in Ireland, raised the condition of the English people and "adjusted the rights and properties of our national industries in a manner which would have prevented that fierce and fatal rivalry that is now disturbing every hearth of the United Kingdom". Instead, he considered that their lack of action on clear principles made inevitable the rise of a new force in the country—AGITATION.

All this was preparing the ground for the challenge of the Young England group in Parliament, and their attempt to imbue the supine Conservative party with active principles. Harry Coningsby himself is supposed to represent George Smythe, although the circumstances of his life have little in common with those of Smythe's, and even his character is not a close parallel. Coningsby is a little too insipid and also too well-balanced for the brilliant, provocative and wayward Smythe, of whom Disraeli said that he was the only man who never bored him. He is drawn again in *Endymion*, as Waldershare, and that portrait is both more lively and more exact, with its attractive eccentricity. Some keys give Lord Lyttelton as the original of Coningsby, but it is perhaps best to regard the hero of the novel as a composite portrait, playing Smythe's leading rôle in Young England but also embodying some of the spirit and ideals of Disraeli himself. The charming character of Lord Henry Sydney, representing Lord John Manners, is far more true to life. Cochrane is represented by Sir Charles Buckhurst.

The personal story of Harry Coningsby is the cement which holds the book together. He was the grandson of Lord Monmouth, a nobleman of vast wealth, polished acumen and indomitable will, who could wield a great influence when he chose, or was goaded, to give himself the trouble to do so. The family was famous for its hatreds and Lord Monmouth had cast off his elder son. When the younger son married against his father's will he was persecuted rather than ignored until, forced to fly from his creditors, he died of fever abroad. His penniless widow had no resource but to apply to Lord Monmouth for support for herself and her only child, Harry Coningsby. Lord Monmouth delivered an ultimatum: if she would give up the child and live in a remote part of England she should be provided with an income of £300 a year, on which her father-in-law—"the shrewdest accountant in England"—

calculated that a lone widow could live with bare decency in Westmorland. Lord Monmouth did not care to see his grandson, but the boy was sent to a homely country school kept by a clergyman, and the poor mother tried to keep her memory alive in his heart by affectionate letters, until her death when the boy was only nine.

Harry Coningsby owed a great change in his life to the fact that Mr. Rigby, a gentleman who had insinuated himself into Lord Monmouth's confidence (although that shrewd nobleman was by no means his dupe) and managed many affairs for him, saw in the boy a further opportunity to increase his own standing in the world. He liked the idea of speaking of Lord Monmouth's grandson as his charge, and his patron made no objection when he proposed to move the boy to a fashionable preparatory school, from which in due course he went to Eton.

Coningsby, a handsome, clever boy with a generous spirit, benefited by the change, but he could not look to Rigby for any fatherly guidance, much less tenderness. Rigby is a masterly portrait of the genus described by Disraeli as "that fungous tribe", men who attached themselves to the powerful noblemen of the day by their assiduity in making themselves useful. He is on a higher plane than Captain Grouse, as he was himself a Member of Parliament, had even held a minor office in a Tory government, and had also won some reputation as the author of "slashing" political articles. This was the climax of a career of pertinacious climbing and he then "set up to be the perfect man of business". He succeeded in this rôle too: "The world took him at his word, for he was bold, acute and voluble: with no thought, but a good deal of desultory information; and though destitute of all imagination and noble sentiment, was blessed with a vigorous, mendacious fancy, fruitful in small expedients, and never happier than when devising shifts for great men's scrapes."

In the course of time Rigby met Lord Monmouth, who soon appraised his quality:

"He was just the animal that Lord Monmouth wanted, for Lord Monmouth always looked upon human nature with the callous eye of a jockey. He surveyed Rigby and he determined to buy him. He bought him; with his clear head, his indefatigable industry, his audacious tongue, and his ready and unscrupulous pen; with all his dates, all his lampoons; all his private memoirs, and all his political intrigues. It was a good purchase. Rigby became a great personage, and Lord Monmouth's man."

Rigby was indeed happy and busy, not least in the prestige he acquired with his party through his control of Lord Monmouth's Parliamentary boroughs, which enabled him to guarantee twelve votes in the House of Commons and occasionally provide a seat for some official who had unexpectedly lost his.

Disraeli's contemporaries, including the victim, at once identified Rigby with John Wilson Croker. Disraeli himself, always chary of admitting that he drew directly from life, professed to see no reason why Croker should "assume that a character in one of my books, which he deemed odious, was intended for himself". Nevertheless, he found it embarrassing when Croker was placed next to him at a political dinner, and was relieved that he behaved like a man of the world, spoke of his friendship with Isaac D'Israeli and made himself generally agreeable. The story has a somewhat pitiful conclusion. Evidently the caricature rankled, and Croker's mind reverted to it in his last illness, when he wrote to Lord Strangford that he had never been able to discover why Disraeli had attacked him, and implied that he would now be glad of some sort of reconciliation. Disraeli deputed George Smythe to manage the affair with due consideration for Croker's "feelings and situation", but he could not face an interview—"It was too late, and my sensibilities, which had been played upon in my earlier life, too much required nursing." He added: "The moral I draw from all this is that men of a certain age like the young ones who lick them."

In "licking" Croker Disraeli was perhaps influenced by the fact that he had been the leader of a group of long-standing contributors to Murray's *Quarterly* who caballed against the appointment of Lockhart as editor, and so he associated him with the wreck of his youthful ambition to help Murray to found a great newspaper.

There are evident parallels between Croker and Rigby. Croker, although no *parvenu*, rose by his own abilities, exercised at the bar and in Parliament, to be First Secretary to the Admiralty at twenty-eight. He associated himself with the third Marquess of Hertford (the original of Lord Monmouth), first acting as his legal adviser and then taking a considerable part in the general management of his affairs. There is plenty of testimony as to the "slashing" character of his articles and speeches. After one of the Reform Bill debates Lockhart wrote to a friend: "Croker was capital and most powerful. I never saw so much horror excited as by his slashing dissection of Lord John Russell: and the House, at first cold and reluctant, became, as he went on, intoxicated with glee. He had some real eloquent declamation too, and his delivery was manly and authoritative, wherever it was not diabolical and vindictive."

On another occasion an article in *Blackwoods' Magazine* described Croker's attack on Jeffery in the House of Commons as "like the wolf dandling the kid". A great lord of the party found it more than he could bear, and, with a whisper of "God-damn-him", he "strode out of the place as if he had been stung by a rattlesnake". Oratory and invective of this kind were evidently genuinely impressive, and of higher quality than Rigby's shallow, insistent volubility, which the august Sidonia deflated with the chilly courtesy of a bow and a murmured, "Perhaps", as he turned to his neighbour to ask if birds were plentiful in Lancashire this season. In fact Croker's abilities were superior to "the sharp talent, the shallow information, and the worldly cunning that make a Rigby" (*Coningsby*). It is not, however, surprising that he made enemies, and Macaulay attacked him with a venom equal to his own.

Croker's biographer (Brightfield) asserts that he took no fees from Lord Hertford and that the legacy he received from him was no more, if as much, than he might have charged for his legal services. The terms of Lord Hertford's will were made public in the year in which *Coningsby* was written, and Disraeli represented Rigby as disappointed by the meagreness of his legacy from Lord Monmouth. As Croker was only three years Lord Hertford's junior he cannot have built great hopes upon a legacy; he had taken his reward in social and Parliamentary prestige, but he was above the mean subservience of Rigby.

Returning to the story of *Coningsby*: in the year 1831 Lord

Monmouth, disgusted by the political see-saw of the Reform Bill agitation, preferred to live in Italy, but a time came when it seemed necessary, if he was to preserve his useful Parliamentary boroughs, to come home and exert his considerable influence in opposition to the Bill. In the House of Lords he met a kinsman, a Duke, whose son, Lord Henry Sydney, was one of Harry Coningsby's greatest friends at Eton. The Duke spoke warmly of the boy, who had stayed at his country house, Beaumanoir, and the next day Lord Monmouth issued a fiat: "Rigby, I should like to see the boy at Eton." He spoke as if it were much the same matter as trying a new horse. The difficulty of procuring leave for the boy at a moment's notice was for Rigby to surmount.

The book actually opens with Rigby and young Coningsby on their way from Eton to Monmouth House. Rigby left Harry in the bleak waiting-room at the Tory party headquarters while he went to ascertain the latest news of the Whig ministry's frantic efforts to force the Reform Bill through Parliament. Coningsby, desperate for occupation, had just mustered courage to straighten a portrait of the Duke of Wellington when Rigby returned. Almost on his heels two men burst in, exclaiming with one voice: "Rigby—Rigby! By G——, they're out!" Their information was that Lord Grey had resigned, but Rigby would not concede superior knowledge to any lesser man and argued ingeniously that time alone made it impossible. Lord Grey could not have been at the Palace before 12 o'clock, it was now only a quarter to one, and he must call his colleagues together on his return before any announcement could be made. He even computed the number of stairs the Minister would have to ascend and descend at the Palace as conclusive support for his argument, and reduced Tadpole and Taper, whose lives were bound up with the minutiæ of political intrigue, to crestfallen doubt. The doubt was resolved when a Duke came in and told them that he had himself spoken to Lord Lyndhurst, a leading Tory peer, as he was stepping into his carriage in full dress to obey the King's summons. Rigby could only recover his poise by remarking that it was pity he had not breakfasted with Lord Lyndhurst that morning instead of going down to Eton.

At Monmouth House Coningsby was again left to wait, but this time in a sumptuously furnished saloon of which the walls were covered with light blue satin and ornamented with portraits of beautiful women by Boucher, set in panels of silver. The coming meeting with his grandfather, the only relative he could claim, began to seem very awful, even more so than a summons to Dr. Keate's study. Yet he could not repress the hope that at last he was to find some family affection, and to take his rightful place as the great nobleman's grandson. A valet came to summon him; he passed through a magnificent bed-chamber into Lord Monmouth's dressing-room and his grandfather rose ceremoniously to greet him, an impressive figure—"superb and icy"—leaning on an ivory cane. Extending his hand Lord Monmouth said conversationally: "How do you like Eton?"

The very naturalness of the question, when the boy's nerves were strung up to breaking point in the expectation of a momentous interview, paralysed his mind for a moment. Then a sudden memory of his Mother overcame him; he could not reply, he sank into a chair, leant his head on a table and burst into tears. Now, indeed, his future trembled in the balance:

"Here was a business! If there were one thing which would have made Lord Monmouth travel from London to Naples at four and twenty hours' notice it was to avoid a scene. He hated scenes—he hated feelings. He saw instantly the mistake he had made in sending for his grandchild. He was afraid that Coningsby was tender-hearted like his father. Another tender-hearted Coningsby! Unfortunate family! Degenerate race! He decided in his mind that Coningsby must be provided for in the Church, and looked at Mr. Rigby, whose principal business it always was to disembarrass his patron from the disagreeable."

Rigby was not unkind; he hustled the boy out of the room, and eventually conducted him to luncheon with the Princess Colanna and her young step-daughter, who were guests in the house. By evening Harry had so far recovered himself that when Mr. Ormsby asked him at the dinner-table "How do you like Eton?" he answered readily enough. Lord Monmouth listened. Presently he began to think his grandson was not merely the amiable spooney he had at first supposed. At least he seemed to have made a good choice of friends at Eton. Finally Harry was dismissed with a handsome tip and his Lordship's promise to come down for Montem.

At Monmouth House we are introduced to various characters representative of the society of the day. Disraeli's contemporaries found it a fascinating game to identify them; Lord Palmerston drew up his own "key". There was Mr. Ormsby, the school, college and club crony of Lord Monmouth, one of whose boroughs he represented in the House of Commons. The friendship had endured because Mr. Ormsby was a millionaire: his Lordship liked his friends to be either very rich, equals who wanted nothing from him and could play with him at high stakes, or very poor, and so glad of any opportunity to amuse or serve him—"there was nothing which he despised and disliked so much as a moderate fortune".

On the same plane as Mr. Ormsby there was Lord Eskdale (who also plays a part in *Tancred*), the urbane, sophisticated peer who could appraise a horse or a man infallibly, and also solve awkward social problems and compose other men's quarrels with masterly tact and skill. He was "a voluptuary who could be a Spartan; clear-sighted, unprejudiced and sagacious". He even appreciated and patronised art and literature, although he only read French novels. In addition he was Lord Monmouth's rival in the country as a proprietor of close boroughs. He was identified as a life-like portrait of the second Lord Lonsdale.

In a different category was Lucian Gay, identified as Theodore Hook, a journalist and novelist, who gained notoriety as the editor of *John Bull*, a Sunday newspaper which deliberately aimed at a *succès de scandale*. He also figured in *Vivian Grey*, as Stanislaus Hoax. As Gay in *Coningsby* he is represented as a scholar and a wit, who had failed to establish himself in a position worthy of his talents, as he lacked money, had no great patronage at his command and could not bear to drudge. He found a patron at last in Rigby, whose slashing articles owed much to Gay's brilliant pen. For some time Rigby jealously kept his protégé from Monmouth House, but when Lord Monmouth alarmed him by signs of boredom he decided to risk introducing Gay to his patron. It was beneath his own dignity to play the rôle of table-wit, but if his

Lordship required a jester Rigby would take the credit of finding him the best in the market. Lucian Gay thus became an habitué at Monmouth House, where his wit, liveliness and aplomb contributed to the success of many dinner-parties, and as Lord Monmouth was generous to those who amused him, Rigby's venture was satisfactory to all parties.

Lucian Gay certainly had qualities in common with Theodore Hook, of whom Jerdan, the editor of the *Literary Gazette*, wrote that his sparkling sallies of wit set the table in a roar. Jerdan claimed more than wit for him; in enumerating his gifts he wrote of "That unflagging mirth which made him the soul and centre of the convivial circle.... That manly sense, acute observation, and accumulated intelligence, which rendered him as instructive when gravity prevailed, as he was unapproachable when festivity ruled the hour." Hook was indebted to Croker for considerable kindness. Through the favour of the Prince Regent, who fell under the spell of his table-talk, he was appointed to the incongruous post of Accountant General and Treasurer of the island of Mauritius, and was involved when some defalcations in the island's accounts were discovered. Croker, then First Secretary at the Admiralty, believed in Hook's innocence and took his part. Hook was grateful, but there does not seem to be any foundation for representing him as Croker's creature.

The stir of the Reform Bill agitation extended to Eton. Coningsby returned from London full of superior information, but before he could begin his story his friend Buckhurst warned him, a little nervously, that he and Lord Henry Sydney had invited an outsider—one Millbank—to join their breakfast party. Coningsby looked pained and presently burst out: "Why should you ask an infernal manufacturer?" Lord Henry replied deprecatingly that the Millbank family had been civil to his in Manchester and his father wished him to pay some attention to the son. This gave Coningsby his opening:

" 'Manchester, indeed!' said Coningsby; 'if you knew what I did about Manchester! A pretty state we have been in in London this week past with your Manchesters and Birminghams!'

" 'Come, come, Coningsby,' said Lord Vere, the son of a Whig minister; 'I am all for Manchester and Birmingham.'

" 'It is all up with the country I can tell you,' said Coningsby, with the air of one who was in the secret.

" 'My father says it will all go right now,' rejoined Lord Vere. 'I had a letter from my sister yesterday.'

" 'They say we shall all lose our estates, though,' said Buckhurst; 'I know I shall not give up mine without a fight. Shirley was besieged, you know, in the civil wars; and the rebels got infernally licked.'

" 'I think that all the people about Beaumanoir would stand by the Duke,' said Lord Henry pensively.

" 'Well—you may depend upon it you will have it very soon,' said Coningsby. 'I know it from the best authority.' "

At that point Millbank came in, asked for Coningsby's news and ventured to say that he must have had a rare lark, to which Coningsby replied:

" 'Yes, if having your windows broken by a mob be a rare lark. They could not break my grandfather's though. Monmouth House is in a courtyard. All noblemen's houses should be in courtyards.'

" 'I was glad to see it all ended very well,' said Millbank.

" 'It has not begun yet,' said Coningsby.

" 'What?' said Millbank.

" 'Why—the revolution.'

" 'The Reform Bill will prevent a revolution, my father says,' said Millbank."

It was perhaps as well that at this moment a small boy (of course "the scion of a noble house") carried in the smoking goose which his seniors had ordered.

Oswald Millbank has been taken as a free study of Gladstone, on the strength of the fact that he came from a Lancashire family whose wealth was derived from commerce. It may be admitted that he has some traits in common with Gladstone; he was grave and a little stern, his intellect was solid rather than dazzling, but there is little else to suggest that Gladstone was his original. The Young England group were Gladstone's juniors by ten years or so, and Disraeli was not yet particularly interested in his great rival of the future. A more likely theory is that, in so far as he represented anyone, Oswald Millbank stood for John Walter, son of the proprietor of *The Times*, who was a friend of Smythe and Manners at Eton.

Millbank had a part to play in Coningsby's political education. His father had little love for the aristocracy and had only sent his son to Eton to prove that he had as good a right to do so as any duke. From young Millbank Coningsby learned that his own view of politics, as a struggle between Whig nobles and Tory nobles for the right to govern the country, was too limited, and that there were other influential classes to be reckoned with. Millbank might not have had the chance to overcome Coningsby's arrogant young prejudice against manufacturers but for a boating accident, in which Coningsby saved his life. This broke down Millbank's reserve and enabled him to show the admiration he had always felt for one who was a leader in the school, and Coningsby himself soon felt a warm and almost proprietary interest in the boy who owed his life to him.

Meanwhile the Reform Bill was passed, and Lord Monmouth left England in disgust, shorn of the twelve boroughs which he had relied upon as one of the levers which were to procure him the dukedom he coveted. In the first election after the Bill the Whigs were returned with a majority of three hundred, which Disraeli considered a source of weakness to them. They not only lost a salutary restraint, but amongst so many aspirants for preferment it was impossible for the leaders to satisfy more than a small proportion and an opposition of discontented elements arose within the party itself. In 1834 the King unexpectedly dismissed the Whig government and sent for the Duke of Wellington. Peel was in Rome at the time and a messenger was at once despatched to fetch him home. The stir and intrigue of this crisis evokes some of Disraeli's best political satire. He describes how people flocked to London. All those who had ever held office, all those who hoped to do so, all those who thought they could press a claim to anything, foregathered in streets and clubs, all professing that of course it was mere accident that they happened to be passing through town, although they were to be met with regularly every day for a month. Amongst them were Tadpole and Taper, in whom Disraeli immortalised a type—the political jobber or wire-puller. Tadpole was never without his memorandum book, full of ingenious day-to-day calculations of promotions, majorities and the relative chances of winning this or that constituency. He had his eye on the Wesleyans as a possible source of new strength, if duly cultivated. Taper's opinion was that all depended on a good cry. He rejected "Ancient institutions and modern improvements" as too cumbersome and inclined to a religious cry, which would mean nothing and not interfere with business when the party was in office. For Tadpole and Taper the be-all and end-all of political life was to obtain office, however subordinate, for its own sake:

"It is a peculiar class, that; £1,200 per annum, paid quarterly, is their idea of political science and human nature. To receive £1,200 a year per annum is government; to try to receive £1,200 per annum is opposition; to wish to receive £1,200 per annum is ambition. If a man wants to get into Parliament, and does not want to get £1,200 per annum, they look upon him as daft. They stare in each other's face and ask 'What can —— want to get into Parliament for?' They have no conception that public reputation is a motive power, and with many men the greatest."

Disraeli cites public reputation where one would have preferred public service, but the motive of public service is not lacking in the votaries of Young England as he pictures them. Tadpole and Taper, however, had other things to think of. They took upon themselves the congenial task of building up the party majority in the House of Commons by hinting at possible promotions and peerages as if they had inner knowledge. Tadpole generously admitted that his friend excelled him in this delicate art and Taper explained his tactics:

"I make it a rule never to open my mouth on such subjects. A nod or a wink will speak volumes. An affectionate pressure of the hand will sometimes do a great deal; and I have promised many a peerage without committing myself by an ingenuous habit of deference which cannot be mistaken by the future noble!" This led them on, however, to the conclusion that a Marquess of Monmouth was no longer "Letter A. No.1", it was now time to devote their attention to the middle class. As to principles, Tadpole felt that Tory governments belonged to the past, what was needed was a sound conservative government. "I understand," replied Taper thoughtfully, "Tory men and Whig measures."

Meanwhile speculation was rife amongst "some brilliant personages who had just scampered up from Melton, thinking it probable that Sir Robert Peel might also want some moral lords of the bed-chamber". A dinner-party given by Mr. Ormsby provided an opportunity to discuss chances:

" 'Do you hear anything?' said a great noble who wanted something in the general scramble, but what he knew not; only he had a vague feeling he ought to have something, having made such great sacrifices.

" 'There is a report that Clifford is to be secretary to the Board of Control,' said Mr. Earwig, whose whole soul was in this subaltern arrangement, of which the Minister of course had not even thought; 'but I cannot trace it to any authority.'

" 'I dare say Rambrooke will have the Buckhounds,' said the great noble musingly. 'Your Lordship has not heard Clifford's name mentioned?' continued Mr. Earwig.

" 'I should think they had not come to that sort of thing,' said the great noble, with ill-disguised contempt. 'The first thing after the Cabinet is formed is the Household: the things you talk of are done last'; and he turned upon his heel, and met the imperturbable countenance and clear sarcastic eye of Lord Eskdale.

" 'You have not heard anything?' asked the great noble of his brother patrician.

" 'Yes, a great deal since I have been in this room; but unfortunately it is all untrue.'

" 'There is a report that Rambrooke is to have the Buckhounds; but I cannot trace it to any authority.'

" 'Pooh!' said Lord Eskdale.

" 'I don't see that Rambrooke should have the Buckhounds any more than anyone else. What sacrifices has he made?'

" 'Past sacrifices are nothing,' said Lord Eskdale. 'Present sacrifices are the thing we want; men who will sacrifice their principles, and join us.'

" 'You have not heard Rambrooke's name mentioned?'

" 'When a Minister has no Cabinet, and only one hundred and forty supporters in the House of Commons, he has something else to think of than places at Court,' said Lord Eskdale, as he slowly turned away."

In the event Peel's government, without a majority in the House of Commons, did not last long.

The time came for Coningsby to leave Eton. Lord Monmouth was still abroad and he had no home where an eager family circle was waiting to welcome him. He had scarcely known the "sweet sedulousness of a mother's love"; for him there had never been "a sister's mystical affection". Apart from his school-friends his only connections had been strangers, whose attitude to him was "calmly and coldly kind". He had, however, been invited by Lord Henry Sydney to stay at Beaumanoir, and he decided to travel the last part of the way, which lay through beautiful woodland scenery, on foot. As Beaumanoir represents Belvoir Castle it was probably Sherwood Forest, and Disraeli writes of it with happy detail. He had a great love of trees and many descriptions of them could be collected from the novels. In his old age, when he was bereft of the wife who had cherished him so tenderly, and was almost too weary with struggle and ill-health to savour the triumphs which had come too late, the trees in his park at Hughenden were still a source of comfort to him and objects for loving care.

In the Forest Coningsby, in pensive mood, reviewed his short life and tried to assess his uncertain future. His meditations were cut short by a sudden storm, in which the trees voiced their individual protests to the buffeting of a gale:

"Soon might be distinguished the various voices of the mighty trees, as they expressed their terror or their agony. The oak roared, the beech shrieked, the elm sent forth its deep and long-drawn groan; while ever and anon, amid a momentary pause, the passion of the ash was heard in moans of thrilling anguish." Coningsby hastened on his way and reached a homely inn before the storm broke in full force. A little later, in the light of a flash of lightning, he saw a rider and his groom dash up to the door.

A flash of lightning is a suitable herald for the arrival of Sidonia, the cosmopolitan Jew of fabulous wealth and complete intellectual mastery of his world, who, no doubt, represents Disraeli's conception of man as he might be with his powers developed to the highest degree and the glorious enablement of unlimited means. Only one thing Sidonia lacked: the law debarred him from the privilege of taking part in the government of his country, although governments often came to him for the means of carrying out their projects. When Coningsby, full of youthful admiration excited by the stranger's talk at the inn, exclaimed that such great thoughts should be matched by heroic deeds, Sidonia replied mournfully: "Action is not for me. I am of that faith that the apostles professed before they followed their Master."

It has been supposed that Sidonia was drawn from a Rothschild. Disraeli had already met various members of the Rothschild family in London and Paris. In the very year in which *Coningsby* was written he described to his sister a fête at Gunnersbury given by "Madame de Rothschild, mère", in a fine park in which stood a villa worthy of an Italian prince, "though decorated with a taste and splendour which a French financier in the olden times could alone have rivalled". This is just the setting which we should expect Sidonia to create for himself, but for a complete picture of a Rothschild country house we must turn to Hainault House in *Endymion*. It is, however, unlikely that Sidonia represents any particular Rothschild. Hesketh Pearson probably comes nearest to the mark when he describes this character as "a fanciful picture of Disraeli in the fortunate ownership of the Rothschild millions". Similarly, Phillip Guedalla names him "Disrothschild". In his youth Disraeli said that Alroy, the Jewish Prince of the Captivity, represented his "ideal ambition"; this is surely far more true of Sidonia.

The first impact of this superman upon Coningsby was dynamic. As they shared a meal at the inn (in which Coningsby ate eggs and bacon while his companion only took bread and wine) Sidonia waxed eloquent upon the subjects of greatness and youth. The disciples of Young England must have exulted in his conclusions:

" 'But when men are young, they want experience,' said Coningsby; 'and when they have gained experience they want energy.'

" 'Great men never want experience,' said the stranger.

" 'But everybody says that experience——'

" 'Is the best thing in the world—a treasure for you, for me, for millions. But for a creative mind, less than nothing. Almost everything that is great has been done by youth.'

" 'It is at least a creed flattering to our years,' Coningsby said with a smile.

" 'Nay,' said the stranger; 'for life in general there is but one decree. Youth is a blunder; manhood a struggle; old age a regret. Do not suppose,' he added, smiling, 'that I hold that youth is genius; all I say is, that genius, when young, is divine.' "

There is an echo of Disraeli's youth in Coningsby's cry, "But everybody says that experience——" How often that cold douche had been turned upon his own young ambitions! He would be no party to inflicting it upon Young England. He makes Sidonia follow up his generalisation by enumerating examples of young genius, from classical history to Don Juan of Austria, who won the great battle of Lepanto at twenty-five, and Bolingbroke and Pitt—"both ministers before other men leave off cricket". When Coningsby asked diffidently, "But what is an individual against a vast public opinion?" the answer was flashed back at him—" 'Divine,' said the stranger."

It is not surprising that George Smythe, fresh from reading *Coningsby*, wrote ecstatically to "Dear Diz" that he was "dazzled, bewildered, tipsy with admiration the most passionate and wild. I never read anything, thought of anything, felt anything, believed anything, before. Thank God I have faith at last!"

The stranger departed, on a superb Arab mare called The Daughter of the Star, without telling Coningsby his name, but they were to meet again at Coningsby Castle.

CHAPTER VIII

Coningsby (II)

THE ducal mansion of Beaumanoir represented a nobleman's country home at its best. Such "palladian palaces" still tempted Disraeli to corresponding grandiloquence and Beaumanoir's Corinthian colonnades were "the boast and pride of the Midland counties", while its gardens were thick with temples which were dedicated to the virtues, or to dead Sydneys, with a few triumphal arches to commemorate the family's military heroes. Beyond the extensive park "the hart and hind wandered in a wilderness abounding in ferny coverts and green and stately trees". The Duke who presided over this paradise was a perfect example of *noblesse oblige*. His bounty to the poor was dispensed with sympathy and kindness; he had, in fact, a very good heart and not a bad head. If his education had not been confined to Latin and English verses he might have been a well-informed man, for he had a natural love of letters, and this despite the facts that "his pack were the pride of England, his barrel seldom missed, and his fortune on the turf, where he never betted, was a proverb. He was good, and he wished to do good; but his views were confused from want of knowledge."

The Duchess was beautiful, dignified and altogether delightful; she never allowed herself to appear bored when another was trying to interest or amuse her. Possibly with some personal feeling, Disraeli wrote: "She was not one of those vulgar fine ladies who meet you one day with a vacant stare as if unconscious of your existence, and address you on another in a tone of impertinent familiarity." The Beaumanoir family party was lively and gracious, the house was a home and not merely an occasional residence, and the ladies knew the cottagers as friends of long standing.

Soon after Coningsby's arrival a conversation arose at table about the new Poor Law, a subject upon which Disraeli had strong opinions. The Poor Law of 1834 represented an extremely severe reaction from a former system under which outdoor relief was given widely to supplement wages, with the result that numbers of labourers were semi-pauperised, while wages were kept at a low level and parish rates rose alarmingly. By the new law parishes were combined into unions, each with its workhouse, and outdoor relief was practically abolished. Whole families were thus driven into the workhouses, and some could never establish independent homes again. To ensure that the workhouse was less attractive than the cottage or the hovel, general rules were drawn up (including silence at meals), and the dietary was said to be scientifically calculated down to the last tablespoonful of gruel, crumb of bread and shred of onion which allowed for a bare sufficiency with no possible waste. When Oliver Twist asked for more he was pitting himself against a deliberate national system. It was a system of which Disraeli said in a speech in 1841 that no other term than that of imprisonment could be given to the confinement which the poor underwent in the Union workhouse.

The Duke had supported the Bill of 1834 in the belief that it would raise the condition of the labouring classes, but now he had misgivings. He was, however, no match for his son-in-law, Lord Everingham, who was a clear-headed, cold-blooded Whig and looked upon the new Poor Law as another Magna Carta. The discussion brings out the characters of the speakers, including that of Lord Henry Sydney, who was such a close study of Lord John Manners. The Duke opened the subject:

" 'By the by, Everingham, you, who are a chairman of a Board of Guardians, can give me some information. Supposing a case of outdoor relief——'

" 'I could not suppose anything so absurd,' said the son-in-law.

" 'Well,' rejoined the Duke, 'I know your views on that subject, and it is certainly a question on which there is a good deal to be said. But would you under any circumstances give relief out of the union even if the parish were to save a considerable sum?'

" 'I wish I knew the union where such a system was followed,' said Lord Everingham; and His Grace seemed to tremble under his son-in-law's glance."

Lord Henry Sydney now came to his father's rescue. He would not listen to statistics, dietary tables, commissioners' rules and sub-commissioners' reports. His contention was that the order of the peasantry—he rebuked his father for speaking 'of the labouring classes'—was as ancient as that of the nobility and equally entitled to its own particular rights and privileges. These were not only matters of economics but bound up with ancient customs, manners and ceremonies. Lord Everingham was scornful:

" 'Henry thinks,' said Lord Everingham, 'that the people are to be fed by dancing round a maypole.'

" 'But will the people be more fed because they do not dance round a maypole?' urged Lord Henry.

" 'Obsolete customs!' said Lord Everingham.

" 'And why should dancing round a maypole be more obsolete than holding a Chapter of the Garter?' asked Lord Henry.

"The Duke, who was a blue ribbon, felt this a home thrust. 'I must say,' said His Grace, 'that I for one deeply regret that our popular customs have been permitted to fall into desuetude.'

" 'The spirit of the age is against such things,' said Lord Everingham.

" 'And what is the spirit of the age?' asked Coningsby.

" 'The spirit of utility,' said Lord Everingham.''

Amongst the guests at table was Mr. Eustace Lyle, a young Roman Catholic landowner, whose portrait was drawn from Ambrose Lisle Phillips. There are few of the novels in which Roman Catholicism is not introduced: it was a subject which had fascinated Disraeli even in boyhood. Ritual and ceremony had a natural attraction for him, and Roman Catholicism seemed to offer one antidote to the utilitarian conception of life which he found so distasteful. Mr. Lyle was drawn into the conversation presently. Looking at his younger daughter the Duke remarked:

" 'Theresa brings me terrible accounts of the sufferings of the poor about us.'

" 'Women think everything to be suffering!' said Lord Everingham.

" 'How do you find them about you, Mr. Lyle?' continued the Duke.

" 'I have revived the monastic customs at St. Geneviève,' said the young man, blushing very much. 'There is an almsgiving twice a week.' "

The ladies thought this extremely interesting, and it was arranged that they should all visit St. Geneviève the following day. This visit gave Disraeli another opportunity to describe one of the stately homes of England, in this case built of glittering white stone, with pinnacles which sparkled gaily against a green background. The inevitable peacocks, sunning themselves on the turrets, spread their gorgeous plumage as if in welcome; little pony carriages were in waiting to carry the guests about the grounds, and before they left the chapel bell announced the hour of the almsgiving. Then a touching procession came in sight: old men led by grandchildren, a widow with her family, sturdy labourers temporarily out of work. Mr. Lyle explained that the rectors of various parishes sent in the names of those in need and his own almoner then visited the homes and signed certificates which the applicants presented to his steward. He admitted shyly to the Duchess that he wanted the people to realise that property was their protector and friend.

Coningsby found Mr. Lyle's political views extremely interesting. The Whig philosophy was uncongenial to him, but the Conservatives seemed to have little to offer:

" 'The Duke talks to me of Conservative principles; but he does not inform me what they are. I observe indeed a party in the State whose rule it is to consent to no change, until it is clamoured for, and then instantly to yield; but those are concessionary, not Conservative principles. This party treats institutions as we do our pheasants, they preserve only to destroy them. But is there a statesman among these Conservatives who offers us a dogma for a guide, or defines any great political truth which we should aspire to establish? It seems to me a barren thing—this Conservatism —an unhappy cross-breed, the mule of politics which engenders nothing.' "

The young men agreed that they would like to see a government which could command love and loyalty, and a religion that was a faith and not a form.

At Beaumanoir Coningsby expanded in the happy atmosphere of family affection, and particularly under the charming attentions of young Lady Everingham. She was a type of woman that Disraeli drew well. He indulged in a panegyric of the coquette: "A coquette is a being who wishes to please. . . . Alas! Coquettes are but too rare. 'Tis a career that requires great abilities, infinite pains, and a gay and airy spirit." In a country house it is she who "provides all the amusement; suggests the riding-party, plans the picnic, gives and guesses the charades, acts them. She is the salt of the banquet." Lady Everingham filled this rôle at Beaumanoir; she was not a celebrated beauty, but something more delightful, a captivating woman. She was a mistress of the art of conversation—"You must originate and you must sympathise. . . . The union is rather rare, but irresistible." She also understood that the way to captivate a man is to talk to him about himself, and when she told Coningsby that his career interested her very much because she liked ambitious men, his heart beat faster. It was all the more disconcerting when the Duke's elder son, the Marquess of Beaumanoir, arrived with his friend Mr. Melton, a young man of fashion and a favourite in society, who soon monopolised Lady Everingham's attention. When the stricken Coningsby overheard her say to the Duchess, "I am so glad, Mamma, that Mr. Melton has come; we wanted some amusement", he felt that it was time to bring his visit to Beaumanoir to an end.

Lord Monmouth was now in England and had bidden his grandson to present himself at Coningsby Castle shortly; with time in hand Coningsby decided to visit Manchester on the way. The wonderful stranger at the inn had met his regret that he had not yet seen the ancient glories of Greece and Rome with the comment: "The age of ruins is past. Have you seen Manchester?" Moreover he had added that adventures were to the adventurous.

To go to Manchester was indeed an adventure to a youth brought up as Coningsby had been. The actual leaders of Young England, Smythe and Manners, made similar expeditions of discovery into industrial areas. Coningsby was almost bewildered. "He had passed over the plains where iron and coal superseded turf and corn, dingy as the entrance to Hades, and flaming with furnaces; and now he was among illumined factories with more windows than Italian palaces, and smoking chimneys taller than Egyptian obelisks. Alone in the great metropolis of machinery itself, sitting down in a solitary coffee-room glaring with gas, with no appetite, a whirling head, and not a plan or purpose for the morrow, why was he there? ... Even his bedroom was lit by gas. Wonderful city!"

Coningsby paid a round of visits to factories and mills and eventually he was directed to Mr. Millbank's works, near Bolton, as the most up-to-date in the neighbourhood. Oswald Millbank was not at home, but his father gave him a welcome befitting the hero who had saved his son's life. Dining in his comfortable mansion with Mr. Millbank Coningsby heard some revolutionary doctrine. The English aristocracy, it seemed, had little to boast of; few noble families were of ancient lineage, most owed their peerages to the spoliation of the Church, the sale of honours by the elder Stuarts or the borough-mongering of modern times. It was time they lost their privileges as hereditary legislators and gave place to men who were distinguished among their fellows for virtues, talents and achievements. Mr. Millbank declared himself a disciple of progress.

Despite the honour shown to him by Mr. Millbank and his beautiful, shy young daughter, Edith, Coningsby sensed some constraint in the mill-owner's attitude. It even amounted to mystery when he asked a question about a picture of a lovely girl which had a strange attraction for him: Mr. Millbank was evidently perturbed and drew his attention to something else. When he hoped that he might repeat his visit there was no response, although father and daughter showed some emotion in bidding him goodbye.

Coningsby duly arrived at Coningsby Castle, a vast castellated building, more magnificent than harmonious, and was received by a crowd of servants. He found the same lack of harmony inside the Castle; this was no home, like Beaumanoir, with evidences of loving occupation scattered about. Some of the grand furniture and fittings had been sent from London for the occasion and seemed to have brought a metropolitan atmosphere with them; there was none of "the sweet order of a country life", such as that he had just left. In fact Lord Monmouth seldom stayed there and had only come down now with the purpose of keeping his political influence in the county alive, since he could no longer dispose of boroughs as private property. His sumptuous entertainments and the affable polish of his manners achieved his object: his neighbours began to discount the stories of his profligacy and to congratulate themselves on having such a truly great nobleman amongst them, interesting himself in local affairs.

Having dressed for the evening, Coningsby entered the largest and most sumptuous saloon he had ever seen, crowded with illustrious strangers, with some trepidation. His grandfather, whom he had not seen for four years, was still a splendid figure, with the garter ribbon across his breast. It took some courage to break into the brilliant circle and present himself. Here Disraeli halts the story to give a brief account of Coningsby's character. Not the least of his charms was a vein of simplicity. He was free from affectation, which was remarkable, for "he had a brilliant imagination, a quality that from its fantasies and the vague and indefinite desires it engenders, generally makes those whose characters are not formed very affected". Once more Coningsby's creator seems to be remembering his own youth. The young man's ingenuous freshness, combined with good looks, a graceful carriage and a charming expression, delighted Lord Monmouth—"his heart was not touched, but his fine taste was gratified". He saw at once that his grandson was an asset, he would be an irresistible candidate for future elections and "a brilliant tool to work out the dukedom".

The house-party at Coningsby Castle affords another galaxy of characters. There were the Prince and Princess Colonna, with the Prince's statuesque, enigmatic daughter Lucretia, who "generally succeeded in conveying an impression to those she addressed that she had never seen them before, did not care to see them now, and never wished to see them again; and all this, too, with an air of great courtesy".

There was Mrs. Guy Flouncey, who might well have been an understudy for Becky Sharp (*Vanity Fair*, 1847). She had amused the Marquess abroad and now embarked upon a career of social conquest, armoured with a truly wonderful wardrobe. The ladies ignored her at first, or confined their notice to the fatal question "Who is she?" The gentlemen, however, were only too willing to ride, dance and flirt with her. She was an adroit flatterer, with a genius for conferring slight obligations, and her quick mind suggested many diversions for his Lordship's guests. In a short time she became the soul of the party—"in a country house the suggestive mind is inestimable"—and in time even the great ladies were obliged to thaw towards her.

There was also a troupe of French comedians to entertain the company. Villebecque, their manager, had married a celebrated actress, now dead, with whom Lord Monmouth had had a liaison, the only one in which she had ever indulged. She had had a daughter by him, whom Villebecque had adopted as his own, and who was with him now, under the name of Flora Villebecque. She was to make her stage début at Coningsby Castle.

. The party was complete when Lord Eskdale and Sidonia arrived. Coningsby now found that the stranger of the inn was a financier of international repute, for whom even Lord Monmouth had a great respect. Here Disraeli indulges in a long account of Sidonia's antecedents. He endowed him with the ancestry he liked to claim for himself, an ancient and noble Spanish family of the purest Jewish descent, driven to fly from the country in which they had lived for generations by the persecution of the Inquisition. To modern minds, with Hitler's theory of racial purity fresh in the memory, there is an ominous ring about Sidonia's claim that "an unmixed race of a first-rate organisation are the aristocracy of nature". He held that a pure race of the Caucasian organisation could not be destroyed by penal laws or physical tortures. The persecutors of mixed race might disappear, but tens of centuries of degradation had not been able to destroy the Jews: not only had their laws and their literature permeated other nations, but "the living Hebrew intellect" still gave them a vast influence all over Europe.

Sidonia had travelled widely for five years before taking his place at the head of the family banking enterprises, and his "penetrative intellect" combined with complete freedom from personal and national prejudice, had enabled him to make good use of his opportunities:

"Sidonia had exhausted all the sources of human knowledge; he was master of the learning of every nation, of all tongues dead or living, of every literature, Western or Oriental. He had pursued the speculations of science to their last term, and had himself illustrated them by observation and experiment. He had lived in all orders of society, had viewed every combination of Nature and of Art, and had observed man under every phasis of civilisation. He had even studied him in the wilderness. The influence of creeds and laws, manners, customs, traditions in all their diversities, had been subject to his personal scrutiny."

As if this were not enough, Sidonia was well acquainted with monarchs and ministers in every country in Europe, and he had strange and various sources of information—"the secret history of the world was his pastime". Furthermore, he was handsome, in the prime of life and a very fine horseman. Princess Lucretia Colonna, so disdainful of lesser men, was subjugated as soon as she met Sidonia. He, however, was "a man without affections", capable of deep feeling but not for individuals; moreover, he held that "passion and polished life were quite incompatible". This trait in his superman leads Disraeli into one of his digressions, a tender panegyric upon married love, which he describes as "the lot most precious to man", and "the most divine of divine gifts, that power and fame can never rival in its delights".

When the time came for Coningsby to leave the Castle for Cambridge he was already firmly established as Lord Monmouth's favoured grandson. He left one devoted heart behind him, that of Flora Villebecque, whom he had kindly befriended when she broke down under the ordeal of her début on the stage.

At Cambridge the little group of Eton friends foregathered and soon they were precipitated into a political campaign. William IV died and the country was plunged into a general election. Coningsby and his friends rallied eagerly to the support of an old Etonian who was standing for Cambridge as a Tory. When it was all over, and their man had been triumphantly "chaired", they began to ask themselves questions:

" 'By Jove,' said the panting Buckhurst, throwing himself on to the sofa, 'it was well done: never was anything better done. An immense triumph! The greatest triumph the Conservative cause has had. And yet,' he added, laughing, 'if any fellow were to ask me what the Conservative cause was, I am sure I should not know what to say.'

" 'Why it's the cause of our glorious institutions,' said Coningsby. 'A crown robbed of its prerogatives; a church controlled by a commission; and an aristocracy that does not lead.'

" 'Under whose genial influence, the order of the peasantry, "a country's pride", has vanished from the face of the land,' said Henry Sydney, 'and is succeeded by a race of serfs, who are called labourers and who burn ricks.'

" 'Under which,' continued Coningsby, 'the crown has become a cipher; the church a sect; the nobility drones; and the people drudges.'

" 'It is the great constitutional cause,' said Lord Vere, 'that refuses everything to opposition; yields everything to agitation. . . .'

" . . . 'By Jove!' said Buckhurst, 'what infernal fools we have made ourselves this last week!'

" 'Nay,' said Coningsby, smiling, 'it was our last schoolboy weakness. *Floreat Etona*, under all circumstances.' "

These views represent the core of Young England's theories; later in the book they are amplified in a long discussion between Coningsby and Oswald Millbank. The Church and the Crown, the age-old and natural protectors of the people, had lost their functions, the one with the suppression of the monasteries in the Reformation, the other in the constitutional revolution of 1688 which, to quote Sidonia, substituted for the king an administrative officer. Thus the only two forces above class—and whose charity could not be degrading—had been fettered by subservience to Parliament. And in Parliament itself the Whigs had created what Coningsby described as "a Venetian oligarchy". The Conservatives, meanwhile, had lost their principles and did not know what they wished to conserve.

In so far as the actual Young England group adopted any definite policy it was to restore the Conservatives to their natural position as the protectors of the people against the harsh forces unleashed by the Industrial Revolution, and encouraged by a utilitarian philosophy which glorified unmitigated competition. To quote Sidonia again: "England should think more of the community and less of the government." In focussing their attention on the community the members of Young England laid a finger on the sore spot in the body politic, but their ideal of a new feudalism, in which the people were to look to a paternal association of King, Church and Aristocracy for the cure of their grievous ills, was already behind the times.

The election of 1837 threw Tadpole and Taper into a frenzy of activity: Taper surpassed himself with the invention of a new cry for the Conservatives—"Our Young Queen And Our Old Institutions." Rigby, meanwhile, was standing for the borough of Darlford, which he confidently expected to hold in Lord Monmouth's interest. It was a great shock when no less a man than Mr. Millbank, with all his local influence, came forward as a "Liberal" candidate. The description of this election has interesting features. Even now only a small proportion of the population of Darlford could vote, but it was still a novelty for the townspeople to have any voice at all in their own representation and large crowds gathered before the hustings to hear the candidates speak. Both sides secretly engaged mob leaders, under whom hired gangs shouted for their candidate and interrupted the other. The meetings were naturally unruly and apt to degenerate into free fights, during which the ladies watching from windows screamed and fainted. The night before polling-day various gangs prowled about the streets disguised with masks, wigs and false noses, keeping watch on each other's machinations. One keen Rigbyite confided to another that he had four Millbankites cooped up, very drunk, and hoped to get them quietly away into the country before daybreak.

Rigby treated the electors to a long speech, well garnished with historical facts, and made great play with the adjective "un-English". Millbank's forthright style was, however, more effective:

"Mr. Millbank was very energetic about resident representatives, but did not understand that a resident representative meant the nominee of a great lord who lived in a great castle (great cheering). There was a lord once who declared that, if he liked, he would return his negro valet to Parliament; but Mr. Millbank thought those days were over. It remained for the people of Darlford to determine whether he was mistaken. 'Never!' exclaimed the mob. 'Millbank for ever! Rigby in the river! No niggers, no valets!'"

Rigby lost the election.

This account has resemblances to the famous election at Eatanswill (*Pickwick*, 1836), where the Buffs and the Blues skirmished in the streets with such gusto. There, too, there was interference with the liberty of voters. Mr. Perker told Mr. Pickwick that Fizkin's people had thirty-three voters in the lock-up coachhouse at the White Hart. When Mr. Pickwick seemed astonished by this information, he explained: "They keep 'em locked up there till they want 'em. The effect of that is, you see, to prevent our getting at them; and even if we could, it would be of no use, for they keep them very drunk on purpose. Smart fellow, Fizkin's agent."

Sam Weller reported that the Blue gangs were "a-hollering themselves hoarse"; he himself, meanwhile, earned a shilling a head for putting "independent" voters, who had slept where they fell the night before at the Peacock, under the pump.

George Eliot also described an election which took place shortly after the Reform Bill in *Felix Holt the Radical*, and she is a conscientious writer who took pains to be correct. Her facts bear out Disraeli's. In the North Loamshire (Staffordshire) election rival brass-bands paraded the streets of Treby, flaunting their colours, and navvies, colliers and stone-pit men flocked into the town bent upon at least making themselves felt by groans and cheers. It was an ordeal indeed to walk up to the polling-booth between lines of vociferous spectators, who commented freely on any peculiarity in an unfortunate voter's appearance. Some of the voters fortified themselves with stiff drinks. Soon the crowd began to hem in the narrow approach to the booth still more closely, and even to demand the payment of toll before they would allow a voter to proceed. Mr. Pink, the saddler, had his coat chalked and was pushed up an alley, from which he could not escape in time to vote. Another voter was so much intimidated by one faction that when he reached the polling-both he gave the name of the candidate he had meant to oppose. There was, of course, no secret ballot then, and the voting was verbal. Polling-day at Treby ended in a fight which reached such a pitch that the Riot Act was read.

Rigby returned to London and presented himself at Monmouth House in great apprehension, but he found that his Lordship had something else to think about besides the defeat at Darlford—he was about to marry the Princess Lucretia Colonna! Rigby had to undertake all the arrangements for the wedding. After some travel Lord Monmouth and his bride settled in Paris and Coningsby was summoned to join them there. From this point the ramifications of the plot thicken, but, in brief, the chief result of the hero's visit to Paris was that he met his fate, in the person of Edith Millbank, now grown into a beautiful woman, who was travelling with relations. Misunderstandings were added to the natural obstacles of youth and dependence, but at last, at home in England, Coningsby won Edith's confession that she loved him. Upheld by this intoxicating assurance he went to open his heart to Mr. Millbank.

Edith's father first pointed out to the eager suitor that he was dependent on Lord Monmouth's capricious favour, and then he spoke of the bitter enmity which existed between Lord Monmouth and himself. It was this which had led him to forestall his Lordship in the purchase of an estate near Coningsby Castle which both coveted, and to oppose Rigby in the Darlford election. Coningsby refused to believe that his grandfather's enmity could be extended to so sweet a being as Edith, and Millbank then harshly reminded him of what his own mother, as sweet and as lovely, had suffered from Lord Monmouth's persecution. Now he learned that his mother had once been pledged to Millbank, but Lord Monmouth's younger son had then appeared upon the scene and stolen her heart. It was her portrait which had attracted her son in Millbank's house. Having told his story, Millbank decreed that Edith must not see Coningsby again.

Under these circumstances Coningsby's position was very painful when Lord Monmouth sent for him and announced that he wished him to contest the borough of Darlford against Millbank in the next election, which seemed likely to take place soon. The scene which follows is one of the best in the book. Lord Monmouth, after regretting that his grandson could not enter Parliament "in the old gentlemanly way", outlined his plans for nursing the constituency. Coningsby thanked his grandfather becomingly but said that he did not wish to enter Parliament. Lord Monmouth, astounded, pressed him for his reasons and he replied that he did not yet feel ready for the responsibility. Lord Monmouth was amused:

" 'Responsibility!' said Lord Monmouth, smiling. 'What responsibility is there? How can anyone have a more agreeable seat? The only person to whom you are responsible is your own relative who brings you in. And I don't suppose there can be any difference on any point between us. You are certainly still young; but I was younger by two years when I first went in; and I found no difficulty. There can be no difficulty. All you have got to do is to vote with your party. . . . As for speaking, if you have a talent that way, take my advice, don't be in a hurry. Learn to know the House; learn the House to know you. If a man be discreet, he cannot enter Parliament too soon.' "

With the courage of desperation, Coningsby declared that his principles would prevent his voting with the Conservative party: before he could support Conservative principles he must know what those principles aimed to conserve, and he then favoured his grandfather with a discourse on Young England tenets.

" 'All this is vastly fine,' said Lord Monmouth; 'but I see no means by which I can attain my object but by supporting Peel. After all, what is the end of all parties and all politics? To gain your object. I want to turn our coronet into a ducal one, and to get your grandmother's barony called out of abeyance in your favour. It is impossible that Peel can refuse me.' "

Warming to his subject, his Lordship expressed his pleasure, and even pride, in the good opinions of his grandson which had reached him, and added that, from what he heard, he hoped he might soon have the satisfaction of promoting his marriage with Lady Theresa Sydney. He concluded, almost coaxingly, "I count on you, boy."

Coningsby replied steadfastly that he would make any personal sacrifice for his grandfather but one—that of his convictions. Upon this Lord Monmouth exploded:

" 'You go with your family, sir, like a gentleman; you are not to consider your opinions like a philosopher or a political adventurer.'

" 'Yes, sir,' said Coningsby with animation, 'but men going with their families, like gentlemen, and losing sight of every principle on which the society of this country ought to be established, produced the Reform Bill.'

" 'D—— the Reform Bill,' said Lord Monmouth, 'if the Duke had not quarrelled with Lord Grey on a coal committee, we should never have had the Reform Bill. And Grey would have gone to Ireland.' "

But Coningsby's young idealism, now afire, could not brook such cynical conclusions; once more he launched upon an oration which he brought to an end in a burst of rhetoric:

" 'What we want, sir, is not to fashion new dukes and furbish up old baronies, but to establish great principles which may maintain the realm and secure the happiness of the people. Let me see authority once more honoured; a solemn reverence again the habit of our lives; let me see property acknowledging, as in the old days of faith, that labour is his twin brother, and that the essence of all tenure is the performance of duty; let results such as these be brought about, and let me participate, however feebly, in the great fulfilment; and public life then indeed becomes a noble career, and a seat in Parliament an enviable distinction.'

" 'I tell you what it is, Harry,' said Lord Monmouth very drily, 'members of this family may think as they like, but they must act as I please. You must go down on Friday to Darlford and declare yourself a candidate for the town, or I shall reconsider our mutual positions. . . . I sent for Rigby this morning. . . . He will be here at 3 o'clock, when you can meet him. You will meet him, I doubt not, like a man of sense,' added Lord Monmouth, looking at Coningsby with a glance such as he had never before encountered, 'who is not prepared to sacrifice all the objects of life for the pursuit of some fantastical puerilities.' "

Immediately after leaving his grandfather Coningsby overheard some talk at his club which led him to think that Edith was betrothed to the Marquess of Beaumanoir, who had paid her court in Paris. There seemed little to live for. He mounted his horse and rode blindly out of town. It was twilight, in a green lane near Willesden, before the tumult in his mind subsided. Now he sternly put aside dreams of power and wealth: he would rely on his own abilities and be true to his own conscience, come what might, and as he reached this conclusion a new hope arose in his heart:

"If the principles of his philosophy were true, the great heart of the nation would respond to their expression. Coningsby felt at this moment a profound conviction which never again deserted him, that the conduct which would violate the affections of the heart or the dictates of the conscience, however it may lead to immediate success, is a fatal error. . . . He devoted himself to a love that seemed hopeless and to a fame that was perhaps a dream."

The desire for fame was not altogether exorcised, but this is a great advance on the attitude of Disraeli's first hero, Vivian Grey: Coningsby had seen ambition and fame in their true perspective. He was soon called upon to practise his new philosophy. Lord Monmouth died unexpectedly. He had previously discovered his wife's secret passion for Sidonia and dismissed her with a jointure; the disposal of his vast fortune was still a matter for speculation. The will was read: Coningsby was only to receive the interest upon £10,000; Rigby, who had lost favour since his failure at Darlford, had a paltry legacy; the greater part of his Lordship's wealth passed to his illegitimate daughter, Flora Villebecque.

The young heiress only wished to bestow this unexpected fortune upon Coningsby, but he refused her generosity with gentle firmness. Mournfully Flora pleaded with him—"Refuse my present offer, and you seal the fate of that unhappy Flora whose fragile life has hung for years on the memory of your kindness." It was of no avail; Flora should be as a dear sister to him, but Coningsby had determined to rely upon himself alone, upheld by the conviction that "nothing is great but the personal". While his friends prepared to take their seats in Parliament he set himself to read for the bar.

Naturally, in a novel by Disraeli, the hero could not be left in comparative obscurity on a meagre pittance. In due time he found out that Edith's heart still was, and always had been, his. Meanwhile Mr. Millbank had heard of the young man's disastrous interview with Lord Monmouth, and Oswald lost no opportunity of pleading his friend's cause with his father. Before long Millbank relented, just in time to withdraw from his candidature at Darlford in Coningsby's favour. He then promised him Edith's hand in marriage and settled upon him the estate near Coningsby

Castle which he had snatched from Lord Monmouth's grasp. Disraeli, however, was not satisfied to leave his hero with only a moderate fortune. Very soon Flora, true to her own prediction, died, leaving the Monmouth wealth to Coningsby. With this princely gesture Disraeli was at last content to bring this long novel to an end.

*   *   *

Coningsby was regarded as the manifesto of Young England and is rather an exposition of theory than a picture of the group in action. We have some sympathy with Coningsby's acquaintance, Mr. Melton, when he was asked what the new policy was:

" 'Well, I don't know what it is,' said Mr. Melton, 'but it has got hold of all the young fellows who have just come out. Beau is a little bit himself. I had some idea of giving my mind to it . . . but it requires a devilish lot of history, I believe, and all that sort of thing.'

" 'Ah! That's a bore,' said his companion. 'It's difficult to turn to with a new thing when you are not in the habit of it. I never could manage charades.' "

Even Coningsby smiled when he heard that Buckhurst had both edified and frightened the electors in his constituency by warning them of the dangers of a Venetian oligarchy.

In actual fact Young England was little more than a brief influence in politics, but it was a pointer towards the social-welfare Conservatism of the future, which was largely moulded by Disraeli. Its votaries naturally supported Ashley (afterwards Lord Shaftesbury) in the numerous bills he brought forward for the improvement of conditions in mine and mill. Lord John Manners wrote *A Plea for National Holydays*, induced his father (the Duke of Rutland) to start a system of allotments and was active in the revival of old pastimes. There is some fascination in the picture of Disraeli accompanying him and George Smythe and the Earl of Eglinton to various country places where they joined "the peasantry" in rustic sports. Perhaps it was now convenient to forget how he had once startled the young officers at Malta by declaring that he had never thrown a ball in his life.

Lord Strangford and the Duke of Rutland were uneasy about

the association of their brilliant sons with Disraeli, especially as this often led them into rebellion against Peel, to whom alone they could look for any advancement. The Duke wrote plaintively to Lord Strangford:

"It is grievous that two young men such as John and Mr. Smythe should be led by one of whose integrity of purpose I have an opinion similar to your own, though I can judge only by his public career. The admirable character of our sons only makes them the more assailable by the arts of a designing person. I will write to John to-morrow, and I shall inquire of him whether there is any truth in the report of his having engaged himself to a great dinner at Manchester under the presidency of Mr. Disraeli."

The dinner in question was a notable occasion in celebration of the opening of the Manchester Athenæum. Disraeli made a fine speech, and Smythe and Manners, who had overcome their fathers' scruples and were present, must have thrilled as they heard him declaim: "The youth of a nation are the trustees of posterity... I tell them to aspire. I believe that the man who does not look up will look down; and the spirit that does not dare to soar is destined perhaps to grovel."

Manners made his own characteristic contribution by exhorting his audience: "Be it yours to render obsolete the taunt that manufactures must produce a dry, harsh, unpoetical and material spirit." Smythe also made a speech which he himself described as a great hit.

Circumstances were too strong for Smythe. The Strangford family finances were at a low ebb; at Cambridge George had lived with companions who spent a pound with as little inconvenience as he spent a shilling, and he had run into debt. Now his father urged him to rehabilitate the family fortunes by a rich marriage. Unfortunately no rich marriage such as he could fancy offered itself, and the only possible professions were the army and diplomacy, both of which were costly rather than lucrative. He complained sadly that his father reproached him for "bringing no honey to the hive". Eventually he towed the line, and in 1846 he accepted from Peel the under-secretaryship of the Foreign Office. The gay, exhilarating intransigence of his Young England days was over; he admitted that he was now "fettered by party ties and muzzled by office". The drudgery of office was uncongenial to him; he was still impatient of control. In 1855 he succeeded his father as Lord Strangford, but his health was failing and two years later he died of consumption. He had written to his father: "Were I to die to-morrow I should occupy three lines in a biographical dictionary as a 'might-have-been'."

Actually, Smythe has three columns in the *Dictionary of National Biography*, in which the brilliant promise of his early years in Parliament is stressed. He broke down in his maiden speech—evidently a considerable ordeal in those days, as Disraeli brought out in *Endymion*—but before long Gladstone rated him as one of the best speakers amongst the younger members of the House. His quick temper often led to trouble and in 1852 he was involved in the last duel to be fought in England. This was almost a comic affair, as a cock pheasant rose between the combatants at the crucial moment! After this curious intervention the quarrel was settled without bloodshed. Smythe made his contribution to the literature of Young England with his *Historical Fancies*, essays upon diverse subjects and full of vivid phrases, such as his description of a constitutional monarch as "a bedizened doll upon a gilded stool". Lord Lyttelton said of him, "Poor George! He was a splendid failure." The charming portrait of him at Hughenden Manor makes it easy to believe Disraeli's remark that he was the only man who had never bored him.

Lord John Manners became First Commissioner of Public Works in 1851, in which capacity he was responsible for the arrangements for the Duke of Wellington's impressive funeral. It is pleasing to find that when Disraeli at last became Prime Minister (1868) he included him in his Cabinet, and again in his second Ministry. A small volume of poems—*England's Trust*—preserves his youthful ideals. Two lines have been quoted derisively:

> Let wealth and commerce, laws and learning die,
> But leave us still our old nobility.

The young Lord John saw the old nobility as a regenerating force in society. He adjured the nobles to raise again "the feudal banner of forgotten days", continuing:

> Then would the different classes once again
> Feel the kind pressure of the social chain,
> And in their mutual wants and hopes confess
> How close allied the little to the less.

The social chain of an idealised feudal system was a young aristocrat's dream and not in keeping with the times, but Lord John should also have the credit of realising the degradation and helplessness to which the Industrial Revolution, and the failure of social responsibility in the governing classes, had reduced the labourer. Lamenting that the old ties had been destroyed, he pictured the plight of the once sturdy peasant:

> Now in their place behold the modern slave,
> Doomed, from the very cradle to the grave
> To tread the lonely path of care and toil;
> Bound, in sad truth, and bowed down to the soil,
> He dies, and leaves his sons their heritage—
> Work for their prime, the workhouse for their age.

Monckton Milnes parodied Lord John's enthusiasm for the revival of old customs in a poem called *Lines to a Judge*:

> Oh! Flog me at the old cart's tail!
> I surely should enjoy
> That fine old English punishment
> I witnessed when a boy!
> I should not heed the mocking crowd,
> I should not feel the pain,
> If *one* old English custom
> Could be brought back again.

There is some interest in comparing Thackeray's sketch of Lord Hartford, as Lord Steyne in *Vanity Fair*, with Disraeli's Lord Monmouth. Disraeli's is the more attractive picture, but he idealised Lord Hertford's physical appearance to suit the impressive figure he needed for his story. There was nothing "superb and icy" about Lord Steyne, whom Thackeray endowed with a bald head fringed with red hair, bushy eyebrows, little twinkling bloodshot eyes and two buck-teeth which "glistened savagely" when he smiled. He was, however, proud of his feet and ankles, and had a habit of caressing his Garter knee. Disraeli allows

Coningsby to find his grandfather entertaining some French actresses, but the dissolute side of Lord Monmouth is not stressed. Thackeray describes "the famous *petits appartements* of Lord Steyne", reached by a back-door in Gaunt House mews. Here were rooms fitted up in ivory and white satin, or ebony and black velvet, and a little private kitchen in which all the utensils were of silver or gold. Here Egalité Orleans and Lord Steyne roasted partridges one night, after his lordship had won £100,000 at ombre. Lord Steyne's country houses were magnificent; at Gaunt Castle there were two hundred silver tea-pots for serving breakfasts. The two lords have other traits in common besides wealth and profligacy. When Thackeray wrote of Lord Steyne that he grinned "as this old cynic always did at any naïve display of human weakness", it might equally well have been Lord Monmouth. Lord Steyne also had his Rigby, in Mr. Wenham, who was "his lordship's vizier and confidential servant, with a seat in Parliament and at the dinner-table". Upon occasion Lord Steyne could assume polished manners as readily as Lord Monmouth; he might bully his daughter-in-law in private but in public he treated her with a distinguished courtesy which charmed everyone. Both noblemen dreaded boredom above all things. When Lord Steyne promised Becky the coveted invitation to Gaunt House he added: "It's not half so nice as here. You will be bored there. I am. My wife is as gay as Lady Macbeth, and my daughters as cheerful as Regan and Goneril."

The real Lord Hertford was dissolute and extremely rich; his dinners and house-parties were magnificent; he was intimate with George IV. Greville gives a repulsive picture of him in his old age, when he was carried by two footmen from his carriage into the brothel. He admits that his faculties were far beyond mediocrity, but they were "wasted and degraded"; the gaiety of the *bon-vivant*, the coolness of the great gambler, were lost in avarice and sensuality and "pride without dignity". Lord Monmouth never sank to these depths. Disraeli, however, drew partly from life; he had met Lord Hertford in society, and shared in the general speculation as to how he would leave his vast property. When the will came out he wrote to Sarah Disraeli: "The Zichy has £150,000 because she saved Lord Hertford from being poisoned by her mother." This clause in the will may have suggested that Lord Monmouth should leave his fortune to Flora.

Thackeray parodied *Coningsby* brilliantly in a burlesque under the title of *Codlingsby*. The weight of his ridicule fell most heavily on Sidonia, whom he called Rafael Mendoza. The hero, Godfrey de Bouillon, Marquis of Codlingsby, penetrated the Jewish quarter of London to visit this great man:

"The occupants of the London ghetto sat at their porches basking in the evening sunshine. Children were playing on the steps. Fathers were smoking at the lintel. Smiling faces looked out from the various and darkling draperies with which the warehouses were hung. Ringlets glossy, and curly, and jetty; eyes black as night—midsummer night—when it lightens; haughty noses bending like beaks of eagles; eager quivering nostrils; lips curved like the bow of Love—every man or maiden, every babe or matron, in that English Jewry bore in his countenance one or more of these characteristics of his peerless Arab race."

Codlingsby reflected that the Jews were but a small people and that they had lost Jerusalem to a Roman army—but had they not taken the world in exchange? He was startled out of his reverie by a voice saying, "D'you vant a nishe coat?" It was Mendoza in disguise. He led his young friend under "an awning of old clothes, tawdry fripperies and greasy spangles", through a sordid shop and into his own apartments. The room they entered by this squalid approach was furnished in "the simple taste of its owner":

"The carpet was of white velvet (laid over several webs of Aubusson, Ispahan, and Axminster, so that your foot gave no more sound as it trod upon the yielding plain than the shadow did which followed you)—of white velvet, painted with flowers, arabesques and classic figures by Sir William Ross, J. M. W. Turner, R.A., Mrs. Mee and Paul Delaroche. The edges were wrought with seed-pearls, and fringed with Valenciennes lace and bullion. The walls were hung with cloth of silver, embroidered with gold figures, over which were worked pomegranates, polyanthuses and passion-flowers, in ruby, amethyst and smaragd. The drops of dew which the artificer had sprinkled on the flowers were diamonds. The hangings were overhung by pictures yet more costly. Giorgione the gorgeous, Titian the golden, Rubens the ruddy and pulpy (the Pan of Painting), some of Murillo's beatified shepherdesses, who smile on you out of darkness like a star, a few score first-class Leonardos, and fifty of the masterpieces of the patron of Julius and Leo, the Imperial genius of Urbino, covered the walls of the little chamber. Divans of carved amber covered with ermine went round the room; and in the midst was a fountain, pattering and babbling with jets of double-distilled otto of roses."

In the midst of this magnificence Rafael's sister Miriam sat on a music-stool of mother-of-pearl at an ivory piano with keys of silver and enamel.

These samples suffice to show how cruelly such a burlesque could wound Disraeli. He might have forgiven the parody of his magnificent settings, which was, indeed, not greatly exaggerated, but the caricature of Sidonia touched him in a tender spot. As in Vivian Grey and Contarini Fleming he had found some compensation for the slights he himself had suffered as a schoolboy, so in the sublime, omniscient Sidonia, a power behind thrones and governments, he had created a dream figure to glorify his slighted race. Brilliant ridicule of Sidonia must have been hard to bear. Disraeli repaid Thackeray in his own coin by the portrait he drew of him thirty-nine years later as St. Barbe in *Endymion*.

CHAPTER IX

Sybil (I)

CONINGSBY is notable for its characters, many of them drawn, with more or less truth, from Disraeli's contemporaries. *Sybil* is distinguished for its scenes, which the author took great pains to picture as faithfully as possible from the life of the "two nations" which, he held, sharply divided England—the RICH and the POOR. Disraeli spent some time in the industrial North garnering material from observation and research. He was in sympathy with the hatred of the new Poor Law of 1834, which was one of the early forces that drove working-men to combine in systematic agitation, stirred by Cobbett's writings and encouraged by some leaders of standing, such as Fielden, a factory owner, and Oastler, who had first denounced child-slavery in the Yorkshire mills. Disraeli studied the report of the Children's Employment Commission (1842) and other documents, and a friend arranged for him to see the correspondence of Feargus O'Connor, a fiery Chartist leader who set the north of England almost literally aflame with his Chartist newspaper, the *Northern Star*.

There is no doubt that in general the background of *Sybil* is neither over- nor under-drawn. The patience of the factory workers, the growth of their slowly mounting anger, the surge of mobs, and the pathetic faith in the People's Charter as a cure for all their ills, are authentic. The slick young town worker, Dandy Mick, his agitator friend, known as Devilsdust, and the pert and lively mill-girls may have a cockney quickness and wit that are not quite in place in Lancashire, but they are living human-beings. The famous scene in the tommy-shop (in which workpeople drew part of their wages in goods supplied by the employer) is one of the most graphic pieces of social evidence in any novel of this type. Disraeli himself claimed that "in *Sybil* I considered the condition of the people". He succeeded so well that for once he emancipated himself from the dominant hero who largely represented his own character; the hero and heroine of

Sybil are little more than lay figures overshadowed by the English People, for whom and by whom the book lives.

Sybil opens on the eve of the Derby of 1837. The first chapters are given to the RICH, and in a London club (Crockford's) we find a number of young men discussing their bets, one of the few excitements of which they have not yet wearied. They dine together; the scene is sumptuous, the talk languid:

"The gleaming lustres poured a flood of soft yet brilliant light over a plateau glittering with gold plate, and fragrant with exotics embedded in vases of rare porcelain. The seats on each side of the table were occupied by persons consuming, with a heedless air, delicacies for which they had no appetite; while the conversation in general consisted of flying phrases referring to the impending event of the great day that had already dawned.

" 'Come from Lady St. Julians', Fitz?' said a youth of very tender years, whose fair visage was as downy and as blooming as the peach from which, with a languid air, he withdrew his lips to make his enquiry of the gentleman with the cane.

" 'Yes; why were not you there?'

" 'I never go anywhere,' said the melancholy Cupid, 'everything bores me so.'

" 'Well, will you go to Epsom with us to-morrow, Alfred?' said Lord Fitzheron. 'I take Berners and Charles Egremont, and with you our party will be perfect.'

" 'I feel so cursed blasé!' exclaimed the boy in a tone of elegant anguish.

" 'It will give you a filip, Alfred,' said Mr. Berners; 'do you all the good in the world.'

" 'Nothing can do me good,' said Alfred, throwing away his almost untasted peach; 'I should be quite content if anything could do me harm. Waiter, bring me a tumbler of Badminton.'

" 'And bring me one too,' sighed out Lord Eugene de Vere, who was a year older than Alfred Mountchesney, his companion and brother in listlessness. Both had exhausted life in their teens, and all that remained for them was to mourn, amid the ruins of their reminiscences, over the extinction of excitement.

" 'Well, Eugene, suppose you come with us,' said Lord Fitzheron.

"'I think I shall go down to Hampton Court and play tennis,' said Lord Eugene. 'As it is the Derby, nobody will be there.'

"'And I will go with you, Eugene,' said Alfred Mountchesney, 'and we will dine together afterwards at the Toy. Anything is better than dining in this infernal London.'

"'Well, for my part,' said Mr. Berners, 'I do not like your suburban dinners, you always get something you can't eat, and cursed bad wine.'

"'I rather like bad wine,' said Mr. Mountchesney; 'one gets so bored with good wine.'"

Presently the hero of the book, Charles Egremont, joined this company. He was, of course, good-looking in a patrician style, and a favourite with both sexes. He was far from mourning over the extinction of excitement, as he had laid bets considerably above his means. The family to which he belonged was not of ancient nobility, its founder had been a confidential servant of one of Henry VIII's favourites and had risen to be a commissioner deputed to take the surrender of various monasteries. He was notably assiduous in this rôle and contrived to enrich himself most satisfactorily. At the beginning of the seventeenth century one of the family achieved the peerage as Baron Marney. The College of Heralds obligingly drew up a pedigree for him, which went back to Norman times, and endowed him with the pleasing family name of Egremont. In the course of time the barony was converted into an earldom. The Marneys had feathered their nest well, although "the country was not indebted to them for a single statesman, orator, successful warrior, great lawyer, learned divine, eminent author or illustrious man of science". The hero of *Sybil* was the younger brother of the Earl of Marney, whose estate in the North included the ruins of Marney Abbey (supposed to be Fountains), which his ancestor had despoiled.

After a graphic description of the Derby (in which Egremont lost heavily) Disraeli interrupts his story with a long digression on the history of England from the latter part of the eighteenth century to the eve of the Reform Bill. The reader who takes up *Sybil* as a novel finds this chapter of pure history disconcerting, but there is some acute observation and good characterisation in it. Disraeli tilts once more against the "Venetian oligarchy" set up by the Whigs who succeeded what Lord Chatham described as the Great Revolution families:

"A people without power or education had been induced to believe themselves the freest and most enlightened nation in the world, and had submitted to lavish their blood and treasure, to see their industry crippled and their labour mortgaged, in order to maintain an oligarchy that had neither ancient memories to soften nor present services to justify their unprecedented usurpation."

There are reflections upon Bolingbroke (a hero of Disraeli's), Burke and Pitt, and a masterly character-sketch of Shelburne, with features that recall Sidonia. Shelburne, we are told, was deep and adroit, a great linguist, versed in both literature and science, and "the earliest and most authentic information reached him from all courts and quarters of Europe". It was he who first realised the rising importance of the middle class and saw that it might be a bulwark for the throne against a powerful oligarchy. The rise of the national debt is denounced. In the consequent over-stimulation of production the moral condition of the people was entirely neglected, and the result was: "A mortgaged aristocracy, a gambling foreign commerce, a home trade founded on a morbid competition, and a degraded people." Passing on, Disraeli asserts that from the death of the younger Pitt to 1825 "the political history of England is a history of great events and little men". At last we come to the Duke of Wellington, who, despite many fine qualities, is said to lack one essential—a knowledge of England.

After this long chapter the story is resumed. Egremont, oppressed by "the horrid phantom of settling-day", went to see his mother, the dowager Lady Marney. This lady, who became Lady Deloraine by a second marriage, is charmingly drawn and said to be modelled on Disraeli's old friend the Marchioness of Londonderry. She now urged her son to forget his naughty horse, as she had important news for him. The King (William IV) was dying; there would be a general election and she had settled with Mr. Tadpole that Egremont should stand for the old family borough of Marbury. Lady Marney buoyantly overrode his objection on account of the expense of a contest: "Oh, I have no doubt that we shall have some monster of the middle class, some tinker or tailor or candlestick-maker, with his long purse, preaching reform and practising corruption ... but we have a capital registration, Mr. Tadpole tells me. And a young candidate with an old name will tell ... And I shall go down and canvass."

Egremont again reminded her of the necessity of powder and shot, and she told him that he must go to see his brother the Earl and persuade him to support his candidature for the honour of the family. As the mother and son talked a note was brought in from Lady St. Julians, a great political hostess and intriguer (representing in some degree Sarah, Countess of Jersey), which assured her friend that the King was only suffering from hay-fever and she was going on with her quadrille. "Poor woman!" exclaimed Lady Marney, "she is always wrong. Her quadrille will never take place, which is a pity, as it is to consist only of beauties and eldest sons."

She was right. Soon Lady St. Julians was "driving distractedly about town, calling at clubs, closeted with red tapers, making ingenious combinations that would not work, by means of which some one of her sons was to stand in coalition with some rich parvenu; to pay none of the expenses and yet to come in first". Meanwhile Lady Marney was able to say serenely that her son had already chosen his borough.

Disraeli now once more launches into historical commentary. He asks what the Reform Bill has done for the country, and concludes that it has increased the worship of Mammon to such an extent that "it has been the breathless business of enfrenchised England" to set up an Utopia of WEALTH and TOIL, until "we are startled from our voracious strife by the wail of intolerable serfage". The only virtue he allows the Bill is that it set men thinking and so led them to study politics. Now, with the death of William IV, perhaps a new era is opening, inaugurated "in a palace in a garden", where the young Queen received the news of her accession to the throne—"Will it be her proud destiny at length to bear relief to suffering millions, and, with that soft hand which might inspire troubadours and guerdon knights, break the last links in the chain of Saxon thraldom?" This passage may well have been founded on Disraeli's meditations as he sat waiting for Lord Lyndhurst, whom he had accompanied to Kensington Palace when he attended the Queen's first Council. The scene, as described by Lord Lyndhurst on the drive back to Westminster, is reproduced in *Sybil*.

Egremont won his election, but the thousand pounds supplied by his mother did not cover his expenses and he was obliged to apply to his brother for a contribution. Lord Marney was capable and not ill-informed, but hard, cynical, pugnacious and obstinate. He was wary and gave the impression that he was "a man who was conscious that you were trying to take him in, and rather respected you for it, but the working of whose cold, unkind eye defied you". There had been an estrangement between him and Egremont, but now, at their Mother's request, the brothers were prepared to make up their quarrel. Lord Marney, however, provided against any show of emotion by coming into the drawing-room only a few minutes before dinner, supported by his ever-ready factotum Captain Grouse and the Vicar of Marney, who also was his puppet. He had invited a neighbour, Sir Vavasour Firebrace, to join them.

At Marney Abbey, as at Beaumanoir, the new Poor Law was a subject of table-talk. Lord Marney expressed himself energetically: what was needed was stringency, if the law were carried out in the proper spirit, as it was in the Marney Union, it would be the salvation of the country. Egremont was doubtful, but he knew nothing of the condition of the people. Sir Vavasour wished the people would take to it a little more, and was inclined to favour some modification of outdoor relief. Lord Marney crushed this weak sentiment by saying conclusively: "The people are very contented here, eh, Slimsey?" "Very," said the obliging Vicar.

Sir Vavasour Firebrace is one of Disraeli's notable oddities. He had his own solution for the problems of society. He believed that, given its due, the baronetage was "the body destined to save this country". The baronets were the hereditary champions of the Crown, the popular branch of the nobles and the natural leaders of the people. The Reform Bill would never have been passed if the baronets had been organised. Encouraged by Egremont's courteous deference to his father's old friend, he enlarged on his theme with enthusiasm. The old prestige of the baronets, and the badge to which they had once been entitled, should be revived. Egremont listened with amazement as he declaimed:

"Picture us for a moment, to yourself, going down in procession to Westminster, for example, to hold a chapter. Five or six hundred baronets in dark green costume—the appropriate dress of *equites aurati*; each not only with his badge, but collar of S.S.; belted and scarfed; his star glittering; his pennon flying; his hat white, with a plume of white feathers; of course the sword and gilt spurs. In our hand, the thumb-ring and signet not forgotten, we hold our coronet of two balls!"

There was much more in the same strain, fitting the eldest sons and the baronets' ladies into the picture.

Lord Marney's boast that the people were very contented in his neighbourhood was not justified. He held that an agricultural labourer could live well on seven shillings a week, and with a certain income he had no cares or anxieties. In case of need he had a resource in the Union workhouse, which was heated with hot air, a luxury they did not enjoy at Marney Abbey. People with no cares did not need a great deal of food; the fact that the labourer usually had a long span of life was proof of this. The labourers, however, obstinately refused to be content with their lot. Amongst other evils was one which had been bred by the old poor law system: landowners were so anxious to avoid having too many paupers on the parish rates that only the genuinely humanitarian would build or repair cottages. Consequently numbers of farm-labourers were forced into the country towns, where they were crowded together in insanitary streets and had to walk considerable distances to their work. The rural town of Marney was an example of this development. In richly wooded country, which was watered by a fine, clear river, it was a cluster of slums. The cottages were falling to pieces, the thatch let in the wind and the rain, the roofs looked like dunghills. The floors were neither boarded nor paved, and channels were often cut in the mud or clay to drain away the water which seeped in or ran down the walls. There was no drainage or sanitation, the refuse was either thrown into the open sewer which ran down the middle of the street or piled in heaps beside the doors. When a door was opened to ventilate an odorous, suffocating room it was not fresh air which came in, but "a mixture of gases from reeking dung-hills".

All these appalling details may be verified in government

reports and blue-books—sanitation had become a public problem by 1840—and in the writings of such sanitary reformers as Dr. Duncan of Liverpool. Mrs. Gaskell and Charles Kingsley give terrible pictures of squalor and destitution in *Mary Barton* and *Alton Locke*. In Greville's *Diary* there are shocking details of the state of the town of Sunderland when cholera broke out there in 1831. Houses were found in which 150 inmates were living "in the lowest state of poverty", five and six huddled in one bed. Conditions in Spitalfields were quite as bad: more than half of the population was living on poor relief and the rest were crippled by the consequent heavy rates. Greville concluded: "The awful thing is the vast extent of the misery and distress which prevails."

Soon Lord Marney was temporarily shaken out of his complacency by the news that his best ricks had been set on fire. He was equally outraged as landowner and magistrate, and determined to quell such symptoms of revolt with a stern hand. Charles Egremont, too, took the conventional view of his class. He asked a "hind" who held his horse what he thought of the fires. The man answered, "I think 'tis hard times for the poor, sir." Egremont made the natural reply, "But rick-burning will not make the times easier, my good man." Nevertheless, he was disturbed. He wandered into the precincts of the ruined abbey and there he asked himself for the first time whether all was well with the English people. The nation was powerful, rich, free and enlightened—why did the people burn ricks?

Presently Egremont saw two strangers. One was dressed in dark velveteen with leather gaiters and might equally well have been a squire or a game-keeper; his face was frank and manly. The other, a younger man, wore faded black, but his linen was clean and his much-worn gloves carefully mended. Egremont spoke to them; the elder man was very ready to talk and gave Egremont his views on the suppression of the monasteries. The monks, he believed, were good landlords. One abbot followed another with no break—"the manor had not to dread a change of lords, or the oaks to tremble at the axe of the squandering heir". The monks granted leases—a thing Lord Marney would never hear of—and their tenants had security. He became eloquent upon the subject: "There were yeomen then, sir: the country was not divided into two classes, masters and slaves; there was some resting-place between luxury and misery. Comfort was an English habit then, not merely an English word." Moreover, the monks knew the people, the poor and the unfortunate could look to them for help. The stranger computed that there had once been about forty such great monastic establishments as Marney Abbey in Yorkshire alone, and he exclaimed: "Try to imagine thirty or forty Chatsworths in this county, the proprietors of which were never absent." After the monasteries had been despoiled the land looked as if it had been invaded by a ruthless enemy, the ravage had never been wholly repaired. The stranger concluded: "I don't know whether the Union workhouses will remove it. They are building something for the people at last. After an experiment of three centuries, your jails being full, and your treadmills losing something of their virtue, you have given us a substitute for the monasteries."

Egremont was deeply interested and confined his objections to a mild suggestion that the monks had their faults, otherwise they might not have been turned out. He was still more impressed when the younger man joined in the talk and argued that England had now become two nations, so different in nurture, habits and thought that there was neither intercourse nor sympathy between them, namely the RICH and the POOR.

The talk was interrupted by a voice of thrilling sweetness, chanting the evening hymn to the Virgin in the ruined lady-chapel. For a moment Egremont saw the singer standing in an archway below the evening star. He thought at first that she wore the dress of a nun, but she had no veil, her glorious fair hair was uncovered. She was more than beautiful, there was an expression of almost divine majesty in her face. Before he could ask a question the vision disappeared, and the two men also slipped away.

This incident seemed little more than a dream when Egremont was confronted with the harsh reality of his position. Lord Marney was not prepared to disburse any money on his behalf, but he proposed that his brother should go with him and his wife on a visit to Mowbray Castle where, if he played his cards well, he might win the hand of Lady Joan Fitz-Warene, a great heiress.

The de Mowbrays, like the Marneys, owed their peerage to an

adventurer. Disraeli pauses to enumerate the types which, in various centuries, had risen to wealth and power: the Turkey merchant, the West India planter, the Nabob, the Loanmonger and the Manufacturer. An obscure ancestor of Lord de Mowbray had made a fortune in India; manufactures in the neighbourhood had trebled the present lord's rent-roll. He had married a Duke's daughter, and his coat-of-arms "was emblazoned on every window, embroidered on every chair, carved in every corner". He was a man of ability, but he had been "over-educated for his intellect". (Disraeli used this phrase again in describing the Prince Consort as a man who had not been over-educated for his intellect.) Unfortunately his heiress, Lady Joan Fitz-Warene, was a sandy girl with little to attract but a good figure, and she was a pedant. She favoured Egremont with an account of the Aztec cities and from Mexico passed on to Egypt, dispatching the phonetic system by the way, and finally invited him to visit her observatory to look at a comet which she had been the first to discover. Egremont found himself unable to fall in with his brother's scheme.

There was, however, much to interest him at Mowbray Castle, and he was glad to meet Mr. Aubrey St. Lys, the Vicar of Mowbray. St. Lys both looked and was an aristocrat, a younger son of an ancient family, and he was not afraid to break a lance with Lord Marney. When his lordship remarked that higher wages would only find their way to the beer-shops, which were the curse of the country, St. Lys deplored the system which herded women into factories for fourteen hours a day and destroyed home life. St. Lys, a high churchman, tried to offer the people some elevating beauty and colour in the church services, but it was up-hill work, despite the fact that Mowbray had a very fine church (identified as Ripon Cathedral). St. Lys may have been drawn from Father Faber, a disciple of the Oxford Movement, whose friendship had influenced the views of Lord John Manners. It has also been suggested that he represents Ambrose Lisle Phillips, already portrayed as Eustace Lyle in *Coningsby*.

In the novel scenes from the life of the rich and the poor alternate, and we must return to the three strangers whom Egremont had seen at Marney Abbey. Walter Gerard, the elder man, was the son of a farmer who had lost his small capital in trying to establish his claim to a great estate. Gerard was now a foreman in Trafford's mill, one of the few model factories in the country. He was a Roman Catholic and his beautiful daughter, Sybil, had been brought up in a convent, of which Mr. Trafford's sister was the Mother Superior. She was motherless and still lived in the convent, to which she owed an education and a refinement unusual in the daughter of a working-man. The younger man, Stephen Morley, was a journalist with radical views; he was interested in Gerard's story and anxious to help him to trace some papers relating to the estate, which had been placed in the hands of a genealogical expert named Hatton, who had disappeared. The three had gone to Marney Abbey to look at the tomb of the last abbot, which bore the name Walter Gerard. This mystery, so characteristic of a Disraeli novel, is a weakness in a book which professes to be dedicated to the condition of the people. Knowing Disraeli, the reader at once jumps to the conclusion that Sybil is not a genuine daughter of the people, will eventually be endowed with rank and wealth, and probably bestow them upon Egremont. The plot of *Sybil*, however, is no more than a thread which holds a succession of scenes together, and now, when Gerard and Morley plunge into the populous working-class quarter of Mowbray, we see something of the life of the POOR.

Saturday night in Mowbray had its gaieties. The jolly Widow Carey at her market stall bantered her customers with hearty relish. Amongst them was Dandy Mick, an impudent, swaggering youth of sixteen, whose Saturday night finery consisted of loose white trousers, a coarse white frock coat, a pink silk neckerchief with a flamboyant pin and a high-crowned brown hat. He greeted the Widow as "Mother", but she retorted tartly: " 'Don't mother me. Go to your own mother who is dying in a back cellar without a window, while you've got lodgings in a two-pair.'

" 'Dying! She's only drunk,' said the youth.

" 'And if she is only drunk,' rejoined Mrs. Carey in a passion, 'what makes her drink but toil; working from 5 o'clock in the morning to 7 o'clock at night, and for the like of such as you.'

" 'That's a good one,' said the youth. 'I should like to know what my Mother ever did for me, but give me treacle and laudanum when I was a baby, to stop my tongue and fill my stomach, by token of which, as my gal says, she's stunted the growth of the prettiest figure in all Mowbray.'

"... 'Well, I never,' said Mrs. Carey. 'No, I never heard a thing like that!'

" 'What, not when you cut up the jackass and sold it for veal cutlets, Mother?'

" 'Hold your tongue, Mr. Imperence!' said the Widow. 'It's very well known you are no Christian, and who'll believe what you say?' "

Dandy Mick was joined by two mill-girls, Caroline and Harriet, with gay handkerchiefs over their hair, coral necklaces and gold ear-rings. They told Widow Carey that they had set up house together and invited her to take a dish of tea with them one day. Dandy Mick rose to the occasion and offered to take the girls to the Temple, the favourite place of entertainment for those who could afford it. As the party moved off Widow Carey reflected that it was a topsy-turvy world, in which the young people got the good wages, while their parents often found it hard to get any work at all.

The Temple of the Muses, presided over by Chaffing Jack, blazed with light; its walls were brightly painted with scenes from Shakespeare, Byron and Scott, and it had a stage on which entertainers appeared at intervals. Harriet, who had never been there before, murmured, "It's just what I thought the Queen lived in; but, indeed, I'm all of a flutter."

"Well, don't look as if you were," said her friend.

"Come along, gals," said Mick; "who's afraid? Here, we'll sit down at this table. Now, what shall we have? Here, waiter; I say, waiter!"

A friend of the Dandy's soon joined them, and was greeted as Devilsdust. At seventeen Devilsdust was a personage, he was a first-rate workman and earned good wages, and was a leading spirit in the Shoddy Court Literary and Scientific Institute. In contrast to his gay and volatile friend, Devilsdust was dark, melancholy and brooding. His had been a strange life. His mother had farmed him out in infancy at threepence a week, and the old woman who took him kept him quiet with Godfrey's cordial until his mother disappeared and the payments stopped. Then, when he could barely toddle, she drove him out into the street "to play", hoping she would not see him again. But the child was tough, and uncannily clever; he never got in the way of the horses and carts and never lost his own. At nights he crept back to the cellar he knew as home. Then the dread cholera swept the district and one night the little creature found the old woman and the last of his companions lying dead. He had shared his bed of straw with a corpse before, but instinct moved him to leave a place where he was the only living thing. He lay down and slept on the steps of a factory. The next morning he followed the workers inside; a child was wanted in the Wadding Hole, to collect the waste cotton from the floor, and the waif was put on the pay-roll. Although he was then five he could not give himself a name; someone called him Devilsdust, and Devilsdust—or Dusty—he had been ever since. He had taken advantage of the factory school, and as he grew up he developed radical views on the rights of labour. After he joined them the young people discussed various places of work. Traffords' was decent and fair, but the mill was in the country, and there was too much schooling and hymn-singing; at Wiggins and Websters' the machinery must be cleaned in the dinner-hour; Shuffle & Screw mulcted their hands of wages by fines and dodges; Truck & Trutt paid partly in goods, and very bad stuff for the money.

Amongst various features of industrial life Disraeli pictures the caller-up, who slipped through the streets and alleys in the cold glimmer of dawn, tapping on windows with a long pole like a shepherd's crook. Not many workpeople had clocks, and they paid a few pence a week for this service, to save themselves the fines that would be deducted from their wages if they were late at the factory.

Perhaps the most famous passage in the book is the one in which Disraeli describes the mine disgorging its slaves at night:

"They come forth; the mine delivers its gang and the pit its bondsmen; the forge is silent and the engine is still. The plain is covered with the swarming multitude: bands of stalwart men, broad-chested and muscular, wet with toil and black as the children of the tropics; troops of youth—alas! of both sexes—though neither their raiment nor their language indicates the difference; all are clad in male attire; and oaths men might shudder at issue from lips born to breathe words of sweetness. Yet these are to be —some are—the Mothers of England! But can we wonder at the hideous coarseness of their language, when we remember the savage rudeness of their living? Naked to the waist, an iron chain fastened to a belt of leather runs between their legs clad in canvas trousers, while on hands and feet an English girl, for twelve, sometimes sixteen hours a day, hauls and hurries tubs of coals up subterranean roads, dark, precipitous and plashy; circumstances which seem to have escaped the notice of the Society for the Abolition of Negro Slavery. Those worthy gentlemen too appear to have been singularly unconscious of the sufferings of the little trappers, which was remarkable, as many of them were in their own employ.

"See, too, these emerge from the bowels of the earth! Infants of four and five years of age, many of them girls, pretty and still soft and timid; entrusted with fulfilment of most responsible duties, and the nature of which entails on them the necessity of being the earliest to enter the mine and the latest to leave it. Their labour indeed is not severe, for that would be impossible, but it is passed in darkness and solitude. They endure that punishment which philosophical philanthropy has invented for the direst criminals, and which those criminals deem more terrible than the death for which it is substituted. Hour after hour elapses, and all that reminds the infant trappers of the world they have quitted and that which they have joined, is the passage of the coal-wagons for which they open the air-doors of the galleries, and on keeping which doors constantly closed, except at this moment of passage, the safety of the mine and the lives of the persons employed in it entirely depend.

"Sir Joshua, a man of genius and a courtly artist, struck by the seraphic countenance of Lady Alice Gordon, when a child of very tender years, painted the celestial visage in various attitudes on the same canvas, and styled the group of heavenly faces—guardian angels!

"We would say to some great master of the pencil, Mr. Landseer or Mr. Etty, go thou to the little trappers and do likewise!"

All this was true of the period of which Disraeli was writing. In the evidence given before the Commission on the Employment of Women and Children in Mines (1842) a little girl described how she sat in the dark from 3.30 a.m. to 5 p.m., opening and shutting the trap-door to let the cages pass. A boy of seven said that he had been a trapper for three years and kept himself awake by smoking a pipe. Another case came up in which a child had been startled by a mouse and failed to close the trap, with the result that a party of miners crashed to their death. This evidence was brought before Parliament and for once it was not necessary for Lord Ashley to labour the case, members were shocked into drastic action and the employment of women and children in mines was forbidden. It was, therefore, a thing of the past by the time *Sybil* was published.

CHAPTER X

Sybil (II)

ONE of the most poignant scenes in *Sybil* is the gathering of workmen's wives on Grand Tommy-Day, when they had to select goods from the employer's shop to be booked against their husbands' wages. It was a wet, gusty morning and a crowd of women, girls and children huddled together waiting until it suited Mr. Diggs to open the shop. They talked of their grievances:

" 'I have been here since half-past four, Mrs. Grigsby, with this chilt at my breast all the time. It's three miles for me here, and the same back, and unless I get the first turn how are my poor boys to find their dinner ready when they come out of the pit?'

" 'A very true word, Mrs. Page; and, by this token, that last Thursday I was here by half-past eleven, certainly afore noon . . . and it was eight o'clock before I got home. Ah! It's cruel work, is the tommy-shop.' "

Others discussed the goods:

" 'The cheese here at sixpence is pretty tidy,' said a crone to her companion; 'but you may get as good in the town for fourpence.'

" 'What I complain is the weights,' replied her companion.

" 'I weighed my pound of butter bought last tommy-day, and it was two penny-pieces too light. Indeed! I have been, in my time, to all the shops about here, for the lads or their father, but never knew tommy so bad as this. I have two children at home ill from their flour; I have been very poorly myself; one is used to a little white clay, but when they lay it on thick, it's very grave.'

" 'Are your girls in the pit?'

" 'No; we strive to keep them out, and my man has gone scores of days on bread and water for that purpose; and if we were not forced to take so much tommy, one might manage—but tommy will beat everything.' "

Here a small boy asked wistfully, "Dame, when will the door

open? I have been here all this morn, and never broke my fast.' The woman asked him what he wanted and he replied, "I want a loaf for Mother; but I don't feel I shall ever get home again, I'm all in a way so dizzy."

Another woman complained that Joseph Diggs had stuck down in her tommy-book things that she had never had; she didn't know figures and her husband had told her that she could no more keep house than a natural born. Her neighbour rounded on her and asked when her husband was going to pay what he owed to hers. She became vehement: "It's a scarlet shame to go to the spout because money lent to a friend is not to be found." The other pleaded with her to be patient a little longer, her poor baby was bound to die soon, and then there would be money from a burial club and the debt should be paid. At last the door of the tommy-shop opened:

"The rush was like the advance into the pit of a theatre when the drama existed; pushing, squeezing, fighting, tearing, shrieking. On a high seat, guarded by rails from all contact, sat Mr. Diggs senior, with a bland smile on his sanctified countenance, a pen behind his ear, and recommending his customers in honeyed tones to be patient and orderly. Behind the substantial counter, which was an impregnable fortification, was his popular son, Master Joseph; a short, ill-favoured cur, with a spirit of vulgar oppression and malicious mischief stamped on his visage . . . For the first five minutes Master Joseph Diggs did nothing but blaspheme and swear at his customers, occasionally leaning over the counter and cuffing the women in the van or lugging some girl by the hair.

" 'I was first, Master Joseph,' said a woman eagerly.

" 'No; I was,' said another.

" 'I was here,' said the first, 'as the clock struck four, and seated myself on the steps, because I must be home early; my husband is hurt in the knee.'

" 'If you were first, you shall be helped last,' said Master Joseph, 'to reward you for your pains'; and he began taking the orders of the other woman.

" 'Oh! Lord have mercy on me!' said the disappointed woman; 'and I got up in the middle of the night for this!'

"... 'Don't make a brawling here,' said Master Joseph, 'or I'll jump over this here counter and knock you down, like nothing. What did you say, woman? Are you deaf? What did you say? How much best tea do you want?'

" 'I don't want any, sir.'

" 'You never want best tea; you must take three ounces of best tea, or you shan't have nothing. If you say another word, I'll put you down four ... Who's pushing on there? I see you, Mrs. Page. Won't there be a black mark against you! Oh! It's Mrs. Prance, is it? Father, put down Mrs. Prance for a peck of flour. I'll have order here. You think the last bacon a little too fat: oh! You do, ma'am, do you? I'll take care you shan't complain in future; I likes to please my customers. There's a very nice flitch hanging up in the engine-room; the men wanted some rust for the machinery; you shall have a slice of that; and we'll say tenpence a pound, high-dried and very lean—will that satisfy you? ... Order there, order; you cussed women, order, or I'll be among you. And if I just do jump over this here counter, won't I let fly right and left?' "

Presently Master Joseph leant forward and struck out in every direction with a yard-stick. A woman cried that he had put out her baby's eye. Master Joseph said, in a softened tone, that he would put her down for half a pound of the best arrowroot, which was the finest thing in the world for babies, and turned to the next victim:

" 'Where's your book, Susan Travers? Left at home! Then you may go and fetch it. No books, no tommy. You are Jones's wife, are you? Ticket for three and sixpence out of eighteen shillings wages. Is this the only ticket you have brought? There's your money; and you may tell your husband he need not take his coat off again to go down our shaft. He must think us cussed fools! Tell him I hope he has got plenty of money to travel into Wales, for he won't have no work in England again, or my name ain't Diggs.' "

At last Master Joseph carried out his threat and jumped over the counter into the crowd, kicking, cuffing and cursing, until a general scream of horror—"A boy killed!"—brought a hush upon the shop. It seemed to be true. The victim was the small boy, sent to get a loaf for his mother, who had felt faint while waiting outside. At that moment Stephen Morley appeared upon the scene. Announcing that he was the editor of the *Mowbray Phalanx*, he took command of the situation. The child still breathed feebly; under Morley's directions he was carried upstairs and laid on a bed. The crowd filed out quietly and the shop was closed.

Disraeli himself claimed that this picture was not over-drawn. No doubt it was true in essentials and working-women were subject to cheating and tyranny under the truck system, but it is difficult to believe in quite such a monster as Master Joseph. In 1831 a Truck Act had made it illegal to force workmen to take payment in goods; as Stephen Morley said to a gathering of miners, they could demand payment in the coin of the realm. In actual practice, however, the law was evaded, especially in the mining districts of Staffordshire and South Wales. Where it was the custom for the butties (themselves miners) to engage men on contract for particular assignments of work it was very common for butties to open shops. By paying their men only once a month they could force them to buy at the tommy-shop on credit, after which they had them in their power. As late as 1871 a Commission was appointed to investigate the truck system and it was at last brought to an end, partly owing to trade union action.

Stephen Morley's search for Gerard's papers carried him to Wodgate, where he had been told that a brother of the vanished Hatton was to be found. Wodgate was a lawless settlement on waste land where squatters could live without interference from landlords or police; it represents an actual district not far from Birmingham. Its business was carried on by master workmen in their own houses, each with his band of apprentices. They had a traditional skill and were famed as nailers and locksmiths, but theirs was a savage community of which neighbouring townspeople lived in considerable fear. Most of the apprentices bore the scars of brutal punishments, but the community was proud of its skill and its thriving trade and the apprentices endured in the hope of becoming masters themselves in time. Masters and apprentices alike worked sixteen hours a day; apprentices slept in lofts and cellars and were often fed on carrion, and sometimes sold from one master to another. The rigours of such a system were, however, made bearable by the fact that for three days a week there was an intermission, on Sunday the masters settled to steady drinking and the rest of the population followed suit, even the babies were drugged with Godfrey's cordial. The apprentices had also a source of recreation and excitement in dog-fighting. There were no public buildings, no schools and no church to break the monotony of the ugly landscape, bare of trees or flowers, and offer an alternative to stark materialism. Ignorance was rife:

"There are many in this town who are ignorant of their very names; very few who can spell them. It is rare that you meet with a young person who knows his own age; rarer to find the boy who has seen a book, or the girl who has seen a flower. Ask them the name of their sovereign, and they will give you an unmeaning stare; ask them the name of their religion, and they will laugh: who rules them on earth, or who can save them in heaven, are alike mysteries to them."

Morley found a haggard, rickety youth working at a file in a doorway and enquired if he knew a man named Hatton. The lad grinned; with a knotty hand he pointed to a deep scar on his forehead and volunteered, "He did that." He added that he would like to have a crown for every time Hatton had cut his head open —"He cut it open once with a key, twice with a lock. . . . He hit me on the head with a hammer once." The recital of such incidents lasted some time but the lad concluded that, take him all in all, Hatton might be a worse master—there was no horse-flesh for his apprentices—and give him a lock to make and it would never be picked. Morley learned that this monster was known locally as the Bishop. The lad then pointed to a girl with a vacant face and a back like a grasshopper, and remarked that the Bishop had married them. Suky had been brought up a Baptist and wanted a proper wedding, but the Bishop had sprinkled some salt on a gridiron, read the Lord's Prayer backwards and written their names in a book, and that was good enough for him. The girl broke in to explain proudly:

"I be a reg'lar born Christian and my mother afore me, and that's what few girls in the Yard can say. Thomas will take it to himself when work is slack; and he believes now in our Lord and

Saviour Pontius Pilate, who was crucified to save our sins; and in Moses, Goliath and the rest of the Apostles."

Morley found Hatton, a thick-set, powerful man, in his workshop, keeping a sharp eye on his apprentices. "Now, boys," he said in a hoarse harsh voice, "steady there, steady. There's a file that don't sing; can't deceive my ear. Don't let me find that one out, or I won't walk into him, won't I? . . . All right! That's music. Where will you find music like twenty files all working at once? . . . Three boys looking about them; what's all this? Won't I be among you?" And he sprang at the first apprentice he could get hold of and wrung his ears until blood spurted. Morley got little satisfaction from him except the knowledge that his brother must be alive because he sent him a £20 note every Christmas, but he had never given him an address.

Meanwhile Egremont had met Sybil once more. He had gone with Mr. St. Lys to see something of the manufacturing district; they made a call at the house of a poor weaver, where they found Sybil, also on an errand of mercy to the starving family. Warner was a hand-loom weaver who had failed to change over to machinery; now he could only make a penny an hour by working at home, and his wife was sick. Egremont and Sybil had not much opportunity to talk, but he was struck by her tender compassion for these poor people, and grieved when she said that she believed the misery of those on the Marney estate was due to the hard hearts of the family who owned the land.

A few days later, when out fishing, Egremont met Walter Gerard and was invited to his cottage, which he found to be furnished in simple good taste. He told his host that his name was Franklin and he was connected with the press. Eventually, after a final quarrel with Lord Marney, Egremont found himself some rooms near Gerard's home. He still had time to fill in before Parliament opened, Sybil was due to leave the convent and take up housekeeping for her father, and he felt that in the companionship of this family and their friend Morley he could develop the new fields of thought which already fascinated him. He was not disappointed. Gerard was well informed and could express himself trenchantly, and there was something sublime about Sybil, softened by a sweet femininity. She told him that she had lived under two roofs only—the convent and the cottage—and each had given her a great idea, under one she had learned the degradation of her faith, under the other that of her race. She concluded: "You should not wonder, therefore, that my heart is concentrated on the Church and the People."

Egremont suggested, a little wistfully, that there were other ideas she might consider, but she replied, "I feel these are enough; too great, as it is, for my brain."

The time came when Egremont must return to London, and there he was soon plunged into the political maelstrom. There was some hope that the Whig government might soon be defeated in the House of Commons and the great political hostesses and the intriguers were all agog. Every possible vote in the House must be secured. Lady St. Julians issued invitations with the skill of a practised strategist. Hearing that a waverer had gone over to the other side she exclaimed with annoyance, "And I have sent his vulgar wife and his great staring daughter a card for next Wednesday!" Tadpole distrusted Mr. Trenchard, perhaps a card for Wednesday might still save him for the Tories—had he a wife? Lady Deloraine thought it open to question that social distinction was Mr. Trenchard's object, but Lady St. Julians dismissed this improbable idea impatiently: "What else can be his object? People get into Parliament to get on; their aims are indefinite. If they have indulged in hallucinations about place before they enter the House, they are soon freed from such distempered fancies; they find they have no more talent than other people, and if they had, they learn that power, patronage and pay are reserved for us and our friends. Well then, like practical men, they look to some result, and they get it. They are asked out to dinner more than they would be; they move rigmarole resolutions at nonsensical public meetings; and they get invited with their women to assemblies at their leader's, where they see stars and blue ribbons, and above all, us, who, they little think, in appearing on such occasions, make the greatest conceivable sacrifice."

Her ladyship continued that anything could be done with such people—a ball or a dinner would command their votes—but it was necessary to take the trouble to recognise their wives at assemblies and call their daughters by their right names.

"You paint them to the life, my dear Lady St. Julians," said Lady Deloraine, laughing, "but with such knowledge and such powers, why did you not save our boroughs?"

Egremont himself came under suspicion; it was rumoured that he had crochets of some sort about the people, which would never do for Peel, who did not like crochety men. Lady St. Julians felt very dubious about him when she heard that he had breakfasted with Mr. Trenchard, and remarked thoughtfully: "Men who breakfast out are generally Liberals. Have you not observed that? I wonder why?"

"It shows a restless revolutionary mind," said Lady Firebrace, "that can settle to nothing; but must be running after gossip the moment they are awake."

Gossip was certainly rife; men asked one another meaningly whether the pear was ripe, but no one would commit himself. "Do you think——" said a diplomatist to Lord Deloraine. "I think that in the long run everything will have an end," said Lord Deloraine. "Ah!" said the diplomatist. "Bah!" said Lord Deloraine as he walked away. All that the gossip amounted to was that "Wishy was down and Washy up".

At last the suspense was over. The government majority sank to five in a division upon the amendment of the constitution of Jamaica and Lord Melbourne decided to resign. The Queen sent for Sir Robert Peel and Conservative activity rose to fever pitch. Tadpole and Taper were here, there and everywhere. Patronage and preferment must be manipulated with the greatest skill but Tadpole advised Taper to be cautious about titles; in some cases a mere non-committal hint would be enough to keep aspirants quiet, if not content, within the party fold. Tadpole concluded earnestly, "If they push you, give a wink and press your finger to your lip." Tadpole himself had been "cooking" the Duke of Fitz-Aquitaine for three years; His Grace wanted Ireland, of which he had not the faintest chance, but he must be sedulously encouraged, and so must Lord de Mowbray, who wanted the Garter, and Lord Marney, who wanted the Buckhounds. "Ours is critical work sometimes, friend Taper," said Tadpole, "but never mind—what we have to do with individuals, Peel has to do with a nation, and therefore we ought not to complain."

The Duke of Fitz-Aquitaine, Lord de Mowbray and Lord Marney met at the Duke's house to discuss their prospects and as they were talking Tadpole was shown in. He was a little dismayed to find himself confronted by all three nobles together, but he knew how to look frank and unsophisticated while he was astutely on the watch for the opportunities he needed. Fortune favoured him. He was able to isolate the Duke and plant his shaft —"I don't pretend to be behind the scenes, Duke," he said frankly, "but it was said to me to-day: Tadpole, if you chance to see the Duke of Fitz-Aquitaine, you may say that positively Lord Kilcroppy will not go to Ireland."

The Duke allowed himself a fleeting smile and Tadpole left it at that. Drawing Lord de Mowbray aside he murmured, "You have heard of Lord Ribbonville?"

"No; what?"

"Can't live the day out. How fortunate Sir Robert is! Two Garters to begin with!"

Then came the turn of Lord Marney:

" 'I don't pretend to be behind the scenes, my Lord,' said the honest gentleman in a peculiarly confidential tone, and with a glance that spoke volumes of State secrecy; 'but it was said to me today, "Tadpole, if you do chance to meet Lord Marney, you may say that positively Lord Rambrooke will not have the Buckhounds." '

" 'All I want,' said Lord Marney, 'is to see men of character about Her Majesty. This is a domestic country, and the country expects that no nobleman should take household office whose private character is not inexpugnable. Now that fellow Rambrooke keeps a Frenchwoman. It is not much known, but it is a fact.'

" 'Dreadful!' exclaimed Mr. Tadpole. 'I have no doubt of it. But he has no chance of the Buckhounds, you may rely on that. Private character is to be the basis of the new government. Since the Reform Act that is a qualification much more esteemed by the constituency than public services. We must go with the times, my Lord. A virtuous middle class shrinks with horror from French actresses; and the Wesleyans—the Wesleyans must be considered, Lord Marney.'

" 'I always subscribe to them,' said Lord Marney.

" 'Ah!' said Mr. Tadpole mysteriously, 'I am glad to hear that. Nothing I have heard to-day has given me so much pleasure as those few words. One may hardly jest upon such a subject,' he added with a sanctimonious air, 'but I think I may say'—and here he broke into a horse smile—'I think I may say that those subscriptions will not be without their fruit.' And with a bow honest Tadpole disappeared."

The Cabinet was in formation, speculations and hopes ran high, when an odd whisper arose in the inner circle of the Conservative party. Lady St. Julians was flushed, Lady Deloraine pale, Lady Firebrace wrote an urgent confidential note to Mr. Tadpole. The clubs were full, even in the morning, and men spoke with bated breath:—

" 'It is true,' said Mr. Egerton to Mr. Berners at Brook's.

" 'Is it true?' asked Mr. Jermyn of Lord Valentine at the Carlton.

" 'I heard it last night at Crockford's,' said Mr. Ormsby."

The dire truth came out—"It seemed that these wrong-headed, rebellious ministers who would not go out, wore—petticoats! . . . Conservatism, that mighty mystery of the nineteenth century—was it, after all, to be brained by a fan!"

This refers to the famous Bedchamber Crisis (1839), when the young Queen indignantly refused to allow her Ladies of the Bedchamber to be changed with the first change of government in her reign. These had always been political appointments and Peel refused to take office shorn of this valuable mark of confidence. The Queen was firm and the Whigs, under Lord Melbourne, returned to power. Lady Deloraine attributed the "Bedchamber Plot" to the fact that it was beyond bearing that Lady St. Julians should hold an office which would bring her into intimate contact with the Queen. Lady St. Julians herself wrung her hands over Her Majesty's unhappy lot, still surrounded by Whig ladies. Ministers who had been disappointed "looked as all men do when they are jilted—embarrassed and affecting an awkward ease". Those who had only had faint hopes of office "complained loudly of their cruel and undeniable deprivation."

Disraeli, who was in Parliament during this crisis, allows himself a digression. Peel, he considered, had lost an opportunity. With the accession of Queen Victoria the time was ripe for raising the prestige and enlarging the functions of the Crown, and this should have been the task of the Conservative party. "But we forget," he wrote, "Sir Robert Peel is not the leader of the Tory party. . . . In a Parliamentary sense, that great party has ceased to exist." And yet, he continued, "even now it is not dead, but sleepeth; and, in an age of political materialism, of confused purposes and perplexed intelligence, that aspires only to wealth because it has faith in no other accomplishment, as men rifle cargoes on the verge of shipwreck, Toryism will yet rise from the tomb over which Bolingbroke shed his last tear, to bring back strength to the Crown, liberty to the subject, and to announce that power has only one duty—to secure the social welfare of the People."

While politicians were absorbed in their great game the discontent of the masses had found a focus in the People's Charter. Disraeli, writing for his own generation, takes for granted his readers' knowledge of the rise of Chartism, but a brief account of it may be helpful to those who read *Sybil* today.

The People's Charter was a document drawn up in the form of an Act of Parliament by the leaders of the London Working-Men's Association in 1838. Its object was to extend political power from a limited class to the whole people, and it embodied the famous Six Points—namely, manhood suffrage, the secret ballot, equal electoral districts, annual Parliaments, abolition of the property qualification, payment of members of Parliament.

The workers in the industrial north had already organised public meetings to protest against the new Poor Law, now such meetings were addressed by Chartist leaders, and the people were persuaded that once the Charter was secured it would be in their own hands to right their wrongs and abolish distress by Acts of Parliament. This propaganda fell on ready ears, the campaign for the Reform Bill had already implanted the idea that the vote was the chief means of enforcing the will of the people. Charles Kingsley brings this out particularly well in his Chartist novel, *Alton Locke* (1850). Kingsley's hero, an intelligent young tailor who had seen the horrors of the sweating system, asked a Chartist friend how a change in Parliamentary representation could abolish such evils, and his friend answered energetically:

"Why, didn't they tell us, before the Reform Bill, that extension of the suffrage was to cure everything? And can you have too much of a good thing? We've only taken them at their word, we Chartists. Haven't all politicians been preaching for years that England's national greatness was all owing to her political institutions—to Magna Carta, the Bill of Rights, and representative Parliaments and all that? ... So, representative institutions are the talismanic palladium of the classes that have them, I dare say; and that's the very best reason why the classes that haven't got 'em should look out for the same palladium for themselves. What's sauce for the gander is sauce for the goose, isn't it?"

Young Alton Locke was easily converted by such arguments: "From that night I was a Chartist, heart and soul—and so were a million and a half more of the best artisans in England—at least I had no reason to be ashamed of my company. Yes; I, too, like Crossthwaite, took the upper classes at their word; bowed down to the idol of political institutions and pinned my hopes of salvation on 'the possession of one ten-thousandth part of a talker in the national palaver'."

With the Charter was associated a National Petition, praying Parliament to adopt it, which was first put forward at a mass meeting in Birmingham and endorsed by many others. In the original Petition one of the Points—equal electoral districts—was dropped, which explains why Disraeli throughout *Sybil* alludes to the Five Points.

A huge demonstration took place on Kersal Moor, at which a quarter of a million people were said to be present. Signatures for the Petition were collected all over the country and eventually reached the figure of 1,200,000. The next step was to set up a National Convention, which became known as the People's Parliament. Under an Act of 1819 political societies with branches were illegal and so delegates to the Convention were elected by public meetings. Excitement spread and was inflamed by the fiery doctrine preached by Feargus O'Connor in the *Northern Star*. He believed that the Charter could never be won without a show of "physical force"; his followers began to collect arms and drill, and tumultuous meetings were held on the moors by torchlight. The government was alarmed and sent troops to the north. Fortunately Sir Charles Napier was in command of these, and he recorded his sympathy with the Chartists: "There is among the manufacturing poor a stern look of discontent, of hatred to all who are rich, a total absence of merry faces: a sallow tinge and dirty skins tell of suffering and brooding over change. . . . Poor fellows!"

Napier did not interfere with orderly meetings, and when he had reason to fear rioting he personally showed the Chartist leaders his guns and persuaded them not to risk open revolt.

In due course the Convention met in London; its principal business was to present the Petition to Parliament, but many delegates regarded themselves as the people's representatives in every sense and proudly wrote M.C. after their names.

In Disraeli's story Walter Gerard and Stephen Morley became Chartist leaders, and Gerard addressed a torchlight meeting on Mowbray Moor, standing on a flat stone known as the Druid's Altar. Amongst his audience were Dandy Mick and Devilsdust, who applauded enthusiastically. Devilsdust confided to his friend that he was not ten years old when he said to himself: "It's a pretty go, this, that I should be toiling in a shoddy-hole to pay the taxes for a gentleman what drinks his port wine and stretches his legs on a Turkey carpet."

Gerard was one of the delegates to the Convention, and Sybil went with him to London. Meanwhile Dandy Mick was persuaded by Devilsdust to join a trade union. His initiation was a fearsome ordeal. First, his eyes were bandaged and he was led through many passages into the dread presence of "The Seven". He found himself in a large room of which the walls were covered with black cloth, and the Seven, robed in surplices and masked, sat at a table above which was a skeleton on a pedestal. On each side of the skeleton was a surpliced sentinel holding a drawn sword, and Mick himself was guarded by two others with battle-axes. He was required to take a solemn oath that he would obey the orders of the majority of his brethren, as issued by the mandate of the Grand Committee, even to "the chastisement of nobs, the assassination of oppressive and tyrannical masters, and the demolition of mills, works and shops that shall be deemed by us incorrigible". He duly swore by Almighty God, kissed the book and was given a surplice and a torch.

This account has been criticised as exaggerated. The ritual was a survival of the period when the Combination Laws made all associations formed to raise wages illegal, and a traitor could bring death or transportation upon his fellows. Surplices, skeletons and battle-axes were then common features of initiation ceremonies; the branch of the Grand National Consolidated Trade Union which met at Tolpuddle in Dorset ordered a figure of Death six feet high. It was at Tolpuddle that six farm-labourers were arrested in 1834 for taking illegal oaths at a trade union meeting, and sentenced to transportation to Australia for seven years. This drastic action followed an outbreak of rick-burning and attacks on threshing-machines. Although the Combination Laws were repealed in 1825 the trade union ritual continued, and reached its most fantastic pitch about 1830. By the time Disraeli wrote *Sybil* such extravagant practices had declined.

Gerard and Morley were deputed by the Convention to call upon a number of members of Parliament to obtain support for the Petition, and the account of their reception by various types of men, such as Mr. Thorough Base, Mr. Kremlin, Bombaster Rip and Floatwell, is good reading. In Lord Valentine they found an attractive young champion of aristocratic rule. He received them in a sumptuous room, wearing a morning robe of Indian shawls, and listened to them courteously. He then expounded his own views: he did not think the great majority were the best judges of their own interests, and he enumerated the services his own ancestors had rendered to the country, concluding:

"You talk of our taxation and our wars; and of your inventions and your industry. Our wars converted this island into an empire, and at any rate developed that industry and stimulated those inventions of which you boast. You tell me that you are delegates of the unrepresented working-classes of Mowbray. Why, what would Mowbray have been if it had not been for your aristocracy and their wars? Your town would not have existed; there would have been no working-classes to send up delegates. In fact, you owe your existence to us. I have told you what my ancestors have done; I am prepared, if the occasion requires it, not to disgrace them; I have inherited their great position, and, I tell you fairly, gentlemen, I will not relinquish it without a struggle."

Gerard pointed to a suit of ancient armour and said, smiling, "Would you combat the people in that suit of armour, my Lord?" Lord Valentine replied: "That suit of armour has combatted for the people before this, for it stood by Simon de Montfort on the field of Evesham."

Gerard then returned to the charge. He pointed out that the aristocracy of England had exercised uncontrolled power for a century and a half and were now the most prosperous class in the world, as rich as Roman senators and furnished by modern science with comforts and conveniences unheard of in the ancient world. He became emphatic:

"Your order stands before Europe the most gorgeous of existing spectacles. . . . You govern us still with absolute authority—and you govern the most miserable people on the face of the globe."

Lord Valentine was not convinced, but he dismissed his callers pleasantly. The next name on their list was Mr. Charles Egremont, M.P.

CHAPTER XI

Sybil (III)

In the later part of *Sybil* the plot gathers force and the series of scenes hitherto slenderly linked by the personal story becomes a drama, full of incident and even excitement. Before the end of the book it reaches the pitch of melodrama. Much of this must be passed over in an account which only professes to be an introduction to this closely-packed novel, but the events that are bound up in the progress of the Chartist movement may be picked out with advantage.

Sybil was deeply shocked by the revelation that the Mr. Franklin to whom she had given a warm friendship was the brother of Lord Marney, and she told him sadly that the gulf between them was impassable. She gloried in being a daughter of the oppressed and had a confident young faith in the People's Parliament, in which delegates expressed their grievances "in language which would not disgrace the conquering race which has in vain endeavoured to degrade them". She believed that God and Truth were on their side and must prevail. Stephen Morley sowed the first doubt in her mind, when he told her of dissensions within the Convention itself. This was true to history; besides minor factions there was a great cleavage between those who relied upon moral force and those who held that only physical force could gain their object, but as long as the National Petition had still to be presented the advocates of moral force were able to restrain the hot-heads. Unfortunately the unexpected resignation of the government over the Jamaica division forced the Convention to postpone the presentation of the Petition, but at last it was conveyed to Westminster, rolled on a huge bobbin and mounted on a triumphal car, which was escorted by the members of the Convention marching two abreast. The debate was not held at once and when it took place the Commons rejected the humble Petition of the People. The blow was all the more bitter because the debate excited little feeling in the House; it was galling to contrast "the interest occasioned by the endangered constitution of Jamaica, a petty and exhausted colony, and the claims for the same constitutional rights by the working millions of England" (*Sybil*). Meanwhile the main body of the Convention had retired to Birmingham, and there serious riots broke out. In *Sybil* we have the reaction of politicians to this development:

" 'Terrible news from Birmingham,' said Mr. Egerton at Brook's. 'They have massacred the police, beat off the military and sacked the town. News just arrived.'

" 'I have known it these two hours,' said a grey-headed gentleman, speaking without taking his eyes off the newspaper. 'There is a Cabinet sitting now.'

" 'Well, I always said so,' said Mr. Egerton; 'our fellows ought to have put down the Convention.'

" 'It is deuced lucky,' said Mr. Berners, 'that the Bedchamber business is over, and we are all right. This affair, in the midst of the Jamaica hitch, would have been fatal to us.'

" 'These Chartists evidently act upon a system,' said Mr. Egerton. 'You see they were perfectly quiet until the National Petition was presented and debated; and now, almost simultaneously with our refusing to consider their Petition, we have news of this outbreak.'

" 'I hope they will not spread,' said the greyheaded gentleman. 'There are not enough troops in the country if there be anything like a general movement. I hear they have sent the Guards down on a special train, and a hundred more of the police. London is not over-garrisoned.'

" 'They are always ready for a riot in Birmingham,' said a Warwickshire peer. 'Trade is very bad there and they suffer a good deal. But I should think it will go no further.' "

The Chartists now fell back on their second weapon and decided to organise a National Holiday, or general strike, to bring the capitalists to their knees, but already many mills were working short time and circumstances were against the project.

In Disraeli's story a committee of Chartist delegates, with Walter Gerard at its head, stayed in London to complete the plans for the next move. Gerard had been converted to the National Holiday scheme, and reluctantly agreed that the people must provide themselves with arms to use in defence in case of need, and the committee proceeded to draw up a proclamation and print pamphlets for general circulation. Meanwhile Sybil, sad at heart, had one consolation: one voice in Parliament had been raised in a plea for consideration of the National Petition, and it was that of Egremont. She reflected with a kindling heart:

"Yes! There was one voice that had sounded in that proud Parliament, that, free from the slang of faction, had dared to express immortal truths: the voice of a noble, who without being a demagogue, had upheld the popular cause; had pronounced his conviction that the rights of labour were as sacred as those of property; that if a difference were to be established, the interests of the living wealth ought to be preferred."

In actual fact, Disraeli himself made a similar speech in the debate upon the Petition, in which he attacked the Reform Bill, as transferring political power to a class which had no corresponding sense of public duty, and denounced the new Poor Law as an outrage upon the social duty of the State. He warned the House that they would be grievously mistaken if they treated this remarkable social movement as "a mere temporary ebullition". Having made his protest Disraeli voted against the Petition, but in a later speech he declared: "I am not ashamed or afraid to say that I wish more sympathy had been shown on both sides towards the Chartists... I am not ashamed to say that I sympathise with millions of my fellow-subjects." In the same speech he indulged in his satirical vein:

"The time will come when the Chartists will discover that in a country so aristocratic as England even treason, to be successful, must be patrician. They will discover that great truth, and when they find some desperate noble to lead them they may, perhaps, achieve greater results. Where Wat Tyler failed, Henry Bolingbroke changed a dynasty, and although Jack Straw was hanged, a Lord John Straw may become a Secretary of State."

Disraeli supported the Radicals in opposing excessive severity in punishing Chartist leaders. He appealed to the Tory party to remember that they were the natural leaders of the people, for "the aristocracy and the labouring population form the nation". This was the doctrine that Egremont preached to Sybil. Before long Sybil was warned, first by Egremont and then by Morley, that Gerard was in danger of arrest. Morley failed her at the crucial moment and she set out alone in a hired cab to seek her father at an obscure address. Disraeli's description of the next scenes is graphic and tense. His picture of the squalid London district which Sybil saw through the window of her cab, as in a nightmare, is Hogarthian:

"Now dark streets of frippery and old stores, now market-places of entrails and carrion, with gutters running gore; sometimes the way was enveloped in yeasty fumes of a colossal brewery, and sometimes they plunged into a labyrinth of lanes teeming with life, and where the dog-stealer and the pickpocket, the burglar and the assassin found a sympathetic multitude of all ages; comrades for every enterprise; and a market for every booty.

"The long summer twilight was just expiring; the pale shadows of the moon were just stealing on; the gas was beginning to glare in shops of tripe and bacon, and the paper lanterns to adorn the stall and the stand. They crossed a broad street which seemed to be the metropolis of the district; it flamed with gin-palaces; a multitude were sauntering in the mild though tainted air; bargaining, blaspheming, drinking, wrangling; and varying their business with their potations, their fierce strife and their impious irreverence, with flashes of rich humour, gleams of native wit, and racy phrases of idiomatic slang."

After sundry unpleasant adventures, Sybil reached her father only in time to be arrested with him. Her one idea was to obtain her own freedom in order to work for her father's, and from the police station she sent a desperate note of appeal to Egremont. Of course he came, with an order for her release and a coach, but after one warm pressure of her hand he mounted beside the coachman and did not obtrude himself upon her. Gerard was shortly released on bail, and received a wonderful ovation on his return to Mowbray, but his trial ended with a sentence of eighteen months' imprisonment.

The idea of the National Holiday, although not taken up all over the country, persisted and led to various sporadic outbreaks. A threatened reduction of wages in Lancashire gave rise to an actual strike known as the Plug Plot, in which workmen marched from mill to mill drawing the plugs from boilers in order to make work impossible. Disraeli had this in mind when, in his novel, he set Wodgate on the march, led by Hatton—the "Bishop"—riding on a white mule and brandishing a hammer. The Hell-Cats, as they were called, terrorised town after town. The Bishop's orders were that every engine must be stopped and men at work after notice should be ducked, and he offered a reward of £50 for every live policeman brought to him. Lancashire strikers had been on the march before, but hitherto they had destroyed rather than plundered, and one form of demonstration was to fill local churches on Sundays. Disraeli describes a real incident which he said came within his personal experience. A body of about two thousand men invaded the park of a local squire and demanded food. The master of the house was out with the yeomanry, but his wife promised to feed them if they would give her time. Carts were sent to the town for provisions, the game-keepers went out with their guns and at last bread and meat were supplied to the waiting mob. When the men had eaten a deputation thanked the lady and asked permission for the people to walk through the gardens. They did so, even passing through the hot-houses, and not a grape was plucked or a flower picked or trampled.

The Hell-Cats of *Sybil* were very different. Their first call was at Diggs' tommy-shop, which they found bolted and barred against them. They marched up to the door with bludgeons and crowbars, and then a window opened and Joseph Diggs looked out, pointing a blunderbluss at the crowd. His father was, however, anxious to appease the Hell-Cats, and for a time he kept them quiet by throwing down bacon and cheese and anything else they demanded. Suddenly someone raised the alarm that Master Joseph was entering all these items against them in the tommy-books. Immediately the crowbars thundered on the door. Master Joseph fired: a woman was wounded and a child killed. Mad with rage, the Hell-Cats collected trusses of straw and plundered a coal barge, and soon the hated tommy-shop was ablaze. For a moment the mob saw Master Joseph on the roof, convulsed and shrieking, but still clasping an account book, before he fell to his fiery death.

Meanwhile in Mowbray the situation was eagerly discussed. The depression in trade had brought Widow Carey and her friends down in the world, and the Temple had been closed, but still Caroline stoutly declared that she would never marry a man who was not for the Five Points. Harriet added, "I should be ashamed to marry anyone who had not the suffrage", and Julia declared that a man without a vote was no better than a slave. The Widow remarked briskly, "Why, at your time of life, my dears, we never even heard of these things, much less talked of them." When Julia replied loftily that there was no march of mind in those days the Widow said:

" 'Lord, my dear, what's the use of all that? What we want is good wages and plenty to do; and as for all the rest, I don't grudge the Queen her throne, nor the noblemen and gentlemen their good things. Live and let live, say I.'

" 'Why, you are a regular oligarch, Widow,' said Harriet.

" 'Well, Miss Harriet,' replied Mrs. Carey, a little nettled, "Tisn't calling your neighbours names that settles any question ... Holly-hock, indeed! Why holly-hock?' "

Devilsdust and Dandy Mick appeared, evidently in a state of suppressed excitement. The Dandy promised Caroline that they would soon have the Temple open again and she exclaimed, "That will be sweet. I often dream of that foreign nobleman who used to sing 'Oh, no, we never!' " Devilsdust, who was of sterner stuff, told them that there was to be a great strike and the people's savings banks, the benefit societies and even the burial clubs were to devote their funds to the support of the strikers in this last glorious struggle. Dandy Mick added gaily, "There shan't be a capitalist in England who can get a day's work out of us, even if he makes the operatives junior partners."

While Mowbray was agitated by this crisis the Hell-Cats marched into the town, with the Liberator, as Hatton now styled himself, at their head. His orders went forth that every engine and boiler was to be put out of action, but at one mill his emissaries met with a rebuff. Mr. Trafford had hoses turned upon them and they retired, drenched and in disorder. The Liberator, much incensed, swore that he would have fire for this water. The fact that Trafford gave his work-people gardens and baths did not soften him, such things only diverted their minds from the Five

Points. He declared sternly. "We will have no more gardens in England, everything shall be open; and baths shall only be used to drown the enemies of the People. I always was against washing, it takes the marrow out of a man."

Trafford's mill was only saved by the courage of Walter Gerard (now released from prison), who appeared on a roof, assured the mob that all work had been stopped and that Trafford would not attempt to interfere with the National Holiday. The Mowbray men responded at once to their old leader, but the Hell-Cats were spoiling for action. Someone suggested that they should march to Mowbray Castle and Devilsdust, moved by Gerard's appeal, clinched the matter by shouting, "Drink a glass of ale with Lord de Mowbray!" On this popular proposal the mob turned and surged towards the Castle.

At the Castle one of the bored youths of the first chapter was now in charge—Alfred Mountchesney had married Lady Joan, the heiress of Lord de Mowbray. For the boredom of London he had exchanged the boredom of the country. He complained bitterly that even the post brought little diversion, Joan only corresponded with philosophers and Maud with clergymen; he himself had never been a letter-writer, as he explained plaintively:

"I never wanted to write or be written to. I always knew what was going on because I was on the spot; I was doing the things that people were writing letters about—but now, not being in the world any longer, doing nothing, living in the country—and the country in August—I should like to receive letters every day, but I do not know whom to fix upon as a correspondent. Eugene de Vere will not write, Milford cannot; and as for FitzHeron, he is so very selfish, he always wants his letters answered."

Mountchesney's boredom was rudely shattered when the Hell-Cats broke into the Castle. Disraeli's account of how this young man, without rising to the heroic, behaved adequately in the emergency is subtly convincing; with the help of some Mowbray men he got his women safely away by a secret passage in the grounds. The whole scene is dramatic and moving. Sybil, in trying to find her father, had been forced to fly before the mob and take refuge in the Castle. When the Hell-Cats, after drinking their fill in the cellar, set fire to the building the ladies had to face the rabble outside. Mr. St. Lys, who had come to help, and Sybil, rallied some of the men who knew them as a bodyguard, to hustle them through the unruly crowd to the entrance of the secret passage. Sybil herself, however, was swept away in the surging mass of men, and was in the grasp of a band of ruffians when an officer of the yeomanry—which had now arrived upon the scene—rushed, drawn sabre in hand, to her rescue. Once more of course it was Egremont, and equally of course he soon routed the ruffians. Then, clasping Sybil to his heart, he said firmly, "We will never part again." "Never," murmured Sybil.

Disraeli now proceeds to finish his story with a holocaust of victims. Hatton was burned to death as he lay dead drunk; Lord Marney, riding at the head of his yeomanry, cut down and killed Walter Gerard, who was leading a band of Mowbray men to the rescue of the de Mowbrays, and was himself stoned to death by Gerard's indignant followers. Stephen Morley was mortally wounded in the muniment room of the Castle, but not before he had found what he was searching for there—a box of precious documents which proved Gerard's claim to the Mowbray estates. This he entrusted to Dandy Mick, with orders to deliver it to Sybil. The Dandy escaped over the roofs and carried the box safely to the convent where Sybil was now living once more.

Egremont now became Lord Marney, and in due time Sybil was established as the rightful heiress of the de Mowbray title and estates. With this crescendo of grandiose improbabilities Disraeli spoiled the end of a book in which he had embodied many pictures that were true to the life of rich and poor in the 'forties, and many human touches. Perhaps the worst flaw is Sybil's great inheritance, which inclines the reader to think that the author could not bring himself to mate Egremont, an aristocrat by nature and nurture (even if his family's nobility was not of the purest water), with a true daughter of the people. The character of Sybil herself is too sublime for warm humanity, but her noble idealism is impressive, and there is a winning touch of womanliness about her, especially when she is overcome by love or fear. As a mine from which valuable nuggets of social history can be dug the book is extremely good; as a novel it lacks unity, the principal characters are not sufficiently life-like and the end degenerates into melodrama. It is, in fact, a clever and vivid piece of book-making rather than a spontaneous creation of art.

*　　　*　　　*

Chartism petered out in fiasco. The Birmingham riots were followed by an insurrection in Newport (Wales), led by John Frost, which was suppressed by troops, and after which four hundred Chartist leaders were arrested. Two more National Petitions, in 1842 and 1848, succeeded the first one; both failed, and the last was held up to ridicule on account of a number of false signatures, such as Snub-Nose, Pug-Nose, Queen Victoria and Duke of Wellington. In 1848 there was a last flash in the pan, when a mass meeting on Kennington Common was planned, but the government had taken formidable precautions and the rally fell far short of the numbers expected.

Two other novels with a Chartist background, published three and five years after *Sybil*, may usefully be compared with it. Charles Kingsley's *Alton Locke* (1850) is written as the autobiography of a young man whose bitter experiences in the tailoring trade made him turn to Chartism. It is a turgid and often tedious book, with an improbable story and long passages of sermonising, but it contains some vivid scenes, including a Chartist mass meeting amongst the ancient stones of a Druid temple. Labourers and even women addressed the meeting in turns and there was some realistic oratory, of which the following is a sample:

"And if you takes turmits or corn, they're yourn—you helped to grown 'em. And if you're put to prison, I tell ye, it's a darned deal warmer, and better victuals too, then ever a one you gets at home, let alone the Union. Now I knows the dodge. Whenever my wife's ready for her trouble, I gets cotched; then I lives like a prince in gaol, and she goes to the workus; and when it's all over, start fair again. Oh, you blockheads!—to stand there shivering with empty bellies—You just go down to the farm and burn they stacks over the old rascal's head; and then they that let you starve now, will be forced to keep you then. If you can't get your share of the poor-rates, try the county rates, my bucks—you can get fat on them at the Queen's expense—and that's more than you'll do in ever a Union as I hear on."

Alton Locke certainly throws light on what went to the making of a Chartist, and Kingsley's account of sweated labour amongst the tailors is supremely good.

Mrs. Gaskell's *Mary Barton* (1848) is a valuable supplement to Disraeli's *Sybil* in that it gives us simple, human scenes based on her own knowledge of working-men's homes in Manchester, which Disraeli could not hope to rival. There are melodramatic features in *Mary Barton*, and too many edifying death-bed scenes, and taken as a whole it is not such a readable book as *Sybil*, but it gives us the authentic voices of the Lancashire poor.

Amongst Mrs. Gaskell's poignant details is the fact that shops were forced to sell such goods as tea and sugar in halfpennyworths, because few working-class women could afford to spend more on one article. The people's touching faith in the National Petition and the Convention is well brought out. John Barton, Mary's father, was one of the Chartist delegates who went to London to escort the Petition to the House of Commons. As Mary was washing his two shirts for the journey neighbours dropped in to wish their delegate luck, and impress their own particular views on him:

" 'So, John, yo're bound for London, are yo?' said one.

" 'Ay, I suppose I mun go,' answered John, yielding to necessity as it were.

" 'Well, there's many a thing I'd like yo to speak on to the Parliament people. Thou'lt not spare 'em, John, I hope. Tell 'em our minds; how we're thinking we've been clemmed long enough, and we donnot see whatten good they've been doing; if they can't give us what we're all crying for sin' the day we were born.'

" 'Ay, ay, I'll tell 'em that, and much more to it, when it gets to my turn; but thou knows there'll be many will have their word afore me.'

" 'Well, thou'lt speak at last. Bless thee, lad, do ask 'em to make th' masters to break the machines. There's never been good times since spinning-jennies came up.'

" 'Machines is th' ruin of poor folk,' chimed in several voices.

" 'For my part,' said a shivering, half-clad man who crept near the fire, as if ague-stricken, 'I would like thee to tell 'em to pass the Short Hours Bill. Flesh and blood gets wearied wi' so much work; why should factory hands work so much longer than other trades? Just ask 'em that, Barton, will ye?' "

The next speaker, a woman, voiced a common grievance against one of the measures intended to lighten the burden of the most helpless class of the industrial community, the Factory Act which forbade the employment of children under nine in cotton mills. She complained:

"I'm sure, John Barton, if yo are taking messages to the Parliament folk, yo'll not object to telling 'em what a sore trial it is, this law o' theirs, keeping children fra' factory work, whether they be weakly or strong. There's our Ben; why, porridge seems to go no way wi' him, he eats so much; and I have gotten no money to send him t'school, as I would like; and there he is, rampaging about the streets a'day, getting hungrier and hungrier, and picking up a' manner o' bad ways and th' inspector won't let him work in th' factory, because he's not right age; though he's twice as strong as Sankey's little ritling of a lad, as works till he cries for his legs aching so, though he's right age, and better."

Another speaker had an ingenious idea:

"My mother comed out o' Oxfordshire, and were under-laundry maid in Sir Francis Dashwood's family... Sir Francis wore two shirts a day. Now he were all one as a Parliament man; and many on 'em, I have no doubt, are like extravagant. Just tell 'em, John, do, that they'd be doing the Lancashire weavers a great kindness if they'd ha' their shirts made o' calico; 'twould make trade brisk, that would, with the power o' shirts they wear."

Another improved upon this:

"There's thousands of poor weavers as have only gotten one shirt i' the world.... though they're turning out miles o' calico every day; and many a mile of it is lying in warehouses, stopping up trade for want o' purchasers. Yo take my advice, John Barton, and ask Parliament to set trade free, so as workmen can earn a decent wage, and buy their two, ay and three, shirts a year; that would make weaving brisk."

When they had all had their say John replied:

"I'm afeard, neighbours, I've not much chance of telling 'em all yo say; what I think on, is just speaking out about the distress that they say is nought. When they hear o' children born on wet flags, without a rag t'cover 'em or a bit o' food for th' mother; when they hear o' folk lying down to die i' the streets, or hiding their want in some hole o' a cellar till death come to set 'em free; and when they hear o' all this plague, pestilence and famine, they'll surely do somewhat wiser than we can guess at now... I'll do my best, and yo see now, if better times don't come after Parliament knows all."

John Barton came home from London a broken man. "Mary," he said, "we mun speak to our God to hear us, for man will not hearken."

Chartism died out after 1848, but its force was not spent. Working-men had learned much, drawn attention to their sufferings and frightened the government, which strengthened the hands of such social reformers as Lord Shaftesbury. With the 'fifties times improved, helped by the railroad boom and the repeal of the corn-laws, and the workers devoted their energies to more practical and realisable objects. The steady consolidation of trade unions, the Short Time Committees and other movements benefited from the experience gained in Chartism; John Stuart Mill spoke its finest epitaph, when he called it "the victory of the vanquished".

CHAPTER XII

Tancred (I)

TANCRED OR THE NEW CRUSADE, the last novel of the trilogy of the eighteen-forties, introduces a new type of hero, a young religious enthusiast who burned to regulate his life by first principles —if only he could discover what they were—and felt impelled to seek inspiration in the Holy Land, where alone God had vouchsafed direct revelation to man. Tancred suffered many vicissitudes in his search for revelation and truth, and the book is divided into two very different parts. The first part of his story has the background of aristocratic English society and the characters and social comedy are in Disraeli's best vein. The second part is set in Palestine and Syria and embodies themes that were very dear to Disraeli's heart, particularly the debt of western civilisation to Jewish theology, law and literature. In this half of the book Disraeli's own travels served him well in picturing the scenery and also the life and conversation of Jews, Arabs and Bedouins, and he himself said that when he wanted to refresh his memories of the East he re-read *Tancred*. The description is, however, subservient to the story; we no longer feel, as in *Vivian Grey* and *Contarini Fleming* that he is more concerned to make use of his knowledge than to develop his theme.

The main situation of the book is piquant. Tancred, Lord Montacute, was the only child of parents who, despite ancient titles and vast possessions, were extraordinarily unversed in the ways of the world. His father, the Duke of Bellamont, had been harshly kept in subjection and seclusion by his own father, and when he succeeded to the dukedom unexpectedly early he was inexperienced and reserved and shrank from society. The intrigues of politics disgusted him—"he wanted nothing, not even the blue ribbon which he was soon obliged to take". He found, however, great domestic happiness in a marriage with his cousin Katherine, and was always at his ease in the country on his own estates.

The Duchess of Bellamont was a woman of character, but as

unworldly as her husband. She had been brought up in Ireland, in an austere circle in which decisive judgment had been passed on "exactly what was true in dogma, what just in conduct and what correct in manners". Consequently she herself had the habit of decision. She was a student of theology, but only in those works whose writers held the opinions which she knew to be the right ones. The Duchess, however, had her charms; her rare smile was sweet and winning, she was frank and simple, and only wished to do her duty to her God and her neighbour.

Tancred was the supreme interest and care of both parents—"from the moment of his birth, the very existence of his parents seemed identified with his welfare. The Duke and his wife mutually assumed to each other a secondary position in comparison with their offspring". They could scarcely bear him out of their sight. On the persuasion of their kinsman, Lord Eskdale, they had "shown him to Eton", accompanied by a private tutor and faithful servants, but a fortunate outbreak of scarlet fever in his first term had given them an excuse to remove him once and for all from such dangers. At eighteen he was allowed to go to Christ Church, but the Duke took a house near Oxford so that he was still under the parental eye.

When Lord Montacute came of age even his parents realised that the heir to such a great inheritance must be suitably presented to the world. They turned to Lord Eskdale for advice. This nobleman (realistically drawn from Lord Lonsdale), whom we have already met in *Coningsby*, was a man of the world of consummate tact, the only man of the world whom the Duke and Duchess of Bellamont both knew and trusted. The first thing he proposed was that he should engage a first class cook to preside in the kitchen at Montacute Castle during the festivities, and the opening chapter of the book consists of a delightful account of Leander, one of the first culinary artists of the age, discussing his dispositions for the occasion with a colleague. Society, all agog over the event, passed the news from club to drawing-room that Leander was going down to Montacute. The house-party assembled, and Disraeli gives us some trenchant sketches of the guests. The celebrations, too, are described in all their sumptuous magnificence, down to the grand transparency which struck awe into the heart of the young footman who told his parents of it beforehand in strict confidence—"like heaven opening; the young Markiss on a cloud, with his hand on his heart, in his new uniform". The festivities were in danger of ending in a disaster when Leander was hurt because, after he had been dressing superb dinners for a week, the Duke had never made a single observation or sent him a single message. The late Lord Monmouth would certainly have sent for him, or written him a letter which would have been preserved in his family; M. de Sidonia would have sent him a tankard from his table; it was inexplicable. Lord Eskdale, who had great sympathy with artists, took the matter in hand. Making his way to the kitchen he took Leander into his confidence: "Why I wished you to come down here, Leander, was not to receive the applause of my cousin and his guests, but to form their taste." Before his Lordship left him Leander was swelling with pride; here was an exciting, an ennobling idea; these people had been like Cossacks in a picture-gallery, but when he had finished with them the barbarians should be impressed with the great truth that there is "a difference between eating and dining".

When the festivities were over Tancred's future had to be considered. The Duchess had already selected a bride for him, a cousin from Ireland, and felt sure he could not fail to fall in love with her; her cup of bliss was full when one of the county members of Parliament offered to resign in Lord Montacute's favour. The Duke, equally gratified, announced the news to his son in his study. Tancred replied that he did not wish to enter Parliament at present. The Duke, crestfallen, urged that such an opportunity was not to be lightly dismissed, the present member might change his mind about resigning, he could not be regarded as a mere warming-pan. Tancred thought it unlikely he would ever want to enter Parliament. Perplexed, the Duke tried to draw his son's views:

" 'I wish I knew what your opinions were, my dear boy, or even your wishes.'

" 'Well, then, to do my duty.'

" 'Exactly; you are a pillar of the State; support the State.'

" 'Ah! If anyone would but tell me what the State is,' said Lord Montacute, sighing. 'It seems to me your pillars remain, but they support nothing; in that case, though the shafts may be perpendicular and the capitals very ornate, they are no longer props, they are a ruin.'"

The Duke strove valiantly to manage the conversation but he was soon out of his depth and the discussion dragged on inconclusively until at last Tancred was betrayed into an outburst. "In nothing," he exclaimed, "whether it be religion, or government, or manners, sacred or political or social life, do I find faith; and if there be no faith, how can there be duty? Is there such a thing as religious truth? Is there such a thing as social propriety? Are these facts, or are they mere phrases? And if they be facts, where are they to be found in England?"

"You are going into first principles," said the Duke gravely.

"Give me then second principles," replied his son; "give me any." Expressing his disgust with the present state of affairs in a country which had ceased to be a nation and become a mere crowd, he besought his father to save him from contributing to the corruption which, he felt, surrounded them. The Duke, mindful of how his own father had thwarted all his impulses, said: "You shall be master of your own actions. I offer you counsel, I give no commands; and, as for the rest, Providence will guard us." Upon this Tancred opened his heart more fully:

"'If an angel would but visit our house as he visited the house of Lot!' said Lord Montacute, in a tone almost of anguish.

"'Angels have performed their part,' said the Duke. 'We have received instruction from one higher than angels. It is enough for all of us.'

"'It is not enough for me,' said Lord Montacute, with a glowing cheek, and rising abruptly. 'It was not enough for the Apostles; for though they listened to the sermon on the mount, and partook of the first communion, it was still necessary that He should appear to them again, and promise them a Comforter. I require one,' he added in an agitated voice. 'I must seek one. Yes, my dear father, it is of this that I would speak to you; it is this which for a long time has oppressed my spirit, and filled me with intolerable gloom. We must separate. I must leave you, I must leave that dear mother, those beloved parents, in whom are concentrated all my earthly affections; but I obey an impulse that I believe comes from above. Dearest and best of men, you will not thwart me; you will forgive, you will aid me!' And he advanced and threw himself into the arms of his father."

The Duke, clasping his son to his breast, tried rapidly to solve the mystery of this distressing ebullition. The boy had been too much at home, he had moped. If only he would have gone into the House of Commons! He would have worked in committees and become practical. Something, however, must be done for him; he supposed he must travel, but it would almost kill his mother, his was such a precious life. However, no doubt their worthy friend, Colonel Brace, could be induced to accompany him, and they must send a skilful physician with him too. Having brought himself to this pitch the Duke had to undergo another shock. Tancred rejected Paris, and even Rome, which his father offered in desperation. Nothing would satisfy his aspirations but the Holy Land. He must emulate the crusading De Montacute of six centuries ago, who had knelt for three days and three nights at his Redeemer's tomb; there alone, in a country sanctified by the revelation of Christ, could he find an answer to the burning questions: "What is DUTY? And what is FAITH? What ought I to DO? And what ought I to BELIEVE?"

It was a sore dilemma. The Duke broke the news to the Duchess by degrees. She was already happily planning her instructions to her son's servant; if the House of Commons sat late he must be sure to have hot coffee and a cold fowl waiting for his young master. When the Duke ventured that Tancred seemed to have a fancy for travel she was aghast: Paris and Rome, she supposed, and the one would imperil his constitution and the other his faith. When the full enormity was revealed to her she cried in anguish, "The Holy Land! Why, if he even reached it, the climate is certain death. The curse of the Almighty, for more than eighteen centuries, has been on that land."

All this was not so extreme as it seems today, when modern hygiene and inoculation have made it possible to travel without any great risk to health, even in the East; Disraeli had seen his sister's fiancé die of smallpox at Cairo.

The Duchess's first line of defence was to request her son to discuss the matter with the Bishop who had confirmed him. This prelate had been appointed to his see by Lord Liverpool, and Disraeli digresses to describe the "Arch-Mediocrity's" idea of a Bishop. His "notion of clerical capacity did not soar higher than a private tutor who had suckled a young noble into university honours; his test of priestly celebrity was the decent editorship of a Greek play. He sought for the successors of the Apostles, for the stewards of the mysteries of Sinai and Calvary, among third-rate hunters after syllables." The Bishop in question was also a bustling man of the world, who "combined a great talent for action with limited powers of thought", and could permit nothing to be done without his interference, and yet he was "one of those leaders who are not guides" and his projects generally ended in a compromise. Disraeli's contemporaries identified him with Dr. Blomfield, Bishop of London, but considered the portrait unkindly exaggerated.

The interview was a failure. When Tancred stated that society, once regulated by God, was now regulated by man, that he preferred divine to self-government and wished to know how it was to be attained, the Bishop replied that the Church represented God on earth. Tancred objected that the Church no longer governed men; the Bishop told him there was now a rising spirit in the Church, and added with conclusive satisfaction, " 'We shall soon see a Bishop at Manchester.'

" 'But I want to see an angel at Manchester.'

" 'An angel!'

" 'Why not? Why should there not be heavenly messengers when heavenly messages are most wanted?' "

The Bishop replied, as the Duke had done, that the missions of angels ceased with the advent of Christ.

"Then why," said Tancred, "did angels appear to Mary and her companions at the holy tomb?" The Bishop was obliged to tell the anxious parents that Lord Montacute was a visionary and he could do nothing for him.

The Duchess was nonplussed, but the Duke said thoughtfully, "I always think the best person to deal with a visionary is a man of the world." This suggested Lord Eskdale and they decided to consult him. He came and listened to the Duchess's tale of woe, with its sad conclusion that Tancred seemed more determined than ever to go to Jerusalem. "Well," said his Lordship, "it is at least better than going to the Jews, which most men do at his time of life." The Duchess answered mournfully, "I cannot agree even to that, for I would rather that he should be ruined than die."

The ever resourceful Lord Eskdale, however, soon evolved a plan of campaign. He elaborated it with enjoyment: "A man cannot go to Jerusalem as he would to Birmingham, by the next train. . . . Your son ought to travel with a suite; he ought to make the voyage in his own yacht. Yachts are not to be found like hack cabs." They should, he continued, insist upon a vessel of considerable tonnage; before their son had got what he wanted he would be interested in yacht building, and probably end by going to Cowes instead of Palestine. Meanwhile they might make it a second condition of their consent to his pilgrimage that Lord Montacute should go into society in London while waiting for his yacht. To this he added the comforting opinion, "Let him but once enter the world, and be tranquil, he will soon find something to engage him."

Tancred could not refuse to accept the conditions imposed by his devoted parents, and soon his time was divided between seeing yachts that were offered for sale and attending receptions, dinners and balls. Society was edified to meet the young heir, but there was much speculation as to what he could possibly find to do in Palestine. Mr. Ormsby had an idea that, according to the Old Testament, there were partridges there in Jeremiah's time, but Lord Milford said positively that there was not a bird in the whole country now. Meanwhile Lord Eskdale's prophecy seemed likely to be fulfilled; Tancred's interest was engaged by Lady Constance Rawleigh, who was said to admire intellect and had refused several "offers of high calibre". In fact it was evident that she would not take a booby, even if "his ears were covered with strawberry leaves". Tancred showed his preference for her society and she obtained an invitation for him to Mrs. Guy Flouncey's great breakfast party.

Another digression from the story here shows us Mrs. Guy Flouncey's triumphant social progress since she had arrived at Coningsby Castle as a nobody eight years ago. She had at last achieved the great step from dinners to a ball, with that glorious and essential corollary—a list. It was a triumph indeed. Disraeli writes feelingly of the obstacles to be surmounted. When you have formed your list you have to get a day, the most difficult thing in the world. When you have chosen one five weeks ahead which seems to be unappropriated, when your preparations are practically complete and Mr. Gunther has "half dressed your supper and made all your ice", the Marchioness of Deloraine sends out cards for a ball on the same night, in honour of some European sovereign who has suddenly arrived in England for a week only, and at whose court Lord Deloraine was ambassador twenty years ago. You perforce postpone your ball, select another day, and then receive a card from Lady St. Julians for that very date. Mrs. Guy Flouncey would never have succeeded but for a fortunate circumstance. A great nobleman who met her at a country house succumbed to her charms; his wife was annoyed, and there was Mrs. Guy's opportunity—"She threw over the Earl and became the friend of the Countess, who could never sufficiently evince her gratitude to the woman who would not make love to her husband." Henceforth all was plain sailing; the Countess engaged her friends to come to Mrs. Guy Flouncey's ball; the list was published and filled two columns of the *Morning Post*; the triumphant hostess was able to say to her husband, who had played his part valiantly as a sporting character, "We have done it at last, my love!"

At Mrs. Guy Flouncey's we meet again Edith Coningsby, now a popular hostess herself. Disraeli gives a long description of her, but the summary is that "she was endued with great vivacity, a sanguine and rather saucy spirit, with considerable talents and a large share of feminine vanity, that divine gift which makes women charming". The great wealth of the Coningsbys carried great obligations. As Lord Eskdale said, the ideal for a man who wanted to enjoy himself at ease was to have ten thousand a year while the world supposed he had only five thousand. Coningsby, however, wished to use his wealth to give him the influence and power he needed to realise his political ideals. He looked to Edith to support him and to keep him informed of what was going on outside the House of Commons. We are told that "as some men keep up their Greek by reading every day a chapter in the New

Testament, so Coningsby kept up his knowledge of the world by always, once at least in the four and twenty hours, having a delightful conversation with his wife".

Tancred followed up the breakfast party by frequent calls on Lady Constance. She was certainly clever—"She talked like a married woman, was critical, yet easy; and having guanoed her mind by reading French novels, had a variety of conclusions on all social topics, which she threw forth with unfaltering promptness, and with the well-arranged air of an impromptu." Tancred was fascinated, and Lady Constance was charmed equally by his intellect and "his pensive beauty and grave innocence". One day she showed him a book called *Revelations of Chaos*, of which he had heard that it had rather a startling theme. The following dialogue is the most often quoted passage in *Tancred*:

"Do you know this?"

"No, I have not seen it."

"I will lend it you if you like; it is one of those books one must read. It explains everything, and is written in a very agreeable style."

"It explains everything!" said Tancred; "it must, indeed, be a very remarkable book!"

"I think it will just suit you," said Lady Constance. "Do you know, I thought so several times while I was reading it."

"To judge from the title, the subject is rather obscure," said Tancred.

"No longer so," said Lady Constance. "It is treated scientifically; everything is explained by geology and astronomy, and in that way. It shows you exactly how a star is formed; nothing can be so pretty! A cluster of vapour; the cream of the milky way, a sort of celestial cheese, churned into light; you must read it, 'tis charming."

"Nobody ever saw a star formed," said Tancred.

"Perhaps not. You must read the *Revelations*; it is all explained. But what is most interesting, is the way in which man has been developed. The principle is perpetually going on. You know, all is development. First, there was nothing, then there was something; then, I forget the next, I think there were shells, then fishes; then we came, let me see, did we come next? Never mind that; we came at last. And the next change there will be something very superior to us, something with wings. Ah! That's it: we were fishes, and I believe we shall be crows. But you must read it."

"I do not believe I ever was a fish," said Tancred.

"Oh! But it is all proved; you must not argue on my rapid sketch; read the book. It is impossible to contradict anything in it. You understand, it is all science; it is not like those books in which one says one thing and another the contrary, and both may be wrong. Everything is proved: by geology, you know. You see exactly how everything is made; how many worlds there have been; how long they lasted; what went before, what comes next. We are a link in the chain, as inferior animals were that preceded us: we in turn shall be inferior; all that will remain of us will be some relics in a new red sandstone. This is development. We had fins; we may have wings."

This was written twelve years before the publication of Darwin's *Origin of Species*, evolution was not yet a familiar word and a common topic. The book in question probably represents *Vestiges of the Natural History of Creation* by Robert Chambers, as Mrs. Disraeli records that they were reading it in 1845 and that "Dizzy is enchanted with it". Darwin himself acknowledged that it prepared the way for his own work. The subject fascinated Disraeli, although he was passionately on the side of faith when science seemed to conflict with it. In his famous speech at Oxford in 1864 he declared that man was born to believe, but that the teachings of science seemed to conflict with those of the Church—"The question is this; is man an ape or an angel? My Lords, I am on the side of the angels." This was received with laughter, but it represented a spiritual reality in Disraeli, he was always a crusader against pure materialism. He recurred to the subject in *Lothair*, in which one of his characters, a Jesuit, arraigns the religion of science: "Instead of Adam, our ancestry is traced to the most grotesque of creatures; thought is phosphorus, the soul complex nerves, and our moral sense a secretion of sugar." In another passage Lothair deplores the lack of clear guidance from philosophers and men of science:—

"How they accounted for everything except the only point on which man requires revelation! Chance, necessity, atomic theories, nebular hypotheses, development, evolution, the origin of worlds, human ancestry; here were high topics on none of which there was lack of argument; and, in a certain sense, of evidence; and what then? There must be design. . . . If there were no design, why it must all be nonsense; and he could not believe in nonsense."

It is interesting to find atomic theories cited in 1870.

As Tancred left Lady Constance he murmured, "I was a fish, I shall be a crow." He felt now that she could be no spiritual mistress for him and wondered how he could ever have indulged in dreams of kneeling at the Holy Sepulchre with her. He decided at once to close with the offer of a yacht which seemed to fit his parents' requirements, and he asked Lord Eskdale for advice as to financial arrangements and an experienced courier. Lord Eskdale sent him to Sidonia.

On his way to Sidonia's office in the City Tancred was able to help a very charming lady who was in distress because her carriage had been involved in an accident. He insisted upon her making use of his and proceeded on foot.

Sidonia was the first person Tancred had met who sympathised with—and even seemed to understand—his longing to go to Jerusalem, and he was able to open his heart to him fully. Sidonia, observing him, saw that he was as ignorant of the world as a young monk, and yet he believed that he had qualities which might enable him one day to control society. (Again, Disraeli could not be content with less than the highest destiny as the natural sphere for his heroes.) Tancred felt uplifted anew when Sidonia said gravely that it appeared that he wanted "to penetrate the great Asian mystery". He left with the promise of a letter of credit and introductions, and an invitation to dine with Sidonia the next night.

On reaching home Tancred found a note from Lady Bertie and Bellair, thanking him for the loan of his carriage. That very night he met the lady at a ball, and found that she was not only meltingly beautiful but a kindred spirit. She had always longed to go to Jerusalem herself, she found society vapid and wearisome beyond bearing, the spiritual alone could satisfy her. Tancred, who had had haunting thoughts from time to time that he might, perhaps, be "the dupe of boyish fantasies", was enchanted. Lady Bertie and Bellair had a soul, she was above "the calculating genius of our reign of Mammon", in which nobody now thought of heaven or dreamed of angels, but concentrated their minds upon steamboats and railways. The ripening of this friendship is delicately described.

Sidonia's dinner-party affords some rich social detail and introduces Coningsby and Edith, Lord and Lady Marney and Lord Henry Sidney. Sybil Marney, after one brilliant season, had found her métier; her house was a focus for those who had the condition of the people at heart. She and her husband were absolutely of one mind and he carried their ideals into Parliament with him. There he found in Coningsby the animating influence he needed to bring out his talents. Tadpole thought Lord Marney little short of insane. "Do you see that man?" he would say, "he might be Privy Seal and he throws it all away for the nonsense of Young England!"

Lord Henry Sidney (now spelled with an "i" instead of a "y") was equally active in promoting the welfare of the people, but his boyish enthusiasm for the revival of ancient pastimes had given place to the deeper pre-occupations of a well informed statesman—"what had been a picturesque emotion had now become a statistical argument"—and he concentrated on the root causes of national disorders, but he still had his ardent mind and gentle disposition. He would have liked to enlist Tancred for his Parliamentary group, but the new crusader was bent upon his pilgrimage to a land "that has never been blessed by that fatal drollery called a representative government, though Omniscience once deigned to trace out the polity which should rule it". Tancred admitted, however, that if a Parliamentary career could save the country Lord Henry would be a public benefactor.

The guests were seated at a round table set with exquisite taste; Sidonia disliked massive plate and obtrusive ornaments at an intimate dinner, and everything was rare and delicate:—

"The dinner was served on Sèvres porcelain of Rose du Barri, raised on airy golden stands of arabesque workmanship; a mule bore your panniers of salt, or a sea-nymph proffered it to you on a shell just fresh from the ocean, or you found it in a bird's nest; by every guest a different pattern. In the centre of the table, mounted on a pedestal, was a group of pages in Dresden china. Nothing could be more gay than their bright cloaks and flowing plumes, more elaborately exquisite than their laced shirts and rosettes, or more fantastically saucy than their pretty affected faces, as each, with extended arm, held a light to a guest."

The food was equally delightful, and the service so perfect and noiseless that it never for a moment impinged upon the conversation. This ranged over the questions of the day, and sometimes went deeper. Sidonia voiced one of Disraeli's own favoured theories in a discourse upon progressive development. After citing the rise and decay of various nations he concluded:

"Is it what you call civilisation that makes England flourish? Is it the universal development of the faculties of man that has rendered an island, almost unknown to the ancients, the arbiter of the world? Clearly not. It is her inhabitants that have done this; it is an affair of race. A Saxon race, protected by an insular position, has stamped its diligent and methodic character on the century. And when a superior race, with a superior idea to Work and Order, advances, its state will be progressive, and we shall, perhaps, follow the example of the desolate countries. All is race; there is no other truth."

Here there is much that is interesting in its bearing on modern times, but Disraeli would have been cut to the heart to see Hitler's application of a theory of race to the persecution of the Jews.

This dinner is the occasion for a portrait of Monckton Milnes (afterwards Lord Houghton) as Mr. Vavasour. Milnes was a well-known figure in London society, in many ways a dilettante, although he had a contemporary reputation as a poet; both Harriet Martineau and Elizabeth Barrett paid tributes to his verse. His breakfasts were famous and there is a story that Carlyle, when asked what he thought would happen if Christ appeared on earth again, replied instantly: "Monckton Milnes would ask Him to breakfast." Milnes was Florence Nightingale's suitor, and she fell under the spell of his undoubted charm sufficiently to record that in refusing him she had sacrificed "the man whom I adore". She even showed some pique when he at last withdrew the special attention he had paid to her for some years. Eventually he married very happily and recognised that he had escaped an ordeal; no doubt life as Florence Nightingale's husband would have been altogether too dynamic for him.

Milnes had toyed with Young England and Disraeli recorded in a memorandum that he came to him with tears in his eyes and complained that he was not represented in *Coningsby*. He wrote a review of *Coningsby* in *Hood's Magazine*, under the title "Real England", in which he argued that the characters were not created but copied from life. He considered the book good but not great, essentially ephemeral, artificial, smart and lacking in real quality. Disraeli was apt to revenge himself upon detractors, but he claimed that he tried to do justice to Milnes in *Tancred*—"I sketched the character of Vavasour, and I made it as attractive as I could consistent with that verisimilitude necessary. I don't know whether he was over-satisfied." The general opinion seems to have been that the portrait was less than fair to Milnes, although unmistakable. It is, at least, painstaking:

"Mr. Vavasour was a social favourite; a poet and a real poet, and a troubadour as well as a member of Parliament; travelled, sweet-tempered, and good-hearted; amusing and clever. With catholic sympathies and an eclectic turn of mind, Mr. Vavasour saw something good in everybody and everything, which is certainly amiable, and perhaps just, but disqualifies a man in some degree for the business of life, which requires for its conduct a certain degree of prejudice. Mr. Vavasour's breakfasts were renowned. Whatever your creed, class or country, one might almost add your character, you were a welcome guest at his matutinal meal, provided you were celebrated. . . . A real philosopher, alike from his genial disposition and from the influence of his rich and various information, Vavasour moved amid the strife, sympathising with everyone; and perhaps, after all, the philanthropy which was his boast was not untinged by a dash of humour, of which rare and charming quality he possessed no inconsiderable portion. Vavasour liked to know everybody who was known, and to see everything that ought to be seen. He also was of opinion that everybody who was known ought to know him. . . . His life was a gyration of energetic curiosity; an insatiable whirl of social celebrity. There was not a congregation of sages and philosophers in any part of Europe which he did not attend as a brother... He was everywhere and at everything; he had gone down in a diving-bell and up in a balloon.... He was the steward of Polish balls and the vindicator of Russian humanity; he dined with Louis Philippe and gave dinners to Louis Blanc."

Vavasour took a lively part in the conversation at Sidonia's dinner-table.

Tancred's yacht was soon ready for him and his suite prepared to sail at a moment's notice. And yet he lingered. It seemed too cruel to depart on his crusade and leave his soul-mate, Lady Bertie and Bellair, almost broken-hearted because she could not accompany him. If only there had been some rare game in Palestine she might have persuaded her husband to take her there! It was unbearable that she should never see Jerusalem. The once eager pilgrim called every day to pore over a volume of Syrian sketches with her; instead of sailing for the Holy Land Tancred of Montacute planned a fish dinner at Greenwich, where his yacht was moored. One object was to introduce Sidonia to Lady Bertie, who was most anxious to meet him, but unfortunately he was not able to come.

One morning when Tancred was with his afflicted friend a note was brought to her. She tore it open, turned pale, shrieked and fainted! As Tancred tried to revive her he could not help seeing the note. It ran: "The Narrow Gauge has won. We are utterly done; and Snicks tells me you bought five hundred more yesterday, at ten. Is it possible?"

As soon as Lady Bertie's maid took charge of her mistress Tancred left the house. He went straight to Sidonia, and from him he learned that Lady Bertie and Bellair was a great speculator in railroads, in fact "the most inveterate female gambler in Europe". She had long been pestering Sidonia for an interview. As soon as he could collect himself Tancred spoke of his letter of credit. Sidonia asked him when he intended to sail. "Tomorrow," said the young crusader, "today if I could."

CHAPTER XIII

Tancred (II)

THE second part of *Tancred* gave Disraeli an opportunity to stress the theme so dear to his heart—that Europe owed its religion and much of its law and culture to the Jews. Even in the first part of the book it occurs in the reflections he interpolates in his story:

"The life of a British peer is mainly regulated by Arabian laws and Syrian customs; but, while he sabbatically abstains from the debate or the rubber, or regulates the quarterly performance of his juridical duties in his province by the advent of the sacred festivals, he thinks little of the land and the race who, under the immediate superintendence of the Deity, have by their sublime legislation established the principle of periodic rest to man, or by their deeds and their dogmas, commemorated by their holy anniversaries, have elevated the condition and softened the lot of every nation except their own."

Tancred did not feel an alien or a stranger in Palestine; his earliest lessons had been from the Bible and from the history of the Jews his young mind had "drawn its first pregnant examples of human conduct and divine interposition, and formed its first dim conceptions of the relations between God and man". In fact his life and conduct were still largely regulated by the laws of Sinai.

The young crusader set out with every possible safeguard and advantage. His parents had insisted that he should be accompanied by the robust and genial Colonel Brace, who had served in the Peninsular war and still largely re-lived it in his conversation, by the irreproachable Mr. Bernard, a clergyman who had been their son's private tutor at Oxford, and by a physician in whom the Duchess of Bellamont had great faith. More important, however, were the introductions he had from Sidonia. Sidonia had written to Adam Besso, the chief banker in Palestine, that Lord Montacute should, on request, receive advances up to "as much gold as would make the right-hand lion on the first step of the throne of Solomon the king". If he required more he was to have as much as would make the lion on the left, and so on, up every stair of the royal seat. In short, Tancred could command unlimited credit. Moreover, Sidonia had provided the perfect courier in Baroni, who had accompanied him on his own travels. Baroni was an example of Sidonia's habit of "enlisting in his service all the rare talent which he found lying common and unappropriated in the great wilderness of the world. . . . He liked to give ability of all kinds its scope. Nothing was more apt to make him melancholy, than to hear of persons of talents dying without having their chance."

Here we have an echo of the note that recurs with poignancy in the early novels, such as the heartfelt reflections in *The Young Duke* upon the unrecognised Caesar and the obscure Napoleon, consumed by anxiety lest their "supernatural energies might die away without creating their miracles".

Tancred disposed of his uncongenial suite by installing them in a furnished house in Jerusalem. Colonel Brace dined at the British Consulate every day, enraptured with such a virgin field for his Peninsular stories; Mr. Bernard was only too happy in constant visits to the English Bishop. As for the doctor, Baroni soon reported that the Governor's wife had sent for him, and, better still, "he has been admitted to the harem; has felt all their pulses without seeing any of their faces, and his medicine chest is in danger of being exhausted before your Lordship requires its aid". Thus free of his encumbrances Tancred presented himself to Alonzo Lara, the Spanish prior of the convent of Terra Santa, to whom Sidonia had commended him. Here he lived in a cell and gave himself up for some time to "unbroken and impassioned reverie, heightened, not disturbed, by frequent and solitary prayers", and only varied by conferences with Lara, in which he strove to "penetrate the great Asian mystery".

The arrival of the young English lord caused a stir in Jerusalem and was discussed in Besso's divan. In describing this Disraeli drew upon his own experience—he had smoked the narghilly in eastern divans on his own travels. The principal subject of conversation was the English lord's vigil at the church of the Holy

Sepulchre, which had been lighted up for his benefit from sunset to sunrise, with special guards posted and only the Prior and two brethren allowed to enter. Such an indulgence must have cost at least ten thousand piastres; the English lord must be rich indeed, in fact the general opinion was that he could be no less a person than the Queen of England's brother. Besso could only tell his friends that he was evidently a very great lord and had brought him such a letter of credit that if he were to tell him to re-build the Temple he must do it. All these details seemed particularly interesting to a young man who was reclining on a pile of cushions, out of which, "like some wily and dangerous reptile, glided the spiral involutions of his pipe". Soon he started up to question Besso, showing a youthful beardless face, with delicate features, a finely arched brow and blue eyes full of fire. This was the Emir Fakredeen, a Prince of the Lebanon, who is one of the best drawn characters in the book, with the particular virtues and vices of the Orient. He was of the opinion that there was some political motive behind the young lord's arrival; the English were not given to making pilgrimages, they might be sure that he had something else to do besides praying at the Holy Sepulchre.

Tancred's first adventure occurred when he made his pilgrimage to Gethsemane and Bethany. The scenery and atmosphere glow upon the imagination when Disraeli writes of Palestine with authentic detail. In this case it was midsummer and the heat seems to exude from the page:

"Bengal, Egypt, even Nubia, are nothing to it; in these countries there are rivers, trees, shade and breezes; but Jerusalem at midday in midsummer is a city of stone in a land of iron with a sky of brass. The wild glare and savage lustre of the landscape are themselves awful. We have all read of the man who had lost his shadow; this is a shadowless world. Everything is so flaming and so clear, that it would remind one of a Chinese painting, but that the scene is too bold and wild for the imagination of the Mongol race."

Tancred had dismissed Baroni so that he might be alone at Gethsemane. When he left the garden the heat of the day was over and he decided to go on by himself to Bethany, but he was led aside from his path by his first sight of a palm tree. It appeared to be in a garden, he could not resist the temptation to enter by the open gate and walk down the alleys of lemon and pomegranate trees, bordered with myrtle and roses. The gentle sound of falling water fell gratefully upon his ears; he walked on and came to a kiosk of white marble, overshadowed by the lofty palm, and looking on to a little hill so thickly covered by bright blue flowers that it looked like a bank of turquoise. Here Tancred sat down to rest and soon, weary with the heat and the emotions of prayer in Gethsemane, he slept. When he woke he found a beautiful girl beside him. She wore an amber vest of gold-embroidered silk, fastened with buttons of precious stones; her wide Mamlouk trousers were made of the finest white cashmere and were fastened round her ankles with clasps of rubies; over these garments were a pelisse of violet silk and an outer cloak of amber cashmere lined with white fox fur. On her head was a small cap richly encrusted with pearls. This was Eva, the daughter of Besso, known as the Rose of Sharon. On her mother's side she was the granddaughter of the great Arab Sheik Amalek. Tancred apologised for his intrusion; they talked and he found that Eva's intelligence was as bright as her beauty. This conversation is interesting and illustrates many of Disraeli's ideas, but is too involved to be represented in extracts. Here again, however, we have the theme of the Jewish influence on western civilisation. It is even carried to modern times, as Eva asked Tancred what was, on the whole, most valued in Europe, and when he shamefacedly replied that it was money, she skilfully drew from him the admission that the richest men in London, Paris and Vienna were Jews.

After Tancred had left Eva's garden he was passed on the road by a young horseman in trousers and jacket of crimson cloth, with a white turban and a shawl round his waist to hold his pistols and sabre. He rode a horse of superb breed, and beside him ran a servant holding a narghilly at which his master took frequent puffs as he rode. It was the Emir Fakredeen, on his way to visit his foster-sister Eva.

Fakredeen, early left an orphan, had been brought up by Besso, but he was now deeply involved in political intrigues in the Lebanon, of which he hoped to become the ruler. Later in the book Disraeli gives a long account of the history of Syria and the

Lebanon, which the general reader may find indigestible in a novel, but history has a considerable influence on the story, and there are some salient facts which must be borne in mind. The Lebanon was divided into fifteen feudal provinces, ruled by Emirs and Sheiks, but they had been subjected to conquest by the Turks and the Egyptians. In the mountain region, where the Shebaab family, of which Fakredeen was a prince, was supreme, the Turkish domination was little more than nominal. When the Egyptians drove out the Turks their yoke was not so light and when they attempted to destroy feudalism there was a general revolt. Some of the Lebanese were Christians and the Christian powers in Europe interested themselves in the situation. Eventually the Turks, favoured by Lord Palmerston, were re-established (1840) and the Emir of the house of Fakredeen, who had governed the Lebanon during the Egyptian occupation, was carried off a prisoner to Constantinople. The next year a civil war broke out in the Lebanon, in which the two leading clans of its mixed population, the Druses and the Maronites, took part with energy and enjoyment. Once more the Great Powers of Europe interfered and Downing Street busied itself with constitution-making. While Turkey only took a passive interest various schemes of government were tried, largely at the instigation of Downing Street. In 1845 another civil war broke out. In this the young Emir Fekredeen played the part of mediator and was one of the Emirs and Sheiks who signed articles of peace by which Maronites and Druses accepted a geographical division of the Lebanon into two spheres of rule.

This situation was one which offered tempting prospects to political intriguers, and Fakredeen, to whom intrigue was the breath of life, plunged into schemes from which he hoped to emerge the ruler of the Lebanon. Since the Egyptian invasion the Turks had refused to entrust power to a prince of the Shebaab again, but Fakredeen believed that his natural right to rule must prevail sooner or later. He opened his heart to Eva, whom he hoped to enlist to persuade her father to give him a loan. The political detail of this chapter is not easy to grasp, but the character of Fakredeen, as revealed in this talk with Eva, is important to the story and interesting in itself.

Eva, whose sound judgment was recognised by both her father and Fakredeen, said decidedly: "You will never succeed. Intrigue will be your ruin, Fakredeen."

"Intrigue!" exclaimed the Prince. "Intrigue! It is life! It is the only thing! . . . Why, England won India by intrigue. Do you think they are not intriguing in the Punjaub at the moment? Intrigue has gained half the thrones of Europe; Greece, France, Belgium, Portugal, Spain, Russia. If you wish to produce a result, you must make combinations; and you call combinations, Eva, intrigue."

He was even ready to change his religion if necessary; he would be of the religion that would give him a sceptre. When Eva was shocked and told him that he had no self-respect, he exclaimed: "No Syrian has; it won't do for us. . . . Self-respect, too, is a superstition of past centuries, an affair of the Crusades. It is not suited to these times; it is much too arrogant, too self-conceited, too egotistical. No one is important enough to have self-respect." He then confessed that he had secured five thousand English muskets, now held by "that Egyptian camel the Scheriff Effendi", who would not hand them over until he received two hundred thousand piastres, which he hoped Eva would coax from Besso. Startled, Eva asked if he would be so rash as to start an insurrection. He explained his scheme eagerly. When both Druses and Maronites had arms they would soon be at each other's throats. He continued with great animation: "And this will make the mountain more unmanageable than ever, and the English will have no customers for their calicoes, don't you see? Lord Palmerston will arraign the minister in the council. . . . The calico merchants will cry out for a prince of the house of Shebaab! . . . And Sir Canning, finding he is in a mess, will sign a fine note of words about the peace of Europe and the prosperity of the Lebanon, and 'tis finished."

Throwing himself on his knees before Eva and kissing her robe, he begged her to plead with Besso for one more loan for him; she was his friend, his ruby, his pearl, his rose, she understood him and would even forgive his faults. When Eva still urged him to give up his project he sprang to his feet and exclaimed with energy: "When I am young and ruined! When I have the two greatest stimulants in the world to action, Youth and Debt! No; such a combination is never to be thrown away. Any young prince ought to win the Lebanon, but a young prince in debt ought to conquer the world!"

Disraeli recurs to this idea again. Later in Fakredeen's story he says that he was fond of his debts, which provided him with excitement and stirred him to action:

" 'What should I be without my debts?' he would sometimes exclaim: 'dear companions of my life that never desert me! All my knowledge of human nature is owing to them: it is in managing my affairs that I have sounded the depths of the human heart, recognised all the combinations of human character, developed my own powers and mastered the resources of others. . . . Oh, my debts, I feel your presence like that of guardian angels! If I be lazy, you prick me to action; if elate, you subdue me to reflection; and thus it is that you alone can secure that continuous yet controlled energy which conquers mankind.' "

Disraeli himself passed much of his life under the burden of debts, but it is difficult to believe that he regarded them as guardian angels.

Finding that Eva had promised her father not to speak to him again on her foster-brother's affairs, Fakredeen confided that he had an alternative scheme. There was, he told her, a young English lord in Jerusalem of the highest rank and rich enough to buy the grand bazaar of Damascus. He must have some secret mission of importance, but meanwhile it was said that he intended to go to Mount Sinai. Fakredeen continued urgently:

"Now lend me that ear that is like an almond of Aleppo! I propose that one of the tribes that obey your grandfather shall make this Englishman prisoner as he traverses the desert. You see? Ah! Rose of Sharon, I am not yet beat. . . . I defy Ibrahim, or the King of France, or Palmerston himself, to make a combination superior to this. What a ransom! The English lord will pay Scheriff Effendi for his five thousand muskets, and for their conveyance to the mountain besides.' "

From this point the story is too complicated and involved with political intrigue to be easily epitomised, but certain episodes stand out and illustrate Disraeli's ability to capture an oriental atmosphere.

Fakredeen succeeded in enlisting the great Sheik Amalek to carry out his plan, and Tancred and his escort were captured in a mountain pass. The description of the Bedouin camp, pitched amidst the ruins of an ancient Idumean city, to which the captive was taken is a vivid picture:

"The pavilion of the chief, facing the sunset, was raised in the arena of an amphitheatre cut out of the solid rock, and almost the whole of the seats of which were entire. The sides of the mountains were covered with excavated tombs and temples. . . . Fragments of columns were lying about, and masses of unknown walls. From a defile in the mountain issued a stream, which wound about in the plain, its waters almost hid, but its course beautifully indicated by the undulating shrubbery of oleanders, fig-trees and willows. On one side of these, between the water and the amphitheatre, was a crescent of black tents, groups of horses, and crouching camels. Over the whole scene the sunset threw a violet hue, while the moon, broad and white, floated over the opposite hills."

Here a swift rider brought news to Amalek that Tancred had been taken. The dialogue has an eastern flavour which is probably based on experience. The rider greeted Amalek:

" 'Salaam, Sheik of Sheiks; it is done; the brother of the Queen of the English is your slave.'

" 'Good!' said Sheik Amalek, very gravely, and taking the pipe from his mouth. 'May your Mother eat the hump of a young camel! When will they be here?'

" 'They will be the first shadows of the moon.'

" 'Good! Is the brother of the Queen with Sheik Salem?'

" 'There is only one God: Sheik Salem will never drink laban again, unless he drink it in Paradise.'

" 'Certainly there is only one God. What! Has he fallen asleep into the well of Nummala?'

" 'No; but we have seen many evil eyes. Four hares crossed our path this morning. Our salaam to the English prince was not a salaam of peace. The brother of the Queen of the English is no less than an Antar. He will fight, yea or nay; and he has shot Sheik Salem through the head.'

" 'There is but one God, and his will be done. I have

lost the apple of mine eye. The Prince of the English is alive?'

" 'He is alive.'

" 'Good! Camels shall be given to the widow of Sheik Salem, and she shall be married to a new husband. Are there other deeds of Gin?'

" 'One grape will not make a bunch, even though it be a great one.'

" 'Let truth always be spoken. Let your words flow as the rock of Moses.'

" 'There is only one God: if you call to Ibrahim-ben-Hassan, to Molgrabi Teuba, and Teuba-ben-Amin, they will not be roused from their sleep: there are also wounds.'

" 'Tell all the people there is only one God: is it the Sheik of the Jellaheens that has done these deeds of Gin?'

" 'Let truth always be spoken; my words shall flow as the rock of Moses. The Sheik of the Jellaheens counselled the young man not to fight, but the young man is a very Zatanai. Certainly there are many devils, but there is no devil like a Frank in a round hat.' "

Tancred, who was suffering from a wound in the arm, was treated as an honoured guest, and Fakredeen in particular offered him every possible service, professing himself a Christian prince and posing as though he had nothing to do with Sheik Amalek's rude conduct. Before long he fell under the spell of Tancred's grave dignity and lofty ideals, and Tancred himself found a great charm in the young Emir's friendship. Soon, however, the pain in the young lord's arm grew worse and then high fever set in. Despite the anxious precautions of the Duke and Duchess of Bellamont it seemed likely that their son and heir might die in a Bedouin camp in the desert, unprotected by Colonel Brace, untended by Dr. Roby and without religious consolation from Mr. Bernard. At this critical juncture Eva arrived, an emissary from her father to reason with her grandfather about the ransom, and she concocted a medicine from herbs which induced a deep sleep and saved Tancred's life.

Disraeli was not content to deny his hero the revelation which he craved and on Mount Sinai Tancred at last had a vision, in which a mighty figure with a radiant star on his brow spoke to him. The spirit's discourse began with the familiar theme which haunts the story:

"Child of Christendom, I am the angel of Arabia, the guardian spirit of that land which governs the world; for power is neither the sword nor the shield, for these pass away, but ideas, which are divine. The thoughts of all lands come from a higher source than man, but the intellect of Arabia comes from the Most High. Therefore it is that from this spot issue the principles which regulate human destiny."

The spirit then spoke of human history and traced the evils from which mankind was suffering to estrangement from God, but the conclusion offered little inspiration for the practical guidance of the young reformer:

"Cease, then, to seek in a vain philosophy the solution of the social problem which perplexes you. Announce the sublime and solacing doctrine of theocratic equality. Fear not, faint not, falter not. Obey the impulse of thine own spirit, and find a ready instrument in every human being."

The readiest instrument at the moment was Fakredeen, and Tancred accompanied him to Canobia, his superb Saracenic castle amongst the mountain crests of Lebanon. This impressed even Freeman and Trueman, two servants who had shared Tancred's adventures and who enliven the story by their comments and their speculations upon what the steward's room at Montacute Castle would have to say about such outlandish doings. Gazing up at Canobia Freeman remarked, "This is the first gentleman's seat I have seen since we left England."

"There must have been a fine coming of age here," rejoined Trueman.

"As for that," replied Freeman, "comings of age depend in a manner on meat and drink. They ain't in noways to be carried out with coffee and pipes. Without oxen roasted whole, and broached hogsheads, they ain't in a manner legal."

Much sumptuous and attractive description follows. Then we are transferred to Damascus, which is feelingly described:

"The rivers of Damascus still run and revel within and without the walls, of which the steward of Sheik Abraham was a citizen. They have encompassed them with gardens, and filled them with fountains. They gleam amid their groves of fruit, wind through their vivid meads, sparkle among perpetual flowers, gush from the walls, babble in the courtyards, dance and carol in the streets; everywhere their joyous voices, everywhere their glancing forms, filling the whole world around with freshness, and brilliancy, and fragrance and life. One might fancy . . . they were the guardian spirits of the city."

Here Besso had his principal home and this provides more sumptuous detail.

Gradually a great conception dawned upon the mind of Tancred, which he confided to Fakredeen. They had spoken of Alexander the Great and Julius Caesar, heroes of Fakredeen, and Tancred exclaimed, "But what are their conquests to those of Jesus Christ? Where are their dynasties? Where their subjects! They were both deified; who burns incense to them now? Their descendants, both Greek and Roman, bow before the altars of the house of David." Kindling to his theme, Tancred declared that Asia alone had been faithless to the Asians, but successive conquests had held the oriental mind in thrall. He concluded rapturously: "Arabia alone has been free and faithful to the divine tradition. From its bosom we shall go forth and sweep away the mouldering remains of the Tataric system; and then, when the East has resumed its indigenous intelligence, when angels and prophets again mingle with humanity, the sacred quarter of the globe will recover its primeval and divine supremacy; it will act upon the modern empires, and the faint-hearted faith of Europe, which is but the shadow of a shade, will become as vigorous as befits men who are in sustained communication with the Creator."

Fakredeen was fascinated and part of his nature responded to the lofty motive, but intrigue was the habit of his life, and he soon sought to turn Tancred's mind—and his wealth—to the over-running of Syria by an army drawn mainly from the Lebanon, as a first step in the resurgence of Asia. He thought the project feasible, but it would be of the first importance to secure the alliance of the Ansarey, a people who held the key to the mountains by which the Turks could enter Syria. These people lived in isolation and would admit no strangers, but at last the astute Baroni obtained permission for Tancred and Fakredeen to visit their Queen. The sojourn in the country of the Ansarey is an interesting part of the book. It was a dramatic moment when the young Queen, whose confidence Tancred had won (and something more), revealed the secret which the Ansarey guarded so jealously—a temple filled with superb statues of Greek gods, brought there long ago from ancient Antioch and worshipped with fervour as the peculiar property of this favoured people.

The story now moves to an exciting climax, in which Tancred, Fakredeen, Eva and the Queen of the Ansarey were involved in a drama of love, jealousy, ambition, capture and escape. Fakredeen over-reached himself in a newly conceived plan to marry the Queen of the Ansarey himself and found a dynasty, and the results were calamitous.

Eventually Tancred returned to Jerusalem, further than ever from guiding the resurgence of Asia. He had not lost faith, but now another thought was uppermost in his mind. He saw in Eva the solace of his heart and the inspiration of his future, with whom alone he might fulfil his ideals. He knew that she was betrothed to her cousin Hillel, but he also knew that the young man was unworthy of her. Eva was now at Bethany, and there Tancred declared his love. First Eva gave him the balm of sympathy: he had thought only of a divine cause, but it had been smirched by the intrigues of politics and the cunning arts of men, he could no longer believe in Arabia. Tancred, throwing himself on his knees, declared that to him she was Arabia—"the angel of Arabia, and of my life and spirit!" He besought her to be his and he could then believe again in the divine cause. Eva tried to recall him to reason—"There are those to whom I belong. . . . This is madness!"—but he urged that nothing should come between them and the "consecrated aim" they could pursue together. If she would but say she loved him he would trample all other ties in the dust.

At last Eva's head fell upon his shoulder, but it is not clear whether it was in willing surrender or a happily, if unconsciously, directed swoon. At this moment voices were heard calling the name of Lord Montacute; Colonel Brace appeared, with Freeman and Trueman and several guides and native servants, and announced that the Duke and Duchess of Bellamont had arrived in Jerusalem. This is the end of the book.

*   *   *

It is difficult to believe that Disraeli originally meant to cut his story short at this point, and yet almost more difficult to see how he could have brought it to a plausible, much less a satisfactory, conclusion. His sister Sarah warned him of the insoluble problem he was setting himself when she had read the first volume: "We are as eager as Tancred to reach the Holy Sepulchre," she wrote, "but, as Sidonia says, when we arrive there, what is to happen? How are these great questions to be answered? When are these mighty truths to be discovered?" It seems likely that the pressure of other business overwhelmed Disraeli and he could not face the difficult task of working out some *modus vivendi* for his new crusader.

Tancred was a favourite with Disraeli himself, as he told Jowett, probably because it embodied his pride in the ancient glories and abiding influence of his race. Only deep feeling could have induced him to write such a book at a time when he needed to placate the prejudices of the Conservatives if he was ever to be their leader. He was already acknowledged as one of the foremost speakers in the House of Commons, but he still had to contend with the mistrust of his race and his exotic personality, and such a novel as *Tancred* was likely to be the reverse of helpful to his ambitions. Monypenny (his biographer) suggests that he had been goaded into revolt and that the book was an "assertion of his detachment and superiority", in which he fortified himself "by the glorification of his race and by the proclamation of the mystic ideas, inherited from the Jews, which marked him out from the commonplace mediocrities around him". Whether this be true or not, *Tancred* expressed the inner mind of Disraeli and some of his abiding convictions. A few years later he expounded these convictions more fully in a chapter which forms a curious interpolation in his *Life of Lord George Bentinck*. There he wrote of Christianity as perfected Judaism, a belief in Calvary consummating the belief in Sinai. He claimed that "the Jews represented the Semitic principle; all that is spiritual in our nature", and that the Hebrew and the Attic races were the two that had done most for mankind.

Tancred provides the best example of the oriental culture and imagery in which Disraeli's mind was steeped, and contains some of his best descriptive passages. The first part of the book is excellent social comedy, but the two halves are so sharply divorced that they seem to represent two different worlds. If these worlds had been brought into closer relations in a third part the book as a whole would have been far more satisfactory.

PART III
THE NOVELS OF A STATESMAN

CHAPTER XIV

Lothair (I)

IN 1834 Lord Melbourne, struck by the young Disraeli's ability, asked him what was his object in life and was startled to receive the reply, "I want to be Prime Minister." The experienced statesman admonished the young man to keep his ambition within the bounds of reason. Late in life Disraeli told the story to Lord Rowton and added, "It was a long speech, and I think I could repeat every word of it still." As reported by Melbourne's biographer it ended, "but you must put all these foolish notions out of your head; they won't do at all". Melbourne did not live to see Disraeli Prime Minister, but when the latter became leader of the Tory party he exclaimed: "By God! The fellow will do it yet!" He did it for the first time in 1868, but after eleven months a Liberal government under Gladstone came into power again, with such a stable majority that Disraeli, now leader of the opposition, found that he could command some leisure. He used it to write *Lothair*.

It was twenty-three years since the publication of *Tancred* and a corresponding change is apparent in the attitude of the author. In the earlier book a vein of bitterness, due to the difficulties and prejudices which he had to surmount, was apt to give venom to his irony. Now he had mellowed to some extent; his satiric quality was still outstanding, but the impish glee with which he gave rein to it in his youth had been transmuted into a more considered, and perhaps richer, style. *Lothair*, too, had not the urgency of a novel with a purpose, but was the fruit of enjoyable observation of the passing show of contemporary life. It had, however, a definite theme, in the conflict in a young man's mind of three rival influences which were brought to bear upon him. The first was his natural environment, as a nobleman with duties to the land and the Church of England; the second was the Roman Catholic Church and the third the international liberation movement, particularly as it concerned the liberation of Italy. This theme was evidently partly suggested by the religious and social sensation caused by the young Marquis of Bute's secession to the Roman Church in 1868; like Disraeli's hero he inherited after a long minority, and Monsignore Capel, the chief agent in his conversion, was drawn in *Lothair* as Monsignore Catesby.

Lothair is one of the richly endowed young heroes in whom Disraeli's soul delighted. He rivalled the Young Duke in his vast estates and wealth, and also resembled him in being a subject of conflict between his guardians, the one a dour Scottish Presbyterian peer and the other a suave and ascetic Cardinal, who had been received into the Church of Rome since his appointment as guardian. The influence of Lord Culloden was predominant in Lothair's youth, and his first taste of highly refined society and gracious family life was due to an Oxford friendship with the son of a Duke, who invited the lonely young man to stay at Brentham, one of his father's mansions in the country.

Brentham rivals Beaumanoir (*Coningsby*) for pride of place amongst the great country houses depicted in Disraeli's novels. Hainault (*Endymion*), which obviously represents a Rothschild mansion, eclipses it in opulence, but is not typical of the English peer's country seat. He had now plenty of models to draw upon for the latter, as he himself had been a guest at Raby, Lowther, Ashridge, Woburn, Stowe and other mansions. In the earlier books he had been forced to rely upon imagination in place of experience; when he visited Belvoir Castle he wrote to his sister that it was not like Beaumanoir (which he intended to represent it) but Coningsby Castle "to the very life". It was the same with Dukes. When *The Young Duke* was published Isaac D'Israeli justly asked, "What does Ben know of Dukes?" But the Duke of Abercorn, who was the model for the owner of Brentham, owed his dukedom to Disraeli; he had now created a duke in fact as well as in fiction.

Brentham obviously represented Trentham, the Staffordshire seat of the Duke of Sutherland, although in *Lothair* he bestowed it upon a different ducal family. The description of this vast, ornate Italian palace of freestone abounds in typical Disraelian phraseology, such as "spacious and graceful chambers", "statued and stately terraces", and "a gardened domain of considerable extent, bright with flowers, dim with coverts of rare shrubs, and musical with fountains". White peacocks spread their tails "in scornful pride" in Lady Corisande's garden. Beyond the gardens stretched a vast park, and "fallow deer trooped among its ferny solitudes and gigantic oaks". The interior was both bright and sumptuous, and the Duchess and her bevy of charming daughters endowed it with something of their own gaiety and grace. The breakfast-room, for instance, was a scene of delightful informality:

"The breakfast-room at Brentham was very bright. It opened on a garden of its own, which, at this season, was so glowing and cultured into patterns so fanciful and finished, that it had the resemblance of a vast mosaic. The walls of the chamber were covered with bright drawings and sketches of our modern masters, and frames of interesting miniatures, and the meal was served on half a dozen or more round tables, which vied with each other in grace and merriment; brilliant as a cluster of Greek or Italian republics, instead of a great metropolitan table, like a central government absorbing all the genius and resources of the society."

The Duke, like the Duke of Abercorn, was extremely handsome, conscious of his duties and a devoted family man, and "every day when he looked into the glass, and gave the last touch to his consummate toilette, he offered his grateful thanks to Providence that his family was not unworthy of him". The daughters all married well after one season; as Hugo Bohun, a friend of their brother's, remarked, "It is a family that marries off quickly. If a fellow is obliged to marry, he always likes to marry one of them." At the opening of the story only Lady Corisande remained unmarried, and she was not yet launched upon society, she was to be presented at Court in the coming season.

The first scene in *Lothair* is set in the morning-room at Brentham and is a charming little period piece:

"The mistress of the mansion sat surrounded by her daughters, all occupied with various works. One knitted a purse, another adorned a slipper, a third emblazoned a page. Beautiful forms in counsel leant over frames glowing with embroidery, while two fair sisters more remote occasionally burst into melody, as they tried the passages of a new air, which had been communicated to them in the manuscript of some devoted friend."

Music was always the chief attraction in the evenings at Brentham, but the Duke liked to collect a party for games that were not billiards played with billiard balls. In the afternoons they rode, and they were a great croquet family; the ladies played in coquettish little hats and the Duchess watched from a Turkish tent.

The ladies in the morning-room were discussing the advent of Bertram's friend Lothair, who was indeed an interesting figure: the Duchess had heard that he had been brought up in the Highlands by a rather savage uncle, but now he would soon enter into possession of as many castles and palaces as the Duke himself. Lothair arrived; he was handsome, with auburn hair and deep blue eyes with dark lashes; the ladies liked him. To him Brentham seemed a world of enchantment; the delightful married daughters made conversation easy, Lady Corisande sang divinely and at night he was initiated into the mysteries of the smoking-room, over which Lord St. Aldegonde presided in an Egyptian robe.

The picture of Brentham is not complete without the sons-in-law. Lord Montairey, a fond husband, enthusiastically abetted his wife in promoting croquet parties; he could not bear to leave her for long. Lord St. Aldegonde, listless and handsome, was heir to a great dukedom, but his eccentric intelligence found an outlet in professing republican views. He was opposed to all privilege, but nevertheless held that all liberty depended on land, and the greater the land-owners the greater the liberty of the country. Unconventional, witty, only afraid of boredom, his favourite style of dress a shooting jacket of brown velvet, with a pink shirt and no cravat, his thick brown hair usually dishevelled, he drifts through the story with nonchalant charm. Bertha St. Aldegonde, his adoring wife, devoted her considerable talents to humouring him—"When he cried for the moon it was promised him immediately"—but often managed to guide him in the right direction. He was not always amenable. He objected to staying with his wife's people in the north in winter—"What I want in November is a slice of cod and a beefsteak, and by Jove I never could get them; I was obliged to come to town. It is no joke to have to travel three hundred miles for a slice of cod and a beefsteak." Yet it was to St. Aldegonde that the Duke turned when he wanted a sound opinion.

Lothair could not conceive any happier way of life than that of Brentham. He was at this time an intense young man who believed that he had already discovered the true objects of life. The Duchess was, however, startled when he asked her permission to propose to Lady Corisande. She tried gentle dissuasion; both Lothair and Corisande should see more of one another, and of life, before such a step, some experience was needed to form sound opinions. Lothair brushed these objections aside; he hated society, he had been to one great party and found it a mass of affectation, malice and falsehood. As for opinions, he had already formed his on every subject of importance and did not expect to change them. The Duchess said mildly, "I could not say that of Corisande." But Lothair was confident that Lady Corisande and he were agreed upon most subjects, although her Church views might be a little higher than his. She would, he was sure, help him to build churches and schools, and sympathise with his first object in life, which was the extinction of pauperism. The Duchess interpolated that this was a vast subject. Lothair, unabashed, said he intended to grapple with it. He believed it was largely a matter of better dwellings, and he already had the designs for building two thousand model cottages on his estates. The Duchess, however, restrained him from speaking to Lady Corisande at present.

Lothair soon went to London, and there his extremely capable lawyer and man of business, Mr. Putney Giles, suggested that the time had come for him to meet his other guardian, Cardinal Grandison. Lord Culloden had kept Lothair in Scotland, sending him to school in Edinburgh, in order to preserve him from the Popish machinations of the Cardinal. The latter had only once interfered decisively in his ward's life, when he insisted upon his going to Oxford, as his father had wished, instead of to Edinburgh University. With his introduction to the Cardinal the second great influence came into Lothair's life.

Cardinal Grandison was drawn from Cardinal Manning, at least in appearance and asceticism, with a few added touches from Cardinal Wiseman. The stir caused when Manning joined the

Church of Rome in 1851 is reflected in a letter Disraeli wrote to Lady Londonderry: "Archdeacon Manning, the spiritual adviser of Sidney Herbert . . . horrible to say, was received not merely by the Oratorians, as Father Newman was—the Oratorians being a sort of Papistical Wesleyans—but by the Jesuits, whom he has joined . . . The whole of the clergy in one of the principal churches in Leeds have gone over in a body, and part of their congregation. The people of this country are really very agitated." From this we see that Disraeli's theme was one which attracted much attention in his own day. How considerable the drift to Rome was is shown by the fact that Bishop Wilberforce's three brothers and two brothers-in-law all seceded to the Roman Church, and his daughter and her husband followed suit as late as 1868.

Cardinal Grandison was tall and thin—"it seemed that the soul never had so frail and fragile a tenement"—and his grey eyes seemed to be sunk into his noble brow, although "they flashed with irresistible penetration". His Eminence did not like to dine out; he said "I never eat and I never drink", which meant that he dined on biscuits and water. Nevertheless, he liked to know something of the world, and he was a great believer in female influence, and also in his own influence over females. True to this belief, he lost no time in introducing his interesting ward to Lady St. Jerome, one of the most enthusiastic votaries of the Roman Church, a woman capable of inspiring crusaders, and yet with all the tact and finesse of a great society hostess. She was ably seconded by her beautiful niece, Clare Arundel, who had expressive deep violet eyes. In due course Lothair was invited to stay at Vauxe, Lord St. Jerome's country seat, an ancient grey stone building of great beauty. At Vauxe there was gracious living indeed, but the chapel was the centre of the household's life, although it was scrupulously indicated to Lothair that he was quite free to absent himself from the services. The benign Jesuit chaplain, Father Coleman, a notable gardener, talked to the young guest delightfully on a number of topics, but it was a rule with him never to press anything. It was Holy Week, and Lothair decided that he would attend Tenebrae. This is described with all Disraeli's sensitivity to beautiful ritual and spiritual symbolism:—

"Manifold art had combined to create this exquisite temple, and to guide all its ministrations. But tonight it was not the radiant altar and the splendour of stately priests, the processions and the incense, the divine choir and the celestial harmonies resounding and lingering in arched roofs, that attracted many a neighbour. The altar was desolate, the choir was dumb; and while the services proceeded in hushed tones of subdued sorrow, and sometimes even of suppressed anguish, gradually, with each psalm and canticle, a light of the altar was extinguished, till at length the Miserere was muttered, and all became darkness. A sound as of a distant and rising wind was heard, and a crash, as it were the fall of trees in a storm. The earth is covered with darkness, and the veil of the temple is rent. But just at this moment of extreme woe, when all human voices are silent, and when it is forbidden even to breathe 'amen'; when everything is symbolical of the confusion and despair of the Church at the loss of her expiring Lord, a priest brings forth a concealed light of silvery flame from a corner of the altar. This is the light of the world, and announces the resurrection, and then all rise up and depart in silence."

Lothair, susceptible to beauty and devotional by nature, was much moved. He talked often to Father Coleman, who spoke of the holy mysteries in a way that could not offend him, and told him "man is on his trial now, not the Church; but in the service of the Church his highest energies may be developed, his noblest qualities proved". Soon another priest joined the household, Monsignore Catesby, a young Jesuit of noble family, who was even more versatile and interesting than Father Coleman. Even more inspiring was the enthusiasm of Clare Arundel, who told Lothair that if she had the command of wealth she would buy some of the squalid streets in Westminster, clear the ground and build a cathedral, where the worship of God could be as gloriously presented to the world as it was in Rome itself. His imagination was fired; to build a cathedral seemed indeed a noble object in life. He found that Monsignore Catesby was an expert on ecclesiastical architecture, and after listening entranced to his discourses on the subject he wrote to an architect and ordered plans for a cathedral.

Before Lothair left Vauxe Cardinal Grandison arrived there.

He asked his ward to walk in the park with him and spoke of Evelyn's *Sylva*, remarking that Mr. Evelyn was a most religious man.

"I wonder," said Lothair, "how any man who is religious can think of anything but religion." This led to a discussion of the decline of religion in England, and presently the Cardinal spoke from his heart, his pale, ascetic face lighted up as if by an inner flame as he said: "I know not a grander or a nobler career for a young man of talents and position in this age, than to be the champion and asserter of divine truth." Dismissing the likelihood of another conqueror, another Dante, another Milton, and discounting statesmen—"whom democracy has degraded into politicians"—he continued:

"The world is devoted to physical science, because it believes that these discoveries will increase its capacity of luxury and self-indulgence. But the pursuit of science leads only to the insoluble. When we arrive at that barren term, the Divine voice summons man, as it summoned Samuel; all the poetry and passion and sentiment of human nature are taking refuge in religion; and he whose deeds and words most nobly represent Divine thoughts will be the man of this century."

"But who could be equal to such a task?" murmured Lothair.

"Yourself," exclaimed the Cardinal, fixing a glittering eye upon his companion—"anyone with the necessary gifts, who had implicit faith in the Divine purpose."

Yet again Disraeli, now far past middle age, could not bring himself to tempt his young hero with anything less than a sublime career as "the man of the century". Lothair, however, could not command implicit faith, and felt that even the Church was perplexed and ambiguous. This the Cardinal denied vigorously; the Church of Christ could never be perplexed; perplexed Churches were "Churches made by Act of Parliament, not by God". He himself had formerly been a parliamentary christian and lived in despondency, until the Divine will brought him to light and rest. And now, having sown his seed, the Cardinal left it to germinate.

Lothair returned to town, and there he found the plans for his cathedral awaiting him, in a magnificent purple leather portfolio ornamented with crosses and coronets. Meanwhile his friends at Brentham had been distressed by a paragraph in the *Morning Post* reporting a rumour that a young nobleman who was shortly to come of age would then enter the Roman Church. Lady Corisande took it bitterly to heart, but her brother told her it was useless to speak to a man about love or religion, as both were stronger than friendship. All that could be done was to draw Lothair into their circle again when the family returned to town, and he had the honour of taking Corisande in to supper at her brilliant coming-out ball, when she was acclaimed as the prettiest débutante of the season.

Lothair was now obliged to attend to the business connected with his coming of age and felt not a little harassed, between his lawyers, his monsignores and his architects. At this juncture a letter from his stud-groom near Oxford offered him a welcome respite from his own perplexities and the attentions of his friends. He decided to go down to Oxford.

Now we come to the third influence in Lothair's life. Already there has been a seemingly irrelevant chapter describing a meeting of the Standing Committee of the Holy Alliance of Peoples, an international society pledged to promote liberation movements in Europe. It was attended by a general who preferred to be known as Captain Bruges, and who is supposed to represent General Cluseret, who afterwards came to the fore in the Paris Commune, but in 1867 was ready to serve with Garibaldi. In another chapter he visited Mazzini, called Mirandola in the novel, but Disraeli failed to bring life and character into this episode. Before the Standing Committee adjourned they drank one toast—"To MARY ANNE." Mary Anne was the name Disraeli adopted for a network of secret societies in France, not as a compliment to his wife, but because it had been mentioned in a Paris protocol in 1856. It is not easy, however, to disentangle truth from fiction in this part of the novel, although revolutionary secret societies were active in Europe at this time, and busied themselves with the Fenian movement in Ireland, republicanism in France and the liberation of Italy. Lothair attended a Fenian meeting in London and was saved from rough handling by Captain Bruges. Disraeli tells us that the Mary Anne societies were founded by a woman, and had been whipped up to enthusiasm by a woman at the time of Garibaldi's unsuccessful attempt to march into Rome in 1862. The rôle then assigned to Mary Anne was to intimidate the French government and prevent their interference in Italy. The Roman Church is represented as a vigilant enemy of these godless secret societies.

Lothair had heard little of international revolutionary activities and did not dream that it was a fateful moment for him when, on his way from Oxford to his stables, he came upon the scene of a carriage accident. Fortunately no one was hurt, but it was clear that the gentleman and lady involved could not use their carriage again, and Lothair sent for his. It soon arrived—drawn by four highly-bred roans and complete with two grooms behind with "folded arms and imperturbable faces"—and before the couple drove away Lothair promised to dine with them in Oxford that night.

This is the introduction of Theodora, an Italian by birth and the inspiration of the Mary Anne societies. Her father and brothers had fallen in Garibaldi's cause; now she was the wife of Colonel Campian, an American of the Southern States, who was still a wealthy man, despite losses in the American Civil War. Theodora is the type of mystical figure which Disraeli could seldom resist bringing into his novels, but she is not without life and character. There was a serene dignity about her. Hers was "a Phidian face", with large grey eyes and dark lashes, her wonderful hair was bound in Grecian fillets, her low, musical voice had a thrilling quality. Lothair soon accorded her a kind of reverent worship, which she never allowed to sink to a lower plane, although she was unfailingly kind to him. On the first evening his heart had leapt gratefully when she rebuked an Oxford Professor (a malicious portrait of Professor Goldwin Smith) who said that he would like to purge Oxford of religion. Theodora said firmly, "I cannot conceive any society of any kind without religion." Lothair had yet to learn that she was not an adherent of any Church and found her God in her conscience; when he did so he came to the conclusion that life was not such a simple affair as he had supposed.

Before long Lothair was driving down every day to Belmont, the Campians' beautiful villa on the Thames. Here he met an entirely new circle. Amongst them was the distinguished painter Mr. Phoebus and his voluptuously attractive Greek wife. Mr. Phoebus, originally sprung from the old nobility of Gascony, was a worshipper of beauty in all physical forms. He could not bear to carry anything so prosaic as a bank-note on his person and when travelling he took small velvet bags of pearls, rubies, Napoleons and gold piastres. He would not visit anyone whose house was lighted by gas. He believed that art was a matter of race, a first-rate race produced first-rate art. When Lothair deplored his own ignorance Mr. Phoebus said that books were fatal, and continued: "Nine-tenths of existing books are nonsense, and the clever books are the refutation of that nonsense. . . . What I admire about the order to which you belong is that they do live in the air, that they excel in athletic sports; that they can only speak one language; and that they never read. This is not a complete education, but it is the highest education since the Greek." Mr. Phoebus dismissed the critics of his art airily—"You know who the critics are? The men who have failed in literature and art."

Surrounded by such society, presided over by a woman with the mien of a Greek goddess, it was small wonder that Lothair began to find the unremitting attentions of Monsignore Catesby somewhat embarrassing. He was told that there was soon to be a supreme function in the Roman Church, a great service over which the Cardinal was to preside. The Cardinal himself expressed a wish that Lothair should attend, in order "to show the world that the sons of the Church will unite for the cause of divine truth". Monsignore Catesby averred that it would be one of the most important days for England in their time; Lady St. Jerome thought of nothing else. On the morning of the great day the Monsignore handed to Lothair a note from Clare Arundel, and seeing that he was evidently moved by it, felt that the battle was won. Before he left, however, he insisted on ordering Lothair's carriage to be ready for him at eight-thirty. But when he stepped into his brougham Lothair's order was "To Belmont", and while the Cardinal was conducting the great service at which his ward was to have been shown to the world in the bosom of the Roman Church, he was sitting at the feet of the divine Theodora.

Despite his preoccupation with the mistress of Belmont, and his entanglement in the net cast about him by his Roman Catholic friends, Lothair was not altogether cut off from the Brentham circle. He heard that a marriage was expected between Lady Corisande and the Duke of Brecon. St. Aldegonde was quite peevish about it and told his wife that in that case he should go to the Indian Ocean. "Why cannot Corisande marry Carisbrooke?" he asked with a reasonable air. "Your father would not like my going to the Indian Archipelago and not returning for five years, perhaps never returning. Why should Corisande break up our society? Why are people so selfish? I never could go to Brentham again if the Duke of Brecon is always to be there, giving his opinions, and being what your mother calls 'straightforward'. I hate a straightforward fellow. As Pinto says, if every man were straightforward, there would be no conversation."

Pinto is one of those character-sketches Disraeli loved to throw off, with no particular bearing on the story, but complete vignettes in themselves. He was "a little oily Portuguese, middle-aged, corpulent and somewhat bald"; no one knew much about him and yet he was generally sought after in society. He might have been expected to be a parasite, but, on the contrary, everybody flattered him and hung on his words. He was not brilliant but his talk was delightful because "he had the art of viewing things in a fanciful light. . . . He was not an intellectual Croesus, but his pockets were full of sixpences." St. Aldegonde enjoyed his company and it even induced him to gratify Mr. Brancepeth by dining with him. Mr. Brancepeth, a grave young man, consecrated his life to his dinner-parties so successfully that to have dined with him was a hall-mark for which every aspirant to social distinction was anxious to qualify. St. Aldegonde alone had held aloof: "not that I dislike Brancepeth", he said, "I rather like him. I like a man who can do only one thing, but does that well. But then I hate dinners."

Lothair drifted in and out of this society like a disembodied spirit. The plans for his cathedral were laid aside; instead he spent a fabulous sum on a string of pearls for Theodora, because he noticed that she wore only one ornament and was told that she had sacrificed some beloved pearls for a great cause which she had at heart. Mr. Ruby, the jeweller, provides another of Disraeli's pleasing vignettes. He told Lothair that pearls were like girls, if they were to keep their complexion they must have air, exercise and sunshine. He himself attended to the Duchess of Havant's pearls every year, and exposed them on a sunny bank in a westerly wind for some days. Disraeli himself used periodically to lay his wife's pearls on the grass by the terrace at Hughenden.

Lothair sent the pearls to Theodora anonymously. She showed them to him and spoke of their superb beauty, but she said that she never wore jewels and could not accept such a present. She then asked him as a favour to take charge of them for her and placed a slip of paper in the case, telling him that, whatever happened, he must not open it for a year. When he tried to protest she exclaimed, "Do not say a word!" She then sealed the packet with her father's seal, which bore the word ROMA, handed it to him and went quickly out of the room.

CHAPTER XV

Lothair (II)

THE celebration of Lothair's coming-of-age provides one of Disraeli's most splendid pictures of aristocratic life. Mr. Putney Giles surpassed himself in the arrangements, and Lothair took his own measure to ensure their perfection by persuading the Campians to join the brilliant galaxy of guests.

Muriel Towers, Lothair's chief country seat, is easily recognised as Alton Towers in North Staffordshire, then belonging to the Earl of Shrewsbury, and not far from Trentham, the original of Brentham. Lothair had only seen Muriel once, as a child, and now he was scarcely able to look about him, as he was met at the station by five hundred horsemen, many of them notables of the county, and a crowd on foot accompanied his carriage. He passed under triumphal arches and between lines of children waving flags and singing songs of welcome. At the park gates he stood up in the carriage and made a speech. Then the postillions were able to speed on, past woods and lawns and a lake gay with green islands and golden gondolas, while the startled deer scudded into the coverts. The steward had galloped on ahead and when Lothair reached the Towers the whole household retinue was gathered on the steps. There were the house-steward, the chief butler, the head-gardener, the chief cook, the head-keeper, the head-forester, the grooms of the stud and of the chambers, and the housekeeper, who was "a grave and distinguished-looking female, who curtsied like the old court". Behind these were the powdered footmen in crimson liveries, and still further back the lesser members of the staff, grouped according to sex. Lothair was impressed, and a little taken aback. "Castles and parks," he thought, "I had a right to count on, and perhaps even pictures, but how I came to possess such a work of art as my groom of the chambers, who seems as respectfully haughty and as calmly graceful as if he were at Brentham itself, and whose coat must have been made in Savile Row, quite bewilders me."

All the grandees of the county, from the Lord Lieutenant and the High Sheriff downwards, were guests at Muriel Towers, and also the Brentham family, the St. Jeromes, the Duke of Brecon, Lord Culloden and the Cardinal, and the Anglican Bishop of the diocese. In this society Colonel and Mrs. Campian were strange phenomena, but Theodora's beauty and gracious dignity soon won golden opinions, and the Duke decided that the Colonel, as an erstwhile landed gentleman of the Southern States, should be treated "as our fathers treated the emigrant nobility of France". St. Aldegonde found him an expert on horses and tobacco, and announced, almost incredulously, to his wife, "I am not bored." The visitors made a tour of the grounds and admired "the parterres blazing with colour, the sylvan background, the undulating paths over romantic heights, the fanes and the fountains, the glittering statues, and the Babylonian terraces". Lothair murmured apologetically, "Perhaps too many temples." The description and the comment could still be applied to the gardens of Alton Towers in the twentieth century.

On the great day the grounds were crowded with people of all sorts and conditions, for whose benefit there were numerous pavilions in which banquets were served continuously from noon to sunset. At 6 o'clock Lothair sat down to dinner in the great hall with two hundred guests. As the sun set the people began to gather in thousands beside the lake to watch Lothair and his party embark in gay barges and gondolas for the central island, where coffee, ices and "whimsical drinks" were served in a pavilion. They were accompanied by a complete orchestra on gold and opal seats in a gigantic floating shell. When it was dark there was a magnificent display of fireworks, and the first rocket was the signal for beacons to be lighted on every height within fifty miles. The festivities ended with a splendid ball. These celebrations resembled those that were actually held at the coming-of-age of the Marquis of Bute, shortly before he joined the Church of Rome.

Meanwhile plots and counter-plots had been agitating the house-party. The Cardinal proposed to celebrate High Mass in the neighbouring town, the episcopal capital of the Anglican see, on the Sunday preceding the coming of age, and this was announced in the leading daily papers. With the announcement was coupled a paragraph stating that the report that Lothair had joined the Roman Church was "premature", as the Cardinal could not countenance such a step while he was still under age. This caused a great flutter in the dove-cote at Muriel Towers. Lady Corisande flew to Theodora in great distress. Theodora confessed that she, too, would be grieved if Lothair fell under the influence of the Roman priesthood, but she added: "I think if they were certain of their prey they would be more reserved." Corisande then unfolded a plan of her own; the Anglican Bishop should be asked to celebrate Holy Communion in the chapel at Muriel Towers on the morning of Lothair's coming of age. He could hardly absent himself, although, she added sadly, her brother Bertram had seen plans for a Popish cathedral which his friend had undertaken to build. Theodora said that many plans were never realised, and when Corisande sighed despondently she exclaimed: "You were not born to sigh. Sighs should be for those who have no country, like myself; not for the daughters of England, the beautiful daughters of proud England."

Corisande found a willing ally in the Bishop. In the description of this prelate Disraeli's contemporaries recognised Wilberforce:

"The Bishop was high-church, and would not himself have made a bad cardinal, being polished and plausible, well-lettered, yet quite a man of the world. He was fond of society, and justified his taste in this respect by the flattering belief that by his presence he was extending the power of the Church . . . The Bishop had no abstract prejudice against gentlemen who wore red hats . . . but in the present instance, however gracious his mien and honeyed his expressions, he only looked upon the Cardinal as a dangerous rival, intent upon clutching from his fold the most precious of his flock, and he had long looked to this occasion as the one which might decide the spiritual welfare and career of Lothair."

The Cardinal suggested to Lothair that it would be unwise to begin an exhausting day with a church service at 8 o'clock, but the Bishop's chaplain had already sent announcements to church papers, and to *John Bull*. The early Celebration duly took place, Lothair communicated and Lady Corisande's heart was uplifted in happy thanksgiving.

In relinquishing his office as guardian Lord Culloden gave some sound Presbyterian advice to his ward. He hoped that Lothair would be firm in the Protestant faith; Popery was more than "the sign of the Cross and music and censer-pots". He warned him solemnly:

"A man should be master in his own house. You will be taking a wife some day, at least it is to be hoped so; and how will you like one of these monsignori to be walking into her bedroom, eh? And talking to her alone when he pleases and where he pleases; and when you want to consult your wife, which a wise man should often do, to find another mind between her and yours? . . . I tell you that if you once embrace the scarlet lady, you are a tainted corpse. You'll not be able to order your dinner without a priest, and they will ride your best horses without saying with your leave or by your leave."

Before the house-party dispersed Lothair met Captain Bruges in the park, on his way to call upon Theodora, but he would not accept an invitation to stay. Theodora did not appear at lunch, but later in the day she received Lothair in her own apartments. She said she must speak to him, although "it is not a subject for the festive hour of your life", adding gravely, "but I cannot resist my fate".

"Your fate must always interest me," murmured Lothair.

"Yes, but my fate is the fate of ages and of nations," she replied, and then continued with some agitation: "Amid the tortures of my spirit at this moment, not the least is that there is only one person I can appeal to, and he is one to whom I have no right to make that appeal."

"If I be that person," said Lothair, "you have every right, for I am devoted to you."

Theodora answered that it was not personal devotion that she needed, but devotion to a cause and one that could mean little to him—"Why should you feel for my fallen country, who are the proudest citizen of the proudest of lands?" She then opened her heart to him. The gist of her story was that the time was now ripe for Garibaldi to make another assault upon Rome, since the French troops upon which the Pope had relied were being withdrawn. The men were at command, the only obstacle was lack of money and arms. She and her husband had already given all they could. When she had finished her story Lothair rose and said: "I am the right person for you to appeal to, the only person . . . I have long resolved, were I permitted, to devote to you my fortune and my life."

* * *

When we next meet Lothair it is as Captain Muriel, serving with the Garibaldi Volunteers, now well armed, under General Bruges. This part of the story is well studied and of some interest, but lacks the life with which Disraeli endowed the scenes of Tancred's eastern adventures. The campaign ended disastrously. Garibaldi was defeated, Theodora's secret visit to the Mary Anne societies did not prevent French troops being hurriedly despatched to Rome. Theodora herself, dressed as a man and acting as secretary to General Bruges, was mortally wounded as she tried to rally the Volunteers in an early skirmish. Before she died she exacted a promise from Lothair that he would not enter the Church of Rome. Lothair, now scarcely caring whether he lived or died, was seriously wounded at the battle of Mentana, which brought the ill-fated venture to an end. It was not until three years later, when the Franco-Prussian war of 1870 made French interference impossible, that an Italian army took Rome.

The story now returns to its main theme. Lothair recovered consciousness in a Roman palace where he was lovingly tended by two veiled women. The first thing that roused him to speech was the distant chant of voices singing vespers. "I have heard the chant of angels," he murmured. Still unequal to asking any questions, he listened daily for the singing of matins and vespers; when a requiem was sung he remembered Theodora and tears poured down his face. The veiled attendant leant over him to bathe his brow and whispered gently: "The Church has a heart for all our joys and all our sorrows, and for all our hopes and all our fears."

The speaker was Clare Arundel. She had been nursing the wounded in a hospital in Rome when a noble-looking peasant woman appeared and led her to a young Englishman who was lying unconscious in an ambulance. She at once recognised

Lothair and had him taken to the palace which the St. Jeromes occupied when in Rome. When he grew stronger Monsignore Catesby took charge of him, and as soon as he could leave his room he was taken into the exquisite Jesuit chapel attached to the palace. Over the altar was a picture of the Virgin which resembled Theodora. Weak from his wounds and mentally prostrated by Theodora's death, he felt that he could now be content to let life glide by him and pass all his days listening to heavenly melodies in this chapel fragrant with incense. He was perplexed by one thing; some of the congregation seemed anxious to kiss his hand, or even merely to touch him. Monsignore Catesby explained that they naturally wished to show their reverence for one so favoured.

"Favoured!" said Lothair. "Am I favoured? It seems to me I am the most forlorn of men." But he was too listless to pursue the matter further.

Soon Lothair joined the St. Jeromes from time to time in their family apartments. He was never left alone, either Monsignore Catesby or Father Coleman was always with him. Then the Cardinal arrived in Rome and treated his ex-ward with tender affection. In due time Lothair was told that there was to be a special service in the Jesuit church of St. George of Cappadocia, at which Miss Arundel was to give public thanks for the mercy vouchsafed to her in saving the life of a fellow-countryman. He felt that he could do no less than offer to be present, if she wished it. It seemed that it was the dearest wish of her heart, with a glowing face she took his hand and murmured earnestly—"And support me, for I need support." That evening the Monsignore said to Father Coleman, "It is done. It is done at last. He will not only be present, he will support her. There are yet eight and forty hours to elapse. . . . He must never be out of our sight; not a human being must approach him."

The day came and Lothair walked in the great procession round the church, led by the banner of the Virgin, followed by two beautiful children dressed as angels, the boy carrying a rose of Jericho, the girl a lily. Acolytes, thurifers, priests and cardinals, Roman princes and veiled ladies came behind them. Lothair's place was behind Clare Arundel, who walked alone, in a veil which touched the ground; a lighted candle was thrust into his hand.

The next morning Lothair found a Roman journal on his table. He took it up and saw that it contained an account of yesterday's service. With utter bewilderment and growing dismay he read the story there given of how the Blessed Virgin herself had led Miss Arundel to her stricken countryman. Many people had testified to seeing the halo round her head. Two priests had followed her when she left the hospital and seen her stop to give a flower to each of two children, and then she had miraculously vanished. The children said that the lady had told them that the flowers would never fade, and today, a month later, they were still freshly blooming. The favoured subject of this miracle had been severely wounded while fighting in the Pope's army on the field of Mentana.

Almost stunned by horror and disgust, Lothair turned to Cardinal Grandison. He was his father's friend, he was an English gentleman; he had been absent from Rome when this story was concocted, surely he would not connive at such a tissue of lies? But the Cardinal said suavely that the report had been drawn up by truly pious men and every statement well considered. As for Lothair's impression that he had fought against the papal army at Mentana, he must remember that he had been very ill and his mind deeply disturbed. When Lothair protested indignantly the Cardinal became positively jocular. "Well, we will not dwell on Mentana," he said. "Your case is no uncommon one. It will wear off with returning health. King George IV believed that he was at the battle of Waterloo, and indeed commanded there; and his friends were at one time a little alarmed; but Knighton, who was a sensible man, said, 'His Majesty has only to leave off curaçoa and rest assured, he will gain no more victories.'"

Passing to a serious tone, the Cardinal adjured Lothair to remember that he was "in the centre of Christendom, where truth, and where alone truth resides", and told him that the Pope himself would receive him into the bosom of the Church of Rome the next day. Then, perhaps, the "divine dream" they had spoken of in the park at Vauxe might one day be realised.

Lothair was in despair. To contradict the facts of the story and discredit the miracle publicly would bring shame and distress on Lady St. Jerome and Clare Arundel, who had so tenderly nursed him back to life. He shrank from an appeal to the British Minister in Rome, who had probably written sarcastically to the Secretary of State describing how "a member of one of the highest orders of the British peerage had carried in the procession a lighted taper, after two angels with amaranthine flowers and golden wings". Night fell. He was actually alone. He slipped out of the palace and wandered until he reached the Coliseum, where he sat down in the vast moonlit amphitheatre to think. There Theodora appeared to him in a vision. She gazed at him with the serene and solemn expression he had last seen on her face, and uttered in her deep, sweet voice the word: "Remember!" It was, perhaps, as well that Father Coleman had been following him and was able to convey his unconscious form back to the palace.

Now, however, Lothair found an ally. Lord St. Jerome said to his wife, "They have over-done it with Lothair, Gertrude," and insisted upon sending for an English doctor. It was settled that the patient was to go back to England as soon as he was fit for the journey; meanwhile a friend of Monsignore Catesby offered him a villa in Sicily for his convalescence. The Monsignore and Father Coleman escorted him there and never let him out of their sight in the daytime. One morning, however, Lothair woke very early and made his way down to the sea. There, in a little cove, not overlooked by the villa, he chanced upon two fishermen with a sailing-boat. Finding that he had an adequate sum of money with him Lothair persuaded them to carry him to Malta at once. The voyage was made safely, despite some risk in so small a boat, but officials made trouble about his landing without papers of any kind. In the midst of this altercation the owner of an English yacht came ashore and to Lothair's great relief he recognised Mr. Phoebus.

Lothair's worst troubles were now over, but there are still a number of episodes to come before the end of the story, involving various characters. One of these cannot be passed over because of the light it throws on Disraeli's attitude to religion, and it also illustrates his predilection for semi-mystical beings. Lothair, like Tancred, needed a Comforter, and he found a more satisfactory one than the ineffectual angel who spoke to Tancred on Mount Sinai. Travelling with the Phoebus family he reached Jerusalem, and once again Disraeli's pen comes to life in attractive description. Here Lothair met a Syrian of distinguished grace and dignity and they talked on the Mount of Olives. Lothair said that he wished to visit the cradle of his faith:

" 'And you would do wisely,' said the Syrian, 'for there is no doubt the spiritual nature of man is developed in this land.'

" 'And yet there are persons at the present day who doubt, even deny, the spiritual nature of man,' said Lothair. 'I do not, I could not; there are reasons why I could not.'

" 'There are some things I know, and some things I believe,' said the Syrian. 'I know that I have a soul, and I believe that it is immortal.'

" 'It is science that by demonstrating the insignificance of this globe in the vast scale of creation has led to this infidelity,' said Lothair.

" 'Science may prove the insignificance of this globe in the scale of creation,' said the Syrian, 'but it cannot prove the insignificance of man.' "

As the talk developed the Syrian denounced the belief in a Creator who is unconscious of creating. Lothair said sadly, "but there are people now who tell you that there never was any creation, and therefore there never could have been a Creator".

"And which is now advanced with the confidence of novelty," said the Syrian, "though all of it has been urged, and vainly urged, thousands of years ago. There must be design, or all we see would be without sense, and I do not believe in the unmeaning. As for the natural forces to which all creation is now attributed, we know they are unconscious, while consciousness is as inevitable a portion of our existence as the eye or the hand. The conscious cannot be derived from the unconscious. Man is divine."

"I wish I could assure myself of the personality of the Creator," said Lothair. "I cling to that, but they say it is unphilosophical."

"In what sense?" said the Syrian. "Is it more unphilosophical to believe in a personal God, omnipotent and omniscient, than in natural forces, unconscious and irresistible? Is it unphilosophical to combine power with intelligence?" Continuing, he cited Goethe's idea that in the centre of space we might find a monad of pure intelligence, and asked if that were more philosophical than "the truth, first revealed to man amidst these everlasting hills, that God made man in His own image"?

"I have often found in that assurance a source of consolation," said Lothair.

"It is the charter of the nobility of man," said the Syrian.

Disraeli here again recurs to his insistence on race. The Syrian quoted "In my Father's house are many mansions", and proceeded, "by the various families of nations the designs of the Creator are accomplished. God works by races, and one was appointed in due season and after many developments to reveal and expound in this land the spiritual nature of man." Later he added: "Why we are here, whence we come, whither we go, these are questions which man is organically formed and forced to ask himself, and that would not be the case if they could not be answered."

When they parted Lothair asked his companion's name and the Syrian replied "My name is PARACLETE."

In Jerusalem Lothair met Bertram and St. Aldegonde, and the former showed him some letters from his sister Corisande, containing anxious and affectionate enquiries about himself. He now returned to England and set himself to clear up several matters which troubled him. He found that Mr. Putney Giles had already acted on his instructions to make it clear that he had not joined the Roman Church, and to use any possible means to discredit the unfortunate story spread from Rome. Mr. Giles had done this handsomely and effectively by building two churches on Lothair's estates and announcing that he would be present at the consecration of both, and by subscribing generously to various Church funds in his name. At the same time he had inserted paragraphs in the papers implying that stories emanating from Rome might lead to a libel action.

A more delicate task was to re-open some sort of friendly relations with the St. Jeromes, to whom he owed his life. He found that they were ready to make it easy for him. Clare Arundel was about to take the veil, as she had intended to do before she had been persuaded that it was her duty to try to win Lothair for her Church by winning his heart for herself. He now had a beautiful cross designed in gold and emeralds, to enshrine some earth which he had brought from the Holy Sepulchre, and sent it to her as a thank-offering.

At last he found himself at Brentham again, and there he told Lady Corisande that his heart had returned to its first love, and found that she loved him. Presently he drew a sealed package from his pocket and asked her to open it. She found a case containing some beautiful pearls and a slip of paper inscribed: "Theodora's gift to Lothair's bride."

*   *   *

In this short account some good minor characters and many episodes have been passed over, and less than justice has been done to various dialogues and discourses. *Lothair* is a leisurely book, in which Disraeli evidently enjoyed drawing upon his ripe experience and now richly endowed memory for character-sketches, reflections and aphorisms. Here and there the language sinks to the style we associate with third-rate romance or melodrama; one review described it as "a mass of verbiage which can seldom be called English". Enough passages have been quoted to show that this was an unfair exaggeration.

The theme of the book was of more interest to Disraeli's contemporaries than to the modern reader. Within the memory of Victorians of 1870 society had been stirred by a series of notable conversions to Roman Catholicism; it was only eleven years since the shock of Darwin's *Origin of Species*, which seemed to bring science into conflict with religion. With England at peace, no harassing international problems, social conditions improved and prosperity spreading, Victorian minds were free to take a deep interest in religious theory and practice. There is a story of how Tennyson, when sharing a room with a travelling companion, lay awake late reading *The Young Stepmother* by Charlotte Yonge. At last his companion heard him exclaim, "I see land! Mr. —— is just going to be confirmed", upon which he put out the light.

As in the other novels, the minor characters are more life-like than the principals. Leslie Stephen, a distinguished critic of Disraeli's books, wrote of the hero: "Lothair reduces himself so completely to a mere passive bucket, to be pumped into by every variety of teacher, that he is unpleasantly like a fool." Yet it is possible to find some charm in Lothair's ingenuous youth, his seriousness and his natural courtesy.

Some reviewers were enthusiastic, others severe. The *Quarterly* condemned the book as a failure and an outrage—"a sin against good taste and justice". Froude, on the other hand, thought it the author's best work, and that it "opened a window into Disraeli's mind, revealing the inner workings of it more completely than anything else he said or wrote". Nevertheless, it is difficult to assess from it his true attitude to Roman Catholicism. The fact that it is introduced into so many of the novels seems evidence that it had a strong attraction for him, although four years after the publication of *Lothair* he sponsored the Public Worship Regulation Bill, designed to check the growth of ritualistic practices in the Church of England, and virtually forced upon the government by the anxiety felt in the country and fully shared by the Queen. On his oriental side Disraeli had some spiritual affinity with the romance and colour, and even the authoritarianism, of the Church of Rome, but the Englishman in him could not tolerate it in the Church of England, where it seemed to him "Mass in masquerade". It was, perhaps, a more or less subconscious conflict in his own nature that led to his preoccupation with the subject, and *Lothair* represented one attempt to resolve this conflict by drawing an extreme picture of the wiles of the Jesuits.

Lothair had a phenomenal success; Disraeli claimed that it had been more widely read in England and America than any book of the last half-century. The name Lothair was adopted for a song, a ship, a colt, a perfume, a dance and a street. Corisande gave her name to Baron Rothschild's filly, a song, a ship and a waltz. One edition of the book quickly followed another and letters of appreciation and congratulation poured in from many quarters. And yet, the biographer Buckle tells us, there were comparatively few congratulations from his Parliamentary colleagues. This is understandable. They may well have been dismayed that this versatile Jew who had lived down his exotic past sufficiently to be accepted as leader of the great Conservative party, which to them was very England of very England, and even to be Prime Minister, should have burst into print again with one of his fantastic novels. It must have been a shock. The twenty-three years which had elapsed since the publication of *Tancred* had led them to believe that he had long outgrown his literary ebullience, but here was the mixture as before—extraordinary theories, injudicious character-sketches of contemporaries, special pleading for the Jews, strange mystical figures and sumptuousness laced with irony. Would the man never reach years of discretion? Once again Disraeli had given proof that he was not solely concerned with political ambition.

CHAPTER XVI

Endymion (I)

IN 1880 Disraeli's second and last term of office as Prime Minister came to an end. Four years earlier he had consented to leave the House of Commons for the House of Lords, as Earl of Beaconsfield, and he thus fulfilled his youthful boast in *The Young Duke* that he intended, if he had time, to give specimens of the two styles of oratory required respectively in the Commons and the Lords. Perhaps if he had not now been a widower he might have been tempted to enjoy a happy retirement at Hughenden, but he shrank from a life of lonely inaction and continued to lead the Conservative opposition. Although he was seventy-six his mind was still lively and inventive, as he wrote to Lady Bradford: "Unfortunately for me my imagination did not desert me with my youth." Now it found one outlet in the production of his last complete novel, *Endymion*, which he had actually begun some years earlier. Disraeli evidently felt that the choice of this strange Christian name for his hero needed some explanation, and in the novel the boy's mother says that Endymion had been a name in her family since the days of Charles I. Lord Rowton (who, as Montagu Corry, had become Disraeli's devoted secretary) said that it was taken from Endymion Porter, a royalist friend of Davenant, Dekker and Herrick, who was an ancestor of Lady Beaconsfield. There is, however, another suggestion. The mythical Endymion was the lover of the moon goddess, Selene, and Selina was the name of Lady Bradford, to whom Disraeli turned after his wife's death for the feminine sympathy and influence which had become indispensable to him. His wife had realised this deep-rooted need in his nature, strengthened by the years of their devotion to one another, and had written in a note she left for him: "Do not live alone, dearest. Someone I earnestly hope you may find as attached to you as your own devoted MARY ANNE." Disraeli found great solace in the friendship of two ladies. One was Lady Chesterfield, a widow two years older than himself, and the other her sister, Lady Bradford, wife of the Earl of Bradford, who was over fifty. The French ambassador said sarcastically that Disraeli's feminine society was *toutes grandmères*. He actually proposed marriage to Lady Chesterfield, with the object of securing the constant society of both sisters, but it was Lady Bradford to whom he really gave his heart. Sometimes she found his demands upon her more than she was prepared to meet. He wrote her 1,100 letters and innumerable little notes dispatched from his seat in Parliament, as he had been wont to send them to his wife. He wrote, in reply to some protest, "I have never asked anything of you but your society." His demands on her society, however, were constant, and in one letter he admitted, "It is not a 'slice of the moon' I want; I want it all." This and other allusions give colour to the theory that in calling his novel *Endymion* he was indirectly dedicating it to Lady Bradford, although one of the few respects in which he found her sympathy wanting was her lack of appreciation of his books.

Endymion certainly illustrates the all-importance of feminine influence in a man's life, in this case both public and private; in fact the hero is little more than a pleasant and sufficiently able puppet, manipulated by his fondly ambitious sister and the great lady of society who became his Egeria. The overweening ambition of Disraeli's early heroes finds a counterpart in that of Myra Ferrars, although hers was concentrated on the advancement of her twin brother; even when she made a brilliant marriage, which also promised to be a happy one, her first thought was, "We have now got a lever to move the world."

Endymion owes even less of its interest to its plot than the other novels, neither does it depend chiefly on its characters (although some of these are memorable portraits of contemporaries) like *Coningsby*, nor on its scenes, like *Sybil*. The outstanding feature of the book is Disraeli's evocation of the atmosphere of political society; in a Preface to a late edition Philip Guedalla describes it as "a *bal masqué* of the great world from Navarino to the Crimea". Disraeli takes us behind the scenes of the political theatre, and in the early chapters he gives us a living picture of the 1830's, a period of which he had garnered vivid impressions in his youth. Some of his generalisations are helpful in setting the stage for his story:

"The great world then, compared with the huge society of the present period, was limited in its proportions, and composed of elements more refined though far less various. It consisted mainly of the great landed aristocracy, who had quite absorbed the nabobs of India, and had nearly appropriated the huge West Indian fortunes. Occasionally, an eminent banker or merchant invested a large portion of his accumulations in land, and in the purchase of parliamentary influence, and was in time duly admitted to the sanctuary. But those vast and successful invasions of society by new classes which have since occurred, had not yet commenced. The manufacturers, the railway kings, the colossal contractors, the discoverers of nuggets, had not yet found their place in society and the senate. There were then, perhaps, more great houses open than at the present day, but there were very few little ones."

And:

"The sympathies of society were more contracted than they are at present. The pressure of population had not opened the heart of man. The world attended to its poor in its country parishes, and subscribed and danced for the Spitalfields weavers when their normal distress had overflowed, but their knowledge of the people did not exceed these bounds, and the people knew very little more about themselves. They were only half born."

The cream of this society gathered in the reception-rooms of Zenobia—"the queen of London, of fashion and of the Tory party"—who, like Lady St. Julians, was modelled on Lady Jersey. Zenobia sat on a sofa in a splendid saloon with a great personage, blue-ribboned and grey-headed, by her side, and an ambassador facing her. She was eager to persuade them that a great re-action was due, in favour of the Conservative party. They deplored the tenacity of the new Liberalism which kept the Whigs in office:

" 'The Church is weary of the present men,' said the great personage. 'No one really knows what they are after.'

" 'And how can the country be governed without the Church?' exclaimed Zenobia. 'If the country once thinks the Church is in danger, the affair will soon be finished. The King ought to be told what is going on.'

" 'Nothing is going on,' said the ambassador; 'but everybody is afraid of something.'

" 'The King's friends should impress upon him never to lose sight of the landed interest,' said the great personage.

" 'How can any government go on without the support of the Church and the land?' exclaimed Zenobia. 'It is quite unnatural.'

" 'That is the mystery,' remarked the ambassador. 'Here is a government, supported by none of the influences hitherto deemed indispensable, and yet it exists.'

" 'The newspapers support it,' said the great personage, 'and the Dissenters, who are trying to bring themselves into notice ... and then there is always a number of people who will support any government—and so the thing works.'

" 'They have got a new name for this hybrid sentiment,' said the ambassador, 'They call it public opinion.'

" 'How very absurd!' said Zenobia; 'a mere nickname. As if there could be any opinon but that of the Sovereign and the two Houses of Parliament.' "

Amongst those who staked all his hopes on the advent of a Conservative government was Mr. Ferrars, who had been an Under Secretary of State in Lord Liverpool's government and was spoken of in Zenobia's circle as "very rising". He was the son of a man who had made his mark in the Treasury under Pitt, who had returned him to Parliament for a Treasury borough, but he had never attained Cabinet rank, and it was his dearest wish to see his son do so. The son duly distinguished himself at Eton and Oxford, and as soon as he left the university an obliging peer placed a borough at his disposal and he entered Parliament. His father was reputed to be wealthy and did not grudge his "very rising" son generous support. Young Ferrars married; his wife, a beauty and an heiress, soon had society at her feet. The Ferrars' dinners were celebrated, their carriages distinguished, they had a house in Hill Street and a villa at Wimbledon. Their family consisted of beautiful twins, Endymion and Myra, whom Mrs. Ferrars dressed in a striking, fanciful style, and who moved about amongst their mother's guests like young gods, a little disdainful of mere mortal company. When they came down to dessert at a dinner-party they caused quite a sensation, the girl with her ringlets braided with pearls and the boy in a black velvet jacket with large silver buttons, a shirt of lace and a waistcoat of white satin. It was a blow when Mr. Ferrars did not receive Cabinet rank as soon as he had hoped, but Mrs. Ferrars entertained still more sumptuously and Zenobia was convinced that her favourite rising man would one day be Prime Minister.

The political under-currents of 1829 and 1830 are described, until a new Whig government came into power with a programme of Parliamentary reform. At first Zenobia laughed heartily at the absurdity of supposing that the House of Commons would pass a Reform Bill; then she pinned her faith on the House of Lords rejecting it, and her optimism kept up the courage of William Ferrars, who distinguished himself notably in speeches against the Bill. When Lord Grey resigned and the King sent for the Duke of Wellington, Zenobia was triumphant, and practically promised William Ferrars the Cabinet. The Duke sent for him and his hopes soared, but then there was a mysterious delay and even Zenobia admitted that there was a hitch, although it could only be temporary. Mr. Ferrars received another summons to Apsley House. The Duke—"calm, easy and courteous"—told him that, since he had requested his co-operation in his ministry, he felt it right to inform him at once that he had been obliged to give up the attempt to form a government.

Now Mr. Ferrars was desperate indeed. His father had recently died and he had discovered that the lavish allowance he had received had been taken from capital; now little remained of either his father's or his wife's fortune. It needed all his honesty and courage to tell his wife, who was first utterly incredulous and then offered to sell her diamonds and reduce the number of her carriages. At last the full horror of the situation dawned upon her and she stormed and wept, but when she saw her husband in tears she rose to the occasion and threw her arms round his neck exclaiming, "O William! If we love each other, what does anything signify?"

Nevertheless, retirement in an isolated old hall in the country, cheap to rent because it was the subject of a Chancery suit, proved a severe trial of the family's fortitude. Myra, in particular, effected an almost permanent expression of "ineffable contempt and disgust", rebuffed her parents' attempts to soothe and interest her, and seemed to live only for her brother. Mr. Ferrars kept a link with the political world by writing articles in Conservative journals. Mrs. Ferrars consoled herself by saying that they were "victims of revolution"—since Mr. Ferrars had lost even his seat in the House of Commons when the Reform Bill abolished close boroughs—and nursing sanguine hopes that one day there would be another Conservative government and her husband's just claims would be handsomely recognised.

In 1834 the King dismissed Lord Melbourne, whose ministry had unaccountably gone to pieces. So unexpected was this crisis that Sir Robert Peel was in Rome. Mr. Ferrars was advised by his political friends to come to London at once. Here, as in *Coningsby*, we have all the anxious stir of those days, while a messenger travelled post haste to Rome and even the Duke was marking time until Peel could get back, which might not be for three weeks. All Mr. Ferrars' old political associates received him kindly and acknowledged his claims, but he felt in some degree a back number amongst his former companions and the new claimants who had come to the fore in the reformed Parliament. He called on Mr. Barron, who had a secret list of constituencies and candidates in case Peel decided on a dissolution. It was a shock when Barron said that there was no certainty nowadays of winning a seat in one's first contest, and of course the expense was considerable, but there were openings even in some manufacturing towns, and no doubt a man who persevered would get in ultimately. The word smote cold on the heart of "this spoiled child of politics, who had always sat for a close borough, and who recoiled from a contest like a woman, when he pictured to himself the struggle and exertion and personal suffering he would have to encounter and endure, and then with no certainty of success". He asked if there were no seats at the government's command, but Barron was afraid they were all appropriated already. Ferrars realised that the expense of a contest would be prohibitive for him, but he had another string to his bow; his wife had suggested that, failing the Cabinet, it would be quite pleasant if he were appointed Governor-General of India.

The great man arrived from Rome and Mr. Ferrars had an

interview with him. He returned home crestfallen, but not hopeless. In reply to his wife's eager enquiries he told her that Peel had not mentioned the Cabinet but had offered him a high post if he could secure his seat, which he feared was impossible. Mrs. Ferrars asked in a low voice whether he had spoken of India, but Mr. Ferrars' courage had failed him. Peel, he said, was "an honourable man, but he is cold, and my manner is not distinguished for *abandon*". His claim to a high post had been acknowledged and he had thought it best to leave the matter there. Meanwhile Peel decided upon a dissolution of Parliament and in the election which followed he failed to win an absolute majority in the House of Commons. Nevertheless, the King asked him to form a government. Shortly afterwards Mr. Ferrars was offered "a second-class West Indian government", but this did not satisfy his wife and he refused it. Then his friend Barron wrote that the government's prospects were not encouraging and he advised Ferrars to come up to town at once and take what he could get. He added, "It is something to have something to give up"; it would at least strengthen his claim in any future Conservative government. Mr. Ferrars went to town, called in Downing Street and spent anxious hours with old colleagues and parliamentary under-secretaries, until he felt almost inclined to accept Sierra Leone or the Gold Coast. But no offer was made and soon all campaigning was brought to an end by the resignation of Peel. All that Mr. Ferrars could show for his pains was the promise of a clerkship for his son in a second-rate government office.

This is the best example of human-political drama in the book, but the inner history of ministries and the political climate in general are a constant background to the story. The account of the Bed-Chamber Crisis is lame compared with that in *Sybil*, but there are interesting character-sketches and reflections in which the elder statesman draws upon his experiences and the opinions he had formed in forty-three years of political life. Amongst the originals who at least gave colour to characters in the novel are Palmerston, Sidney Herbert, Napoleon III (then in exile), Bismarck, Cardinal Manning, Baron Rothschild, George Smythe and Thackeray. The story is mainly told from the Whig standpoint, a curious fact which puzzled Queen Victoria and others.

The state of parties in 1837, after the spate of reformist legislation in the early 'thirties, is commented upon in a conversation between Waldershare (George Smythe) and Mr. Sidney Wilton (Sidney Herbert):

" 'Well, I go upon this,' said Waldershare. 'It is quite clear that Peel has nothing to offer the country, and the country will not rally round a negation.' . . .

" 'Yes, that is all very well,' replied Mr. Wilton, 'but we are the Liberal shop, and we have no Liberal goods on hand; we are the party of movement, and must perforce stand still. The fact is, all the great questions are settled. No one will burn his fingers with the Irish Church again; in this generation certainly not, probably in no other; you could not get ten men together in any part of the country to consider the corn laws. . . . As for the ballot, it is hardly tolerated in debating societies. The present government, my dear George, will expire from inanition. I always told the Cabinet they were going on too fast. They should have kept back municipal reform. It would have carried us on for five years. It was our only *pièce-de-résistance*.' "

Amongst the imaginary minor characters of the political world are Mr. Bertie Tremaine and his brother Mr. Tremaine Bertie, whom Disraeli drew with lively satire. The combination of names may have been suggested by Edward Bulwer Lytton (who placed Lytton after Bulwer on inheriting property) and his brother Henry Lytton Bulwer. Mr. Bertie Tremaine was a young man with an estate, ample means and a parliamentary borough of his own, who aspired to political distinction; with more vanity than talent, he intended to found "the party of the future". The young Endymion, invited to one of his recherché dinners, was startled by the sweeping character of the table-talk. Mr. Bertie Tremaine professed to understand philanthropy but found patriotism unmeaning. Mr. Tremaine Bertie, who was as sympathetic as his brother was autocratic, whispered apologetically to Endymion that it was a fact that "the idea of patriotism was entirely relinquished, except by a few old-fashioned folk who clung to superstitious phrases". Once in Parliament, Mr. Bertie Tremaine collected a youthful group which sat aloof on "the mountain" and reserved their fire, as far as speaking was concerned, while they circulated their views in a journal called *The Precursor*. The editor sometimes found it difficult to interpret his patron's theories, but Mr. Bertie Tremaine explained that he only had to show that "democracy is aristocracy in disguise, and aristocracy is democracy in disguise". Meanwhile. Mr. Bertie Tremaine had his own secret list of ministers for the party of the future, and when a new member made a good speech he invited him to dinner and hinted at a high post when he himself came into office. He cultivated a ceremonious manner befitting the dignities and honours he expected to attain, and after the abolition of his close borough he believed that he won a popular seat by "the manner in which I gave my hand, when I permitted it to be touched". Mr. Tremaine Bertie acted on a different principle and believed in being "hail fellow, well met!" in a democratic world, but his brother warned him that he would find this habit of familiarity awkward when he sent him to an embassy in St. Petersburg or Vienna. Eventually Mr. Bertie Tremaine accepted a minor office in a short-lived Protectionist government, but it carried the dignity of a privy councillorship. He then adopted Sir William Temple's plan for vesting the real authority of government in the Privy Council, and *The Precursor* was converted into *The Privy Council*.

The necessity of conciliating the Radicals is brought out in the episode of Mr. Jorrocks. Jorrocks had been given office by the Whigs when the party was strengthened by a reconstruction in 1835. He was duly invited by Mr. Sidney Wilton to a Christmas house-party at Gaydene. Lord Roehampton (Palmerston) was one of the guests, and so were various ambassadors, who always found the English Christmas trying, as they had no country homes of their own. Lord Roehampton often received one of them after a shooting-party; he found this a convenient way of keeping the interview within a time limit, and used to say, "the first dinner-bell often brings things to a point". Here Disraeli was probably writing from experience.

A difficulty arose about Jorrocks. The Prime Minister was due and the Blue Ribbon Covert had been kept for him, although he was not a keen sportsman. It was a family tradition that only Knights of the Garter should be asked to shoot this covert. Jorrocks was not only unqualified by the Garter, but he was a "pretentious, under-bred, half-educated man, fluent with all the common-places of middle-class ambition, which are humorously called democratic opinions, but at heart a sycophant of the aristocracy". He was, however, important, and his promotion was looked upon as a masterpiece of political management on the part of the Whigs. Mr. Sidney Wilton was reluctantly forced to outrage his family tradition and allow the Blue Ribbon Covert to be desecrated by Jorrocks' gun. No doubt such unpleasant specimens cropped up in the evolution of radicalism in an age in which aristocracy and privilege were still dominant.

After the drama of William Ferrars the plot of *Endymion* is subordinated to a discursive retrospect of the times and their chief personalities. That early drama ended in tragedy. Mrs. Ferrars pined and died; William Ferrars committed suicide. Endymion had to depend upon his own diligence in a junior clerkship at Somerset House. Myra determined to dedicate all her resolution and ability to restoring the family prestige and, in particular, to securing the advancement of her less ambitious and resolute twin brother. As a first step she took a post as companion to the only daughter of the great banker, Mr. Neuchatel (Baron Lionel Rothschild), in which she was treated with courtesy and consideration, and her beauty, intelligence and good manners soon won her a position almost equal to that of a second daughter of the house.

Endymion's introduction to the circle of his fellow clerks at Somerset House is described with realistic detail. Amongst his companions was St. Barbe, who combined journalism with his official work. This character represents Thackeray. St. Barbe was bitter, inordinately jealous, ambitious and a snob at heart, but brilliant and amusing. The portrait is unkind, but Thackeray at least inspired some of the best dialogue in the novel.

St. Barbe considered his clerkship a degradation. It was shocking to think of the incomes some men were making, who could no more write an article in *Scaramouch* (*Punch*) than fly, while he and his companions earned little more than a butler. He was both envious and contemptuous of a fellow-writer called Gushy, who obviously represents Dickens. When he and Endymion were dining at Canonbury Tavern he burst out:

"A fellow might get a good chapter out of this scene. I could do it, but I will not. What is the use of lavishing one's brains on an ungrateful world? Why, if that fellow Gushy were to write a description of this place, which he would do like a penny-a-liner drunk with ginger-beer, every Countess in Mayfair would be reading him, not knowing, the idiot, whether she ought to smile or shed tears, and sending him cards with 'At Home' upon them as large as life. Oh, it is disgusting! Absolutely disgusting. It is a nefarious world. You will find it out some day. I am as much robbed by that fellow Gushy as men are on the highway. He is appropriating my income and the income of thousands of honest fellows. And then he pretends he is writing for the people! The people! What does he know about the people? Annals of the New Cut and Saffron Hill. He thinks he will frighten some lord, who will ask him to dinner. And that he calls Progress. I hardly know which is the worst class in this country—the aristocracy, the middle class, or what they call the people. I hate them all."

This pæan of hate is too extreme, but there was some reason for it in the fact that Dickens, Thackeray's junior by one year, had an assured literary position and an easy self-confidence before Thackeray's genius was even recognised. There was also little in common between the two men; whereas Dickens was exuberant, sentimental and warmly human, Thackeray's fastidious and selective mind tended to satire, and even cynicism, and he was inclined to self-distrust. It is more surprising that Disraeli should represent Thackeray as a snob, when the snob was his favourite butt, especially in *Punch*. Anthony Trollope, however, in his life of Thackeray, suggests that snob-hunting became an obsession with him, and this may have been because he was conscious of a weakness in that respect in himself. Sergeant Ballantyne described him as "very egotistical, greedy of flattery and sensitive to criticism to a ridiculous extent". Thackeray died seventeen years before the publication of *Endymion*, so it can only have been for his own satisfaction that Disraeli took his revenge for *Coningsby*, with its burlesque of Sidonia. His portrait is generally considered exaggerated, but Thackeray himself did not spare his fellow-authors, and in particular decried Edward Bulwer, a friend of Disraeli's, mercilessly.

When Endymion procured an invitation for St. Barbe to a dinner at the house of the great banker, Mr. Neuchatel, his friend waxed almost lyrical about the food, the plate and the company:

"I declare when I was eating that truffle, I felt a glow about my heart that, if it were not indigestion, I think must have been gratitude; though that is an article I had not believed in. He is a wonderful man, that Neuchatel. If I had only known him a year ago! I would have dedicated my novel to him. He is the sort of man who would have given you a cheque immediately. He would not have read it, to be sure, but what of that? . . . There are some top-sawyers here to-day, Ferrars! . . . Now I daresay that ambassador has been blundering all his life, and yet there is something in that star and ribbon; I do not know how you feel, but I could almost go down on my knees to him . . . And there is a Cabinet Minister; well, we know what he is; I have been squibbing him for these two years, and now that I meet him I feel like a snob. Oh! There is an immense deal of superstition left in the world."

When St. Barbe found that Endymion had risen in the world and now lived in the Albany he took it almost as a personal affront:

"'You live in the Albany!' repeated St. Barbe, with an amazed and perturbed expression. 'I knew I could not be a Knight of the Garter or a member of White's—the only two things an Englishman cannot command; but I did think I might some day live in the Albany. It was my dream. And you live there! Gracious! What an unfortunate fellow I am!'"

He supposed that Endymion owed his luck to his sister marrying a lord, and continued bitterly: "I wish I had been a woman. Women are the only people who get on. A man works all his life, and thinks he has done a wonderful thing if, with one leg in the grave, and no hair on his head, he manages to get a coronet; and a woman dances at a ball with some young fellow or other, or sits next to some old fellow at dinner and pretends she thinks him charming, and he makes her a peeress on the spot. Oh! It is a disgusting world; it must end in revolution."

Success did little to mellow St. Barbe. When Endymion congratulated him on the fame of his last book he was not gracious:

"'Its success is not owing to your friends,' said St. Barbe tartly.

" 'My friends!' said Endymion; 'what could they have done to prevent it?'

" 'They need not have dissolved Parliament,' said Mr. St. Barbe with irritation. 'It was nearly fatal to me; it would have been to anybody else. I was selling forty thousand a month; I believe more than Gushy ever reached; and so they dissolved Parliament. The sale went down half at once—and now you expect me to support your party!' "

St. Barbe was now, however, able to pick and choose amongst his invitations. He refused the "small and earlies" with scorn: "How I hate a 'small and early'! Shown into a room where you meet a select few who have been asked to dinner, and who are chewing the cud like a herd of kine, and you are expected to tumble before them to assist their digestion! . . . No, sir; we only dine out now, and we think twice, I can tell you, before we accept even an invitation to dinner."

Endymion had another circle in the house in which he lodged. This was kept by Mr. Rodney and his pretty wife Sylvia, who had been respectively protégés of Mr. and Mrs. Ferrars in the days of their magnificence. Sylvia's sister Imogene lived with them, a beautiful young girl who combined a sweet nature with considerable intelligence. One floor of the house was occupied by Mr. Waldershare, an attractive young man who was a younger son of a noble family and had a moderate income of his own and a seat in Parliament. This portrait is closely drawn from George Smythe. Waldershare had been the leading light in his debating society at Cambridge and his friends believed that he must some day be Prime Minister, but he was as capricious as he was versatile. When under the influence of the Oxford Movement he was extremely high church—"he prayed and fasted, and swore by Laud and Strafford". A sojourn in Paris moderated this ardour, and in later life he considered that sensible men all had the same religion; when asked what that was he replied "sensible men never tell". Waldershare plunged into English society with zest, but social success soon palled upon him. He had no particular principles by which to govern his life:

"Waldershare was profligate, but sentimental; unprincipled, but romantic; the child of whim, and the slave of an imagination so freakish and deceptive that it was always impossible to foretell his course. He was alike capable of sacrificing all his feelings to worldly considerations or of forfeiting the world for a visionary caprice."

The original comments of this wayward and brilliant young man light up the succession of political episodes all through the book. He was a great admirer of the Stuarts for various reasons. "I must say," he remarked on one occasion, "it was a grand idea of our kings' making themselves sovereigns of the sea. The greater portion of this planet is water; so we at once become a first-rate power. We owe our navy entirely to the Stuarts."

One of Waldershare's whims was to educate Imogene, chiefly by conversation; he regarded her as a work of art in which he was determined to excel. In pursuit of this object he often joined the Rodney family party in the evenings. Endymion also formed the habit of spending his evenings with them, and young men of fashion whom Mr. Rodney met on the race-course dropped in. The young Earl of Beaumaris drove the whole party down to the Derby in his coach. One of Mr. Rodney's friends was a fashionable tailor, who often entertained his aristocratic clients at his fine Thames-side villa. Mr. Vigo recognised Endymion's quality—"There are two things which I think I understand," he said, "men and horses. I like to back them both when I think they ought to win." Accordingly he insisted upon dressing Endymion, only stipulating that he should be as careful not to stint himself in drawing upon him as to avoid needless extravagance; he wished his experiment to have a fair chance. It was important, he said, to dress suitably for his age, his pursuits and his object in life. In youth "a little fancy" was permissible, but if he aspired to a political career this should be dropped after the age of twenty-one. Disraeli himself might have benefited from this advice in his twenties. Mr. Vigo added the solemn warning: "What all men should avoid is the shabby genteel. No man ever gets over it. You had better be in rags." Endymion thus received the first impulsion towards a successful career; he was a young man who innocently attracted such attentions.

The principal floor of Mr. Rodney's house was occupied by a Colonel Albert, a foreigner, although he spoke English perfectly.

His dress, his manners and his fine horses marked him as a man of distinction, but for a long time he was a mystery to the other inmates of the house, with whom he did not mix. This character represents Prince Louis Napoleon, afterwards Napoleon III. Disraeli drew upon the incidents of Louis Napoleon's early life for his account of Prince Florestan (alias Colonel Albert), although he was not exact as to dates and sent Florestan to Eton, whereas Louis Napoleon was educated in Switzerland. To play his rôle in the novel Florestan had to be handsome, but according to the diarist Charles Greville, Prince Louis Napoleon was "a short, thickish, vulgar-looking man". Apart from these divergencies it is evident that Disraeli's own memories of Louis Napoleon provided detail for the portrait. He had met him when he was in exile in London and an intimate of Lady Blessington's circle, and also at one of Monckton Milnes' breakfast-parties. On another occasion Louis Napoleon undertook to row Disraeli and his wife up the Thames to breakfast with Edward Bulwer at Craven Cottage. He landed them on a mud-bank in the middle of the river and Mrs. Disraeli told him that he should not attempt things which he could not do, and added, "You are always, sir, too adventurous." Disraeli thought that the Prince took his scolding well. The following year (1840) he proved himself too adventurous on a larger scale by a rash attempt to "invade" France with inadequate support. He was captured and condemned to life-imprisonment in the fortress of Ham, but after five years he escaped and returned to London. It is recorded that he acted as a special constable at the time of the alarming Chartist rally on Kennington Common. He was a familiar figure in London society and his house in Carlton Gardens, his Arabian horses and excellent cook are reproduced in Prince Florestan's establishment after he left Mr. Rodney's. Describing Florestan at his own dinner-table, Disraeli wrote: "The Prince never spoke much, but his remarks always told. He liked murmuring to women, but when requisite, he could throw a fly over the table with adroitness and effect."

Prince Louis Napoleon returned to France after the upheavals of 1848—a revolutionary year in Europe—and became President of the Republic. Within four years he established himself as Emperor, with the title of Napoleon III. Disraeli was content to endow his Prince Florestan with a mere kingdom, and he gave him an English Queen.

Another character in the Book, Job Thornberry, deserves mention because he represents a conscientious attempt to draw a Radical without malice. Job was a farmer's son with progressive views who became a mill-owner and was a keen supporter of the Anti-Corn-Law League. He has features suggestive of Cobden and Bright, but he remains a somewhat artificial figure.

CHAPTER XVII

Endymion (II)

HAINAULT HOUSE, the mansion near London where Mr. Neuchatel entertained distinguished guests of banking and political circles, was a glorified picture of Gunnersbury, a Rothschild house where Disraeli often stayed. The conservatories rose like a city of glass and produced most of the fruits and flowers of the tropics, the chef was of European celebrity. The house was correspondingly splendid, but its mistress sighed for the simple life, professed to despise wealth and dislike display, and seldom wore the magnificent jewels which her husband presented to her every year as a matter of routine. The Neuchatel's only child, Adriana, was a sweet and gentle girl, obsessed by the idea that her father's vast riches would prevent anyone marrying her for love.

In this household Myra Ferrars was in her natural element, and her brother Endymion was soon admitted to the family circle. Amongst the regular guests was Colonel Albert. Myra fell under the spell of his charm, enhanced by the mystery which obviously surrounded him, but when the Neuchatels returned to town she found the panorama of high society too fascinating to allow her mind to dwell upon one individual, however romantic. At a brilliant dinner-party, where all the ladies except Mrs. Neuchatel wore "dazzling tiaras and flashing rivières", the queen of the evening was Lady Montfort, the famous Berengaria, who was "the Queen of society and the genius of Whiggism". Myra was deeply interested in this fascinating woman who was little, if at all, older than herself, and who had startled society by capturing the aloof, eccentric Lord Montfort, when he returned to England after living for years in Paris. Lord Montfort had soon reverted to his eccentric habits, and on the plea of ill-health he shut himself up at one or other of his mansions, only requiring of his wife relays of extraordinary people, such as explorers, scientists and engineers, to amuse him. The beautiful Berengaria had to play the brilliant game of social politics, in which she was an adept, alone, but there was never a breath of scandal against her.

Myra noticed a distinguished-looking man who wore the Garter ribbon paying court to Lady Montfort and realised that he was no less a person than Lord Roehampton, the most famous of England's Foreign Secretaries, at whose pronouncements kings and governments trembled all over Europe, and even in the East. Lord Roehampton was modelled on Palmerston and Philip Guedalla, the author of a life of Palmerston, allows this to be a good portrait. He is described as Myra first saw him:

"He was somewhat advanced in middle life, tall and of a stately presence, with a voice more musical even than the tones which had recently enchanted everyone"—Adriana had been singing—"His countenance was impressive, a truly Olympian brow, but the lower part of the face indicated not feebleness, but flexibility, and his mouth was somewhat sensuous. His manner was at once winning, natural, and singularly unaffected, and seemed to sympathise entirely with those whom he addressed."

This is a just rendering of Palmerston's charm in society. As a younger man he had been nicknamed Cupid, but although he behaved with delightful gallantry to various ladies worthy of his bow, he paid particular court to Lady Cowper for many years. This charming woman, a sister of Lord Melbourne, had a husband who suffered from ill-health and became something of a recluse, and she never neglected his welfare. Eventually, after Lord Cowper's death, she married Palmerston, when she was fifty-two and he fifty-five, and it was an ideally happy marriage. Lady Montfort answers in some respects to a description of Lady Cowper, but, as we shall see, Disraeli diverged widely from Palmerston's actual life in his novel.

Lady Montfort, bravely determined to be altruistic, decided that her dear friend Lord Roehampton must marry Adriana, whose fortune would be of service to him, and when he accepted an invitation to stay at Hainault she regarded the matter as practically settled. His charm and his surprisingly young manner would overcome the disparity in age, and the banker's daughter was not likely to refuse such an opportunity of becoming a *grande dame*. Meanwhile Mr. Neuchatel had planned that Lord Roehampton should meet Prince Florestan at Hainault. The great banker was a good friend to the Prince and gave him some useful advice, social as well as financial, such as: "Put on a good countenance. Nobody should ever look anxious, except those who have no anxiety." Mr. Neuchatel knew that a word from Lord Roehampton in the right quarter would probably secure the Prince a fortune which was unjustly withheld from him. Prince Florestan's identity was now known to Myra and Mr. Neuchatel believed that she would be the best person to enlist Lord Roehampton's interest on his behalf; the great statesman evidently liked her, and he was never severe with ladies, even when he refused their requests. The banker felt that his position as host made it awkward for him to bring up the subject, and he explained, somewhat ruefully, to Myra:

"I like Lord Roehampton and, between ourselves, I wish he were first minister. He understands the Continent, and would keep things quiet. But, do you know, Miss Ferrars, with all his playful, good-tempered manner, as if he could not say a cross word or do an unkind act, he is a very severe man in business. Speak to him on business, and he is completely changed. His brows knit, he penetrates you with the scrutiny of that deep-set eye; he is more than stately, he is austere. I have been up to him with deputations—the Governor of the Bank, and all the first men in the City, half of them M.P.s, and they trembled before him like aspens."

Myra soon had an opportunity to see the difference between the statesman and the man. Lord Roehampton received the Prince with stately courtesy, but during dinner she was struck by his "lofty grace and somewhat haughty mien", a great contrast to the "frolic and fancy, and even tender sentiment", which he had shown with her and Adriana in the morning.

Disraeli is surprisingly kind to Palmerston in his portrait, since he was a pillar of strength to the party which kept his own out of office for so long. Many of Palmerston's contemporaries, both Liberal and Conservative, resented his autocratic way of taking decisions on his own authority, and thought that he sometimes blundered. Greville believed that he owed much to good luck—"He is a man blessed with extraordinary good fortune and his motto seems to be that of Danton, *'De l'audace, encore de l'audace, et toujours de l'audace.*' " Disraeli brings out the advantage which his long and intimate knowledge of leading foreign statesmen gave him; he had learned to gauge the men who governed the world at the Congress of Vienna. Hence his superiority to the type of statesman who never left his chair in Downing Street except to kill grouse. Disraeli puts into the mouth of the Count of Ferroll (a portrait of Bismarck) a piece of advice to the young Endymion which stresses the same point: "You will find it of the first importance in public life to know personally those who are carrying on the business of the world; so much depends on the character of an individual, his habits of thought, his prejudices, his social weaknesses, his health. Conducting affairs without this advantage is, in effect, an affair of stationery; it is pens and paper that are in communication, not human beings."

This is an interesting commentary on the conduct of foreign affairs in the nineteenth century; today the rapid changes in the political scene, the iron curtain, and the greater range of personalities in the governments of modern democracies, make such intimate experience as Palmerston's less possible.

Lady Montfort's scheme for her friend's marriage with Adriana came to nothing, to the young lady's great relief. It was Myra Ferrars who won Lord Roehampton's heart. She did not hesitate to accept him. She was frank with her brother Endymion: what she had longed for was now within her grasp, their degradation was over—"I see a career, ay, and a great one; and what is far more important, I see a career for you." Endymion, who was of a softer nature, urged her to think only of herself at such a moment. She replied that Lord Roehampton had "every quality and every accident of life that I delight in"; she even included his sweet disposition and tender heart. As for the great difference in age, he claimed to be, and really seemed, the younger in spirit of the two. In fact these qualities in her husband soon inspired genuine devotion in the young wife and it was a happy marriage for both. There are some charming little scenes in the Roehampton ménage. Disraeli confers most of Palmerston's habits upon Lord Roehampton, and in particular his absorption in his work:

"He wrote his own dispatches, whenever they referred to matters of moment. He left to the permanent staff of his office little but the fulfilment of duties which, though heavy and multifarious, were duties of routine. The composition of these dispatches was a source to Lord Roehampton of much gratification and excitement. They were of European fame, and their terse argument, their clear determination, and often their happy irony, were acknowledged in all the cabinets, and duly apprehended."

An endless succession of red boxes containing papers poured from the Foreign Office into the house, and often Lord Roehampton was closeted with them far into the night. It was so that death came to him before the end of Disraeli's story; his wife found him leaning back in his chair at a desk upon which the candles had almost guttered out.

After Myra's marriage Endymion had two powerful feminine influences working upon him. The second was Lady Montfort, who adopted him as her particular protégé; she needed an object for her talent and ambition. In discussing with Endymion the possibility of his widowed sister marrying Mr. Sidney Wilton she exclaimed, "For my part, I think to have a husband who loved you, and he clever, accomplished, charming, ambitious, would be happiness." Lord Montfort neither could nor would satisfy such aspirations. In him Disraeli gives us one more picture of a nobleman of the old régime, for which Lord Hertford again provided features:

"Lord Montfort was the only living Englishman who gave one an idea of the nobleman of the eighteenth century. He was totally devoid of the sense of responsibility, and he looked what he resembled. His manner, though simple and natural, was finished and refined, and, free from forbidding reserve, was yet characterised by an air of serious grace. . . . There was no subject, divine or human, in which he took the slightest interest. He entertained for human nature generally, and without any exception, the most cynical appreciation. . . . No one could say Lord Montfort was a bad-hearted man, for he had no heart. He was good-natured, provided it brought him no inconvenience; and as for temper, his was never disturbed, but this not from sweetness of disposition, rather from a contemptuous fine taste, which assured him that a gentleman should never be deprived of tranquillity in a world where nothing was of the slightest consequence."

Lord Montfort found constant conjugal affection wearying; he preferred—and exacted—vivacious letters from his wife to her company. She strove valiantly to minister to his strange tastes, and also to keep up appearances. As long as she was under his roof—or one of his roofs—the world could not say that they had separated, however little they saw of one another. She diligently kept up the supply of guests who might amuse him, and consequently his dinner-table, in London or the country, was never dull. On one occasion a notable civil engineer was the guest of the evening, and the conversation was chiefly of suspension bridges. A gentleman from the British Museum "made some remarks on the mode in which the ancient Egyptians moved masses of granite, and quoted Herodotus to the civil engineer. The civil engineer had never heard of Herodotus, but he said he was going to Egypt in the autumn by the desire of Mehemet Ali, and he would undertake to move any mass that was requisite, even if it were a pyramid itself."

Endymion's first promotion was to become private secretary to Mr. Sidney Wilton, then a Cabinet Minister, and Disraeli gives a pleasing account of the relationship between the young man and the great statesman, which was probably founded on Montagu Corry's to himself. Sidney Wilton was confident that Endymion had it in him to rise to a distinguished position: he had perseverance and tact, the two qualities most valuable for those who would mount—Disraeli might well have interpolated "And who would not?"—and, especially for those who have to step out of the crowd. "Without tact you can learn nothing," said Mr. Wilton; "tact teaches you when to be silent. Inquirers who are always inquiring never learn anything.

The character of Sidney Wilton has points in common with Sidney Herbert, and Wilton was the chief seat of Sidney Herbert's family. The likeness, however, does not go much further than a similar background of ancient lineage and wealth, a similar charm and undisputed probity and integrity. Sidney Wilton was a bachelor, in love with Lady Roehampton; Sidney Herbert was happily married. There is no counterpart in Sidney Wilton's life of Sidney Herbert's devoted team-work with Florence Nightingale, which is said to have been partly responsible for his premature death.

By the end of 1840 various currents were gathering force in politics and Tadpole said that the government was dancing on a volcano. The ferment of these years, when national distress inexorably drove the unwilling Peel towards the repeal of the corn-laws, lives for us again in these chapters. When a dissolution of Parliament seemed likely in 1841 both Myra and Lady Montfort felt that it was time for Endymion to enter the House of Commons. They were sure that their united interest could procure him a seat, which should not cost him a shilling. Lady Montfort said it would be no bad thing for him to form himself in opposition, and then, later on, she would entertain in his interest and never rest until he was Prime Minister. But Endymion refused to stake his future on the uncertainties of a political career, in which his livelihood must depend upon holding office. He told Lady Montfort gently: "I think if one is patient and watches, all will come of which one is capable"—surely a comment on Disraeli's own life—"but no one can be patient who is not independent. My wants are moderate, but their fulfilment must be certain."

Myra was in despair: after all her efforts to provide her brother with great opportunities she found that she had failed in the one essential; her own happiness and prosperity were but cold comfort. Lady Montfort, who was prepared to sell her diamonds to further her object, was hurt and shocked to find that Endymion was not clay in her hands, as she had supposed. Endymion himself was very much depressed by the cruel necessity of wounding Myra and offending, even estranging, Lady Montfort. In this mood he listlessly took up a business letter: it informed him that £20,000 in consols had been purchased in his name by an anonymous donor. It was a long time before he discovered that the gift came from Adriana Neuchatel.

The next problem was to find a seat. It proved unexpectedly difficult. A borough which Lord Montfort's interest could usually command was to be contested by a nominee of Lord Beaumaris, who had as great a local influence. Lady Montfort called at the party headquarters, confident that a safe seat would be forthcoming at her request. She reported the result indignantly to Myra: "When I go to them and ask for a seat, I expect a seat, as I would a shawl at Howell & James's if I asked for one. Instead of that they only make difficulties." Endymion, however, had yet another feminine influence in his favour: the lovely Imogene had justified the pains which Waldershare had taken to educate her by marrying Lord Beaumaris. An amicable arrangement was soon made by which the Beaumaris candidate was withdrawn from the borough, which was otherwise safe for anyone supported by the Montfort interest. It is not surprising that when Lady Montfort told Endymion, "Everything in this world depends upon will", he replied, "I think everything in this world depends upon woman."

It was with a sense of awe that Endymion took his place in the House of Commons, that great assembly with its traditions of genius, eloquence and power which had for so long fascinated and inspired him. The state of the country was still a source of great alarm and distress, and the defenders of the corn-laws were fighting a losing battle. Mr. Neuchatel observed that no mere measures were likely to be effective; what was wanted was a new channel. He was justified when the railroad boom swept the country like a blind force of nature and made the calculations of statesmen, the activities of the Anti-Corn-Law League and the People's Charter fade into insignificance. The value of land rose, trade was stimulated, blast furnaces were re-lit, fortunes were made. Endymion's friend Mr. Vigo, the tailor, became a Railroad King. Mr. Bertie Tremaine, much impressed by his spectacular activities, placed him on his list of men of the Future and remarked: "When this excitement is over, I hope to induce him to take India."

In Parliament Endymion benefited by his connection with Lord Roehampton and, in fact, became his secretary and understudy. The party was in opposition, but Endymion's position was important, as the spokesman of Lord Roehampton in the House of Commons. It was an agitating moment when Lord Roehampton suggested that the young man should ask his first question in the House. Disraeli's description of his feelings is graphic: "When he got on his legs his head swam, his heart beat so violently that it was like a convulsion preceding death, and though he was only on his legs for a few seconds, all the sorrows of his life seemed to pass before him. When he sat down he was quite surprised that the business of the House proceeded as usual, and it was only after some time that he became convinced that no one but himself was conscious of his sufferings, or that he had performed a routine duty otherwise than in a routine manner." This account, written with such poignancy in old age, carries the mind back to the disastrous scene of Disraeli's maiden speech and emphasises what he must have suffered then.

Endymion's question was followed up by a reasoned speech a week later, when Lord Roehampton and Lady Montfort were in the gallery. Again he almost wished he were dead and was only sustained by dogged despair, but once on his feet his powers returned to him and the speech was very well received. The Prime Minister himself rose to answer him, thereby depriving Waldershare, who was now Under Secretary for Foreign Affairs (as George Smythe was), of an opportunity which he considered his own prerogative. Disraeli's comment is: "The Minister was wrong. He was not fond of trusting youth." However true of Peel, it was not an accusation that could be made against Disraeli himself.

Myra next turned her attention to Endymion's marriage: if only he would propose to Adriana, who already loved him, he could command a secure and brilliant future. She urged upon him that she had married to further the great object of raising the family from poverty and shame, but she was not a Ferrars, only he could add lustre to the name. She wanted him to be something infinitely greater than Lady Roehampton's brother or Lord Roehampton's brother-in-law, and he had only to marry an angelic being to have every glorious possibility within his grasp. Endymion did not respond. On one occasion he remarked that at twenty-five there was no need to commit himself as yet. Myra answered scornfully, "Great men should think of Opportunity, and not of Time. Time is the excuse of feeble and puzzled spirits. They make time the sleeping partner of their lives to accomplish what ought to be achieved by their own will." But Endymion's heart was already given—to Lady Montfort.

The long progress of Disraeli's story at last brought Endymion both his heart's desire and a success which satisfied even Myra; no less was to be expected for a Disraelian hero. Lord Montfort died and in due time the beautiful and dynamic Berengaria bestowed her hand upon Endymion, thus providing both the social position and the stimulus that he needed. True to her boast, she did not rest until he was Prime Minister. Myra eventually married King Florestan and found a fitting apotheosis as a Queen. At the time of that marriage Mr. Sidney Wilton, then Prime Minister, was nursing his gout in morose seclusion: but then, as Lady Montfort said, "all prime ministers have the gout". Disraeli himself was no exception. Adriana was consoled by the wayward Waldershare, who made a better husband than might have been expected—"Waldershare had really a good heart, though a bad temper, and he was a gentleman." He also had a healthy respect for his father-in-law, now Lord Hainault.

Endymion has some of Disraeli's own qualities. In describing his oratory the author might be writing of his own: his voice had power and melody; he was ready without being too fluent; there were light and shade in his delivery; he repressed his power of sarcasm, although when unjustly attacked he could be keen. This is not enough to justify the suggestion that in this hero Disraeli re-created his own youth; the young gusto of Vivian Grey's ambition seems to have more in common with their author's than Endymion's sweet reasonableness. Endymion's was a malleable character, young Disraeli's was the reverse, like Vivian Grey and Contarini Fleming he aspired to mould men and affairs himself.

Two more characters must not be passed over. The Count of Ferroll has the characteristics of Bismarck, whom he resembled in appearance:

"The Count of Ferroll was a young man, and yet inclined to be bald ... Though not to be described as a handsome man, his countenance was striking; a brow of much intellectual development and a massive jaw. He was tall, broad-shouldered, with a slender waist." Prince Florestan recognised him as a man of the future and told Endymion: "He is a man neither to love nor to detest. He has himself an intelligence superior to all passion; I might say all feeling; and, if in dealing with such a being, we ourselves have either, we give him an advantage." He was, moreover, a man who seldom made a mistake. His identity with Bismarck is confirmed by his remark to Lady Montfort that Germany could only be welded into a nation by blood and iron. She exclaimed, "My dear Count, you shock me!" He replied, "I shall have to shock you a great deal more, before the inevitable is brought about."

The Count of Ferroll had all the qualities to make him a favourite in English society: he was of noble birth, distinguished in appearance, munificent and frank, a dead shot and the boldest of riders. He took part in the jousting at the magnificent tournament which Berengaria staged at Montfort Castle, where Prince Florestan was his chief antagonist. The Count, as the Black Knight, was an imposing figure, Prince Florestan a resplendent one, in blue damascened armour inlaid with silver roses. The Prince remarked that he and the Count of Ferroll would have to contend for many things more precious than the golden helm of the victor of a tournament before they died. Prince Louis Napoleon did actually take part in the famous Eglinton Tournament of 1839, which was obviously Disraeli's model. Bismarck visited England in 1842, but never held a diplomatic post in London, as the Count of Ferroll did.

In a letter to Lady Bradford, the year before the publication of *Endymion*, Disraeli reported that the French ambassador at Berlin had found Bismarck amusing himself during a period of ill-health by "reading over again all Lord Beaconsfield's novels." Only the year before the two great statesmen had sat in the Congress of Berlin, in which Bismarck met his match for the first time, and which inspired his famous dictum—"The old Jew, that is the man." Disraeli commented to the Queen on the change in the German Chancellor's appearance since he had last seen him, sixteen years before: "A tall, pallid man with a wasp-like waist, was now represented by an extremely stout person with a ruddy countenance, on which he is now growing a silvery beard. In his manner there was no change, except perhaps he was not quite so energetic, but frank and unaffected as before."

Another foreign statesman, Baron Sergius, is a well-drawn character in the novel, and has been credited with some resemblance to Metternich.

The Roman Catholic interest is not lacking in *Endymion*. Nigel Penruddock, the son of the vicar of Hurstley, the scene of the

Ferrars family's ignominious retirement, is another, and juster, portrait of Cardinal Manning. This young priest's enthusiasm for high church principles was a driving force which carried him far. Discussing politics with Endymion he said contemptuously: "I know nothing about Whigs or Tories or Liberals ... Nor do I know, or care to know, what Low Church means. There is but one Church, and that is catholic and apostolic, and if we act on its principles, there will be no need, and there ought to be no need, for any other form of government." When Endymion made some objections to the Athanasian creed Nigel answered impatiently: "The Athanasian creed is the most splendid ecclesiastical lyric ever poured forth by the genius of man. I give to every clause of it implicit assent. It does not pretend to be divine; it is human, but the Church has hallowed it, and the Church ever acts under the influence of the Divine Spirit. St. Athanasius was by far the greatest man that ever existed."

Nigel Penruddock's single-minded fanaticism carried him first into a London pulpit and then into the Roman Catholic Church. He returned to England as Papal Legate, bearing the title of Archbishop. Disraeli makes this the occasion for a lively account of an actual episode in 1850 known as "the Papal Aggression". The Pope issued a Bull setting up a Roman Catholic hierarchy in England, to the great indignation of Lord John Russell, then Prime Minister, who objected to the division of the country under Roman Catholic bishops and archbishops, bearing territorial titles. Russell's famous open letter to the Bishop of Durham, denouncing both the Pope's aggression and the practices of the Puseyite high churchmen, caused a furore in the country. According to Disraeli in *Endymion*, corporations and universities sought audiences with the Queen upon the subject, county and municipal authorities were stirred up and nearly seven thousand public meetings were held to protest against the Pope's infringement of the Queen's sovereignty. This is borne out by passages in Greville's *Diary*, such as: "The whole country is up: meetings everywhere, addresses to Bishops and their replies, addresses to the Queen; speeches, letters, articles, all pouring forth from the press day after day with a vehemence and universality such as I never saw before." Disraeli wrote to Lord Londonderry in a lighter vein, "The people are very much alarmed in this country. Even the peasants think they are going to be burned alive and taken up to Smithfield instead of their pigs."

The agitation came to a tame end. The Pope's action could not be considered illegal, a similar hierarchy had been permitted in Ireland; some members of Lord John Russell's own party felt that he was throwing over the hallowed Whig principles of civil and religious liberty. Lord John had to content himself with a Bill which forbade Roman Catholics to take territorial titles in the United Kingdom. The incident is chiefly interesting to students of Disraeli's novels because it influenced his attitude to Roman Catholicism, and was probably partly responsible for his attack upon the Jesuits in *Lothair*. Cardinal Wiseman represented the Pope very ably during the crisis, and in the novel Nigel Penruddock played his part, although in other respects he was more like Cardinal Manning. Disraeli's description of the refined beauty of his face, his calm and radiant expression, and the height that made his emaciation all the more noticeable, fits Cardinal Manning.

Thus Disraeli in this last discursive novel introduced many of the dominant figures of his lifetime, but he allowed himself considerable licence in adapting their lives to the purposes of his story. The running commentary on political life by one who had himself been a leading actor on the political stage for forty-three years remains the chief distinction of the book, but other interests are represented. In particular, *Endymion* contains two loving descriptions of trees, which show that Disraeli was no less susceptible to the beauty of the English countryside than to the exotic and colourful landscapes of the East. They are worth quoting in full:

"It was a still mild day in November, a month which in the country, especially on light soils, has many charms, and the whole Ferrars family were returning home after an afternoon ramble on the chase. The leaf had changed but not fallen, and the vast spiral masses of the dark green juniper effectively contrasted with the rich brown foliage of the beech, varied occasionally by the scarlet leaves of the wild cherry tree, that always mingles with these woods. Around the house were some lime trees of large size, and at this period of the year their foliage, still perfect, was quite literally golden. They seemed like trees in some fairy-tale of imprisoned princesses or wandering cavaliers, and such they would remain, until the fatal night that brings the first frost."

And:

"The woods were beginning to assume the first fair livery of autumn, when it is beautiful without decay. The lime and the larch had not yet dropped a golden leaf, and the burnished beeches flamed in the sun. Every now and then an occasional oak or elm rose, still as full of deep green foliage as if it were Midsummer; while the dark verdure of the pines sprang up with effective contrast amid the gleaming and resplendent chestnuts."

CHAPTER XVIII

Falconet

DISRAELI wrote to Lady Bradford when he was nearly seventy that his imagination had not deserted him with his youth. It was in full vigour until the end. When *Endymion* was finished he started upon yet another novel, which is usually called *Falconet*, after its hero. He only laid down his pen after the opening paragraph of the tenth chapter because he was too ill to go on. The fragment is tantalising because it is obvious that the hero, Joseph Toplady Falconet, was to be modelled upon Gladstone, who, almost alone of Disraeli's great contemporaries, had not appeared in any of his novels. Perhaps, after all, it is as well that it was not published in his lifetime! The chapters were printed in *The Times* in 1905, and are to be found at the end of Vol. V of Monypenny & Buckle's biography.

Falconet was, as far as Disraeli was concerned, a modern novel, although he took his usual licence with characters adapted from life by representing Gladstone as a young man. In the opening chapter we are introduced to a peculiar coterie at Clapham. Here rich merchants and bankers and commercial magnates of old standing lived in substantial red brick houses with old-fashioned gardens, glorified by extensive glass-houses. This society was marked by its traditions of philanthropy and piety. The hero's father, Mr. Wilberforce Falconet, was a godson of William Wilberforce, of whom his wife's father had also been a close friend. The Wilberforce Falconets had a large family. The elder sons entered their father's counting-house; one, who professed a reprehensible leaning to the Army, was hustled into the Church. The daughters were all pretty and pious, and the eligible young men of their circle soon succumbed to "the blended spell of religious devotion, female charms, and the most comfortable and piously luxurious domestic establishment in the whole neighbourhood".

The youngest son, Joseph, was precociously clever. He was a grave boy, deficient in a sense of humour, but of a disputatious nature, with a wonderful flow of language at his command. At the University he distinguished himself in undergraduate debates and won the proud distinction of senior wrangler. His ambition, however, was centred in religious leadership, the only sphere of action worthy of man's highest energies. He knew his own mind:

"Firm in his faith in an age of dissolving creeds, he wished to believe that he was the man ordained to vindicate the sublime cause of religious truth. With these ardent hopes, he had renounced the suggestion which he had once favoured of taking Orders. It was as the lay champion of the Church that he desired to act, and believed that in such a position his influence would be infinitely greater than in that of a clergyman, whatever his repute."

A seat in the House of Commons seemed to be indicated, and in taking up a parliamentary career he would be following in the footsteps of the great Wilberforce. Although the period of close boroughs was now ancient history, certain noble lords still wielded great influence, fostered by kindly patronage of local charities and religious and horticultural functions, which secured election for candidates who had their support. One of these, Lord Bertram, was under obligations to Mr. Wilberforce Falconet's firm. His own son, who had held the borough in question, had recently changed his politics, and, after the manner of opinionated young men, had made this known in an unnecessarily offensive address and then resigned the seat. Lord Bertram placed it at the disposal of Mr. Falconet. Joseph was invited to attend a meeting in the borough and made a most impressive speech on the revival of the slave trade in the Red Sea. It was afterwards discovered that there was no foundation for the rumours of such a revival, but the speech had served its turn.

There is a delightful scene in which Lord Bertram—himself an eminent statesman—dined with the Falconets. Mrs. Falconet liked her parties to end in psalmody, but in this case her husband curbed her and they compromised for an unusually long grace before and after the dinner. The noble lord praised everything; he thought Clapham Common worthy of *As You Like It*. The only rift was when Joseph said that he thought of bringing forward the affair of the slave trade in the Red Sea in Parliament. The Earl replied: "I think I would leave the Red Sea alone. It was a miracle that saved us from being drowned in it before." Mrs. Falconet looked grave and her husband quickly changed the subject.

The society of Lord Bertram's town house, to which Joseph was now admitted, is described with vivacity. Lady Bertram, whose receptions were distinguished, is supposed to suggest Lady Palmerston, but without very much foundation. Lord Bertram's son by a former marriage—Lord Gaston—is the last of Disraeli's gallery of disillusioned and intransigent young men. When Lady Bertram regretted his giving up Parliament he expounded his views:

" 'I am not. Parliaments are worn out.'

" 'But you say that of everything,' said Lady Bertram.

" 'And it is true of everything; but of the whole affair nothing is so exhausted as the human race itself.'

" 'But what, then, is to happen?' inquired Lady Bertram.

" 'Many things may happen. I do not suppose that because man is worn out even this little planet which we call ours has not yet some future. The mistake which our self-conceit has always made has been to suppose that this planet was made for man. There never was any foundation for such a belief, and now we know it is mere folly. The fact is that man has really never very much taken to this globe. And no wonder. It clearly never was intended for him. It consists of more water than land, and of that land a great portion is uninhabitable desert.' "

Lady Bertram's daughter by a former husband, Lady Ermyntrude, said that the handsome and fascinating Lord Gaston's professed wretchedness was on such a scale that it amounted to the sublime.

This brings us to the second motive in these chapters. No less than four characters seem to be devotees of a theory that the sooner the extinction of man takes place the better; they only differed as to the time and the means necessary to achieve this desirable end. One, obviously a great personage, remains a mystery. He invaded a great society reception, suitably decked with a star in brilliants, and flattered Lady Bertram by confiding strange doctrines—but not unlike Lord Gaston's—to her sympathetic ear. She thrilled to the communication that "society is resolving itself into its original elements", but she could not discover who the mysterious stranger was, even the hostess did not know. The other two exponents of this philosophy of annihilation were a wealthy scholar who had left Germany for Clapham and a Buddhist missionary from Ceylon, who softened the rigour of the new creed by saying, "Death is only happiness, if understood."

It is difficult to see how Disraeli could have developed this theme satisfactorily; he was setting himself a problem even more intractable than the one he left unsolved in *Tancred*. He may have been influenced by the Nihilist conspiracy in Russia, which led to the assassination of the Czar Alexander while he was writing this fragment.

Falconet is worth reading for its touches of social comedy and a few Disraelian aphorisms. It is trying to have Joseph Falconet's story cut short so early in his parliamentary career. Needless to say, he had created an impression by his oratory, although the House was still waiting for him to deliver himself upon some subject of practical interest. Meanwhile he gathered a following of substantial men who, while confident as to their own judgment on financial and commercial matters, were "incapable of grappling with the great questions that touch the convictions and consciences of nations." In this sphere they felt that they had found in Joseph Falconet "a commanding expounder of opinions" whom they could support. In fact, we are told, Joseph Falconet was essentially a prig, and as there is an unfailing freemasonry amongst prigs, all the other prigs in the House spoke of him as the coming man. Philip Guedalla comments that it was "not by coincidence that Joseph Toplady Falconet was decorated by a sardonic author with two names, one of which had been borne by the writer of *Rock of Ages*, and the other by Joseph Surface. It was his final repartee."

EPILOGUE

If Disraeli's novels were represented by a contour map two undulating mountain ranges would run across it with few breaks. One would represent a quality, ambition, and the other a presence, the House of Commons. A string of peaks might stand for England's great country houses, black patches for the Industrial scenes of *Sybil*, a volcanic cone for the Reform Bill of 1832, a depression for the Poor Law of 1834, red flags for the massed Chartist rallies. Over all these should be the patina of England's wealth, prestige and splendour, covering the depths of degradation to which her people sank in the 1840's, which Greville described as "the rotten foundation on which the whole fabric of this gorgeous society rests". A large purple patch should be added to represent the oriental scenes. All these features are to be found in the eleven novels, and from the English ones emerged the principles of Tory democracy as Disraeli shaped them: reconciliation of "the two nations" (Rich and Poor) in a commonwealth upon which the living wealth of the country, its people, should be the first charge, and the fusion of the scattered British colonies into an empire conscious of union under one Queen.

The drama of the novels is both personal and political. In the early books, with their element of autobiography, the personal predominates. In these ambition is a keynote. After Disraeli had achieved power he told Lady Derby that in his youth he had been devoured by an irresistible ambition, and had had no means of satisfying it. He was never ashamed of ambition, to him it was a healthy mainspring of life. Only once did he disparage it, when he was still smarting from his failure in the project of *The Representative*. The passage is in *The Young Duke*: "I am one, though young, yet old enough to know Ambition is a demon; and I fly from what I fear. . . . When all is gained how little then is won! And yet to gain that little how much is lost!"

Nevertheless, to Vivian Grey, Contarini Fleming and Harry Coningsby, life without ambition would have been savourless. Even as a schoolboy Contarini only found it tolerable because of the ambition and desire of distinction which, we are told, raged in his soul. Alroy thirsted to be a hero and to restore the glory of his race. In Coningsby's case "absolute, not relative, distinction was his noble aim". Even the mild Endymion admitted, but with a blush, that he would like to have power. Lady Montfort asserted that everybody wanted power, even if they did not know what to do with it. Probably this was Disraeli's own opinion; with the imagination and capacity to wield power himself, he discounted those negligible beings who were afraid of it, and could find happiness, and even fulfilment, in the faithful discharge of routine duties. In every case the ambition of Disraeli's heroes was founded on the inner conviction of capacity; the supreme tragedy of life was to be conscious of powers which were not matched with opportunity. It was this which nerved him in his own battle with circumstances, and his is a more brilliant success-story than that of any of his heroes. Not one of them was a Jew. He was not exaggerating when, in later life, he wrote to Queen Victoria that he had been "vilified and decried for upwards of forty years", and had thereby learned "patience, self-control and some circumspection". In the end he achieved a success beyond even the dazzling dreams of his youth. He was Prime Minister, he swayed European powers and was a guest of honour at magnificent banquets in the Congress of Berlin; he became Earl of Beaconsfield and a Knight of the Garter. Even an imperial crown was his to bestow, when he advised the Queen to take the title of Empress of India. His sovereign visited his grave and had the vault opened so that she might look at his coffin. As Buckle summed up in the great biography he completed after Monypenny's death: "The 'Jew boy', the despised adventurer, the oriental mystery-man, had reached the summit of place and power."

The young man who had been avid for political and social success, the novelist who had revelled in picturing splendid mansions, had had his fill of all that Parliament and society could offer him, and at seventy-five he wrote to Lady Bradford: "For myself I could live in a garret provided it was well white-washed, and very clean." He had, in fact, experienced in his own life the poignancy of which he wrote so feelingly in *Henrietta Temple*

EPILOGUE

when he was thirty-three. He argued then that no prosperity of manhood, no splendour of old age, could compensate for a crippled youth—"In youth, of all seasons, we require power, because we can enjoy everything that we can command." In the splendour of his own old age, when he could command even more than he had ever dreamed of, he thought that he could be as happy in a garret. This was highly improbable, but it emphasises the fact that place and power came to him too late. His devoted Mary Anne felt the pity of it keenly. When he first achieved high office she wrote: "You don't know my Dizzy, what great plans he has long matured for the good and greatness of England. But they have made him wait and drudge so long—and now time is against him." He himself, on becoming Prime Minister for the first time, said that it was twenty years too late. Again, in the year of his great triumph at the Congress of Berlin, he said: "Power! It has come to me too late. There were days when, on waking, I felt that I could move dynasties and governments; but that has passed away." He had also lost his zest for living magnificently.

The boundless visions, the exultation, and the frustration of Disraeli's youth can be recaptured in *Vivian Grey* and *Contarini Fleming*. The heroes of these novels represent his own ambition, naked and unashamed, but in Disraeli himself ambition was never mean, or purely self-seeking, as it was in Vivian Grey. The great ends that he felt he could serve acted upon him as a driving-force and stiffened him to withstand prejudice and obstruction. It is significant that Gladstone, called upon to pay a last tribute to his chief antagonist in the House of Commons, singled out for praise his great Parliamentary courage. Lord Salisbury emphasised the same quality in his tribute in the House of Lords, but he called it "splendid perseverance", a perseverance which overcame all obstacles and proved that there was "for every Englishman, however humble, an open career leading to the highest positions under the Crown". *For every Englishman*: but Disraeli, although English (and baptised) was a Jew. He did not try to discount his race or live it down, but, as a study of the novels makes clear to us, he used it as a weapon of attack. He would not rise in spite of his Jewish birth, rather he claimed that Jewish birth was a source of strength and pride, and that all Englishmen were in spiritual and intellectual debt to Judaism. Sidonia and Tancred were proud gestures; he did not demean himself or his race by making concessions to the anti-semitic prejudices of the English country-gentlemen he aspired to lead. A mere careerist would not have published such a novel as *Tancred* just when that coveted leadership was almost within his grasp.

Lord Salisbury, to his honour, stressed another aspect of the great statesman's complex character when he said: "Zeal for the greatness of England was the passion of his life." The novels give us an incomparable picture of England when our country was indeed the arbiter of the civilised world, and to this greatness the author made his own contribution, not least in raising the condition of the working people.

There was never any doubt in his own mind, or in the minds of most of his heroes, as to the supreme object of ambition. No one questioned that the House of Commons, then the most august and influential assembly in Europe, was the grand theatre for those who aspired to power and fame. Vivian Grey "panted for the Senate"; when Endymion Ferrars entered Parliament he felt that "the greatest opportunity that can be offered to an Englishman was now his—a seat in the House of Commons".

This brings us to the second mountain range in a contour map of the novels. A fascinating picture of the evolution of the House of Commons in the middle decades of the nineteenth century can be culled from these books. In *Endymion* there is a digression in which Sir Fraunceys Scrope, the father of the House, who had in his youth ridden up to Westminster from his seat in Derbyshire to support his dear friend Charles Fox, tells Endymion how different the House had been fifty years ago:

"Up to Easter we rarely had a regular debate, never a party division; very few people came up indeed. . . . After Easter there was always at least one great party fight. This was a mighty affair, talked of for weeks before it came off, and then rarely an adjourned debate. We were gentlemen, used to sit up late, and should have been sitting up somewhere else if we had not been in the House of Commons. After this party fight, the House for the rest of the session was a mere club. . . . There was not much

EPILOGUE

business in the country then. The House of Commons was very much like what the House of Lords is now. You went home to dine, and now and then came back for an important division."

Sir Fraunceys supposed that Latin quotations would be the next thing to disappear. In a House of Commons of which almost all the members were public school men who had spent at least five years of their lives in an intensive study of the classics, it was *de rigueur* to quote Latin to illustrate or drive home arguments. Sir Fraunceys, however, said that Fox drew the line at Greek, and held that no English poet should be quoted unless he had completed his century.

The pace of Parliamentary life quickened steadily with the advance of the nineteenth century, but a member looking back nostalgically to the days before the Reform Bill could say: "Ah! Those were the good old gentlemanlike times when members of Parliament had nobody to please, and Ministers of State nothing to do" (*Sybil*). They were the days, too, when most of the members belonged to one of two or three famous London clubs, when, in fact, a man could step into Parliament as if he were stepping into a club (*Endymion*). It was small wonder that the aristocracy felt themselves to be victims of revolution when their close boroughs were taken from them and no one could enter Parliament without submitting to the hideous vulgarity of a contest.

The apprehension of old members when the new men, mostly representatives of the middle class, took their seats after the Reform Bill is well brought out in *Endymion*. The House of Commons had been regarded as "a queer place", which no one could understand until he was a member of it. The incursion of reporters had first violated its sacrosanct quality, but the new invasion was more serious. The Reform Act "suddenly introduced into the hallowed precincts a number of individuals whose education, manners, modes of thought, were different from those of the previous inhabitants", and these individuals were in a majority. To the relief of the great hereditary political families the old material acted as leaven in the new mass; within five years the House had recovered much of its "serene, refined and even classical character". There was no other incursion on a great scale within the period dealt with in the novels. *Endymion* did not cover the Reform Bill of 1867, which Disraeli himself sponsored, and which brought the artisan into active partnership with the aristocracy and the middle class in Parliamentary elections.

Two features of Parliamentary life in Disraeli's period strike the modern reader. Party discipline was evidently less strict, and men changed sides oftener. There was no extreme ideological difference between the two great parties, and the personnel of both belonged to the same world, especially before the Reform Bill. The other notable feature was the importance of what Disraeli called social politics. It was a period when snobbery was rife, and an invitation to a great house was a useful weapon in the political armoury. The receptions and balls given by Lady St. Julians (*Sybil*), and by Zenobia and Berengaria (*Endymion*), were functions of importance in the campaigns of their parties. This continued even after the Reform Bill. In real life Holland House, so well portrayed in Macaulay's letters, was almost a political institution, and Lady Palmerston's famous parties were more than great social occasions. Philip Guedalla, in his charming book *Bonnet and Shawl*, said that for a quarter of a century Lady Palmerston's parties helped to govern England. At Cambridge House members of all political parties met on the staircase, and "an awkward interview with Mr. Cobden could end in a civil murmur that 'Lady Palmerston receives to-morrow evening at ten'". A statesman could thus pay a civility to an opponent or a waverer in his wife's name without committing himself to anything. In *Endymion* Lord Roehampton was unwilling to make any personal advance to Prince Florestan, but decided that there was no objection to the Prince receiving a card from Lady Roehampton.

Apart from the general pattern of social-political life, the novels afford some interesting side-lights on the great actors, such as the Duke of Wellington, Peel and Palmerston.

The splendour of society, the noblemen's town mansions and country seats, received full justice from the ecstatic pen of the young Disraeli. It is sometimes suggested that he exaggerated the luxury and magnificence, but it was a period when "the rich became almost too rich for reason" (Arthur Bryant, in *The Age of Elegance*). Lady John Manners, in *Some Personal Recollections of*

EPILOGUE

the Earl of Beaconsfield, defended him from this charge on the ground that many of those who most appreciated him, and in whose houses he was an honoured guest, lived with "a certain amount of state, and even magnificence". She explained that they "could not forgo these accessories without being faithless to traditions of the past, and without condemning to idleness and penury many of those dependent on them". She then cited various great houses, including Knole, with its antique chambers and eighty staircases, Trentham with its terraced gardens, and Hatfield, where a suite of tapestried rooms was set apart for Lord Beaconsfield's use.

Lady John Manners's account can be confirmed by reading the letters of Thomas Creevey, an inveterate visitor to splendid mansions during the eighteen-twenties and thirties. Creevey bears out the necessity of keeping a host of dependents in his description of the numerous servants at Stoke, who could not be interfered with, much less dismissed, because they were "all bred upon the spot and all related to each other". Disraeli's "palladian palaces", set in magnificent parks, have actual counterparts in Creevey's pages. At Stoke the dining-room was sixty feet long, with a wainscot carved by Grinling Gibbons, and it was well lighted every night by innumerable wax candles. When Lord Derby read prayers at Knowsley the guests gathered in the library and beyond the open door the hall was filled with servants kneeling round the billiard table, and behind them a few late comers listened through the drawing-room door. Creevey describes the galleries of pictures by such masters as Vandyke, Reynolds and Romney at all these great houses. Food was supplied on a lavish scale. At breakfast at Croxteth, the seat of the Earl of Sefton, there were four silver covers containing hot dishes—"kidneys at the top, mashed potatoes at the bottom, three partridges at one side, with bread sauce, crumbs, etc., Pattys at the other". The next morning there were mutton cutlets, an "omlet" and a pheasant.

Some of Creevey's sketches are good companion-pictures to characters in Disraeli's novels. Lady Foley, for instance, was a very fitting hostess for old Lady Cork, whom Disraeli drew as Lady Bellair (*Henrietta Temple*), and who was a fellow-guest with Creevey at Witley Court, Worcestershire, where Lord Foley kept the best house and planted more oaks than any man in England—"without a halfp'orth of income". Lady Foley never degraded herself by putting on either a pair of gloves or a ribbon a second time, and always had four ponies ready saddled and bridled for any excursion that might take her fancy. When she chose to come into her drawing-room a groom of the chamber prepared her great chair, draping it with a shawl and a large white satin cloak. A table covered with red velvet with a deep gold fringe was placed beside the chair, and on it her watch, smelling-salts and other "bijouterie". In the evening the same table was used for her game of hazard, and a gold tray was brought containing piles of gold and silver money, every piece of which had been carefully washed and cleaned by the butler.

Such true pictures are certainly in the same *genre* as the imaginary ones in Disraeli's novels, of which many samples have been given, and they prove that the splendours he delighted to describe are not greatly overdrawn. The contrast between them and the lives of the second nation (the Poor)—to which Disraeli did equal justice, in *Sybil*—is deeply shocking. The rotten foundation of a gorgeous society, to use Greville's phrase again, forced itself upon the attention of governments in time; both Dickens and Disraeli helped to expose it, and during their lifetime conditions improved steadily. Child-labour, dark, damp hovels with no drainage, the tommy-shop, and such firms as Shuffle & Screw, became at last "old, unhappy, far-off things". It was then the turn of the gorgeous society to fall into decay. The process was slow and Disraeli, perhaps, scarcely realised it; Hainault House in his last novel is as splendid as Château Désir in his first. His pictures of great houses are, however, something more than merely gorgeous; they preserve for us the elegant and the exquisite, as exemplified in the perfection of their equipment and services. In many cases pictures, porcelain and gold and silver plate which used to grace daily life have now passed from homes into museums, and only on public or state occasions is a banquet served with the old magnificence. The noiseless perfection of the waiting at Sidonia's table is rare in an age in which "self-service" is the common rule.

In *Endymion* we are told that every dinner at Hainault House was a banquet. At first it seems shocking that jaded palates should have been titillated by a chef of European fame, but as we read of the recherché dinners given by Sidonia, Mr. Neuchatel, and even by Mr. Bertie Tremaine, it is hard to repress a regret that today we cannot hope to learn from an artist like Leander that "there is a difference between eating and dining". In fact the democratic bosom is not always proof against the seductive culinary dreams called up by such passages as this invocation to the ortolan in *The Young Duke*:

"Oh! Doff, then, thy waistcoat of vine-leaves, pretty rover! And show me that bosom more delicious even than a woman's. What gushes of rapture! What a flavour! How peculiar! Even how sacred! Heaven at once sends both manna and quails. Another little wanderer! Pray follow my example! Allow me. All Paradise opens! Let me die eating ortolans to soft music."

"*Pray follow my example! Allow me*"; almost the swooning imagination accepts the invitation. But the ortolan is not for us. How many people to-day have even tasted a quail? How many know what an ortolan is? We recall ourselves sternly to a higher and saner ideal—fair shares for all. But they will not be shares of quails and ortolans.

No one can regret the passing of the surfeit of luxury which Disraeli represented by young Alfred Mountchesney throwing away his almost untasted peach in an agony of boredom, and wanting to drink bad wine to relieve the monotony of good wine. Yet it is evident that individual wealth did command great and genuine artistry, in which the artist was gloriously untrammelled by considerations of cost. Disraeli's novels have embalmed the fine finish which art gave to luxury in living pictures which no array of museum pieces or suites of disused "state apartments" can call up for us.

Disraeli was not blind to the vices of his high society, as we have seen in his gambling scene at Brighton. It was a society in which patronage was an accepted institution, and which inevitably bred the toady and the snob, of whom there are numerous examples in the novels. Disraeli even introduces snobbery amongst the Gods in his lively satire *Ixion in Heaven*. Mercury, who is bearing Ixion to Heaven, points out a star in their course and

Ixion asks who lives there. Mercury replies contemptuously: "The Fates know, not I. Some low people who are trying to shine into notice. 'Tis a parvenu planet, and only sprung into space within this century. We do not visit them."

The great houses Disraeli drew—Château Désir, Beaumanoir, Coningsby Castle, Brentham, Muriel Towers, Hainault House—are almost personalities in the novels. Their fate illustrates the sweeping change which has been wrought in English society since Disraeli's day. Only a few are still the family seats of noblemen; some serve useful purposes as schools, institutions, headquarters of National Boards or centres for conferences; the parks and gardens of others are public pleasure-grounds. Brentham, the great ducal mansion of *Lothair*, stood for Trentham, the Staffordshire seat of the Dukes of Sutherland. Most of the house has been pulled down and the grounds are now an entertainment park for the Potteries. In what remains of the mansion there is an Amusement Hall, full of slot machines with cryptic captions such as "Oh, Mother, look!" and "Answerite". The lady visitor can take advantage of an ingenious method of photography in which she puts her head through a frame and is shortly presented with a finished photograph showing her with the appropriate dress and background of a bathing belle, or some other glamorous figure of her choice. A loud-speaker splays popular music over the lawns, a miniature railway carries parties to the lake and swimming-pool. Disraeli used to stay at Trentham. We can imagine his ghost on the terrace, perhaps impaling a bit of orange peel or a toffee paper on his elegant stick and murmuring, "We must educate our masters." Yet he had discarded the feudal ideals of Young England long before he took his "leap in the dark" by enfranchising the town labourer. He believed in the fundamental soundness of the English people.

Alton Towers, the Muriel Towers of *Lothair*, and its ornate gardens (" 'Perhaps too many temples,' murmured Lothair") also became a resort for pleasure-parties from the Potteries, with canteens and bars in some of its empty rooms. During the last war it was used as an officers' training school.

The world which Disraeli passed in review in the period covered by the novels (1826–80) has certainly changed even more than

EPILOGUE

his prescient imagination could have conceived; but he, too, changed with the times during his life. His early manhood is fitly symbolised by the peacock, of oriental origin and brilliant plumage. It had been domesticated in a land which was not its natural *habitat*; Disraeli, too, even in his old age, gave the impression of being still a foreigner. Maurois illustrates this in one of his brilliant flashes of description, in which he compares him to other exotic birds: even when he gave up his dandyism in favour of sober black, the cast of his face alone made him noticeable amongst his colleagues, as if an ibis or a flamingo had strayed into an English poultry-yard. When the sun fell on the Tory benches all the other faces looked pale, but his grew darker.

Disraeli admitted that he had a fondness for peacocks. When he bought Hughenden Manor the long sunny terrace seemed to call out for them, and he said to a visitor: "My dear lady, you cannot have terraces without peacocks." Almost all the country houses in the novels were provided with them. The year before his death he wrote to Lady Bradford that he was watching half a dozen peacocks basking on the lawn, but he now sometimes found it trying when they strutted about, making love or war, and screamed.

Disraeli never quite outgrew the peacock in his nature. After making his last speech in the House of Commons, when he was about to enter the House of Lords, he left the scene of a long and colourful career leaning on the arm of Montagu Corry and wearing a long white overcoat and lavender kid gloves. Henry Baerlein records (in *Squire of Piccadilly*) how William Stone, passing from Hughenden Manor to the church in Disraeli's funeral cortège, noticed that the peacocks on the lawn were screeching, and felt that a peacock's feather would be a more suitable emblem to wear in his button-hole than a primrose. It was, however, the primrose which was to be permanently associated with Disraeli. Two references to primroses in the novels have often been quoted. The first is from *Coningsby*, when the hero was served with "hissing bacon and eggs that looked like clusters of primroses". The other occurs in *Lothair*: " 'They say primroses make a capital salad,' said Lord St. Jerome." There is, however, a third reference, which seems to have been overlooked. In the opening of the second chapter of *Venetia* there is a passage which happily combines peacock and primrose:

"The dewy vistas of Cherbury sparkled in the sun, the cooing of the pigeons sounded around, the peacocks strutted about the terrace and spread their tails with infinite enjoyment and conscious pride. . . . The air was scented with the violet, tufts of daffodils were scattered all about, and though the snowdrop had vanished, and the primroses were fast disappearing, their wild and shaggy leaves still looked picturesque and glad."

This is more than a casual allusion, the wild and shaggy leaves which looked glad is an original touch of observation such as one finds in Dorothy Wordsworth's Journal.

The Queen used to send primroses to her dear Lord Beaconsfield every spring; once he acknowledged them as "an offering from the Fauns and Dryads of the woods of Osborne". He found other graceful phrases with which to thank the Queen for successive gifts; he could do no less when "the Faery" (his private name for her) honoured him with the bounty of her own beloved woods. Yet there is no reason to doubt that he was sincere when he told visitors to Hughenden that the great bowls of primroses on his dinner-table came from the Queen—"As she knows it is my favourite flower." He was always particular that the primroses in his own woodlands should be fostered.

When Disraeli died in the month of April the Queen sent a wreath of primroses, bearing the inscription: "His favourite flowers." To many people this seemed an incongruity; they would have expected him to prefer a more gaudy flower. A suggestion was even made that the Queen's inscription referred to the primrose being the Prince Consort's favourite flower, but there seems to be no foundation for this. Lady John Manners tells us that Disraeli delighted in flowers. In particular he loved the signs of spring and wrote that he could not live without cuckoos, nightingales and pink may: the passage quoted from *Venetia* is followed by Lady Annabel exclaiming: "This is spring, my child, beautiful spring!"

On the first anniversary of Lord Beaconsfield's death London florists were surprised by the number of customers who came in to ask for buttonholes of primroses, afterwards known as Beacons-

EPILOGUE

field buttonholes. These were spontaneous gestures on the part of individuals who wanted to commemorate the day. "Dizzy" had taken a firm hold on the national imagination. In 1883, when the Beaconsfield statue in Parliament Square was unveiled, primroses were in evidence everywhere. This suggested the observance of Primrose Day on April 19th, and from that arose the Primrose League, founded to keep alive the principles of Conservative democracy which were Disraeli's legacy to the party which he had revivified.

Primroses are still placed at the foot of Lord Beaconsfield's statue on April 19th; he is accepted as a great Englishman for whom this most English of flowers is no unfitting emblem. As Walter Sichel expressed it: "He understood England, but it took a long time for his countrymen to understand him." Bismarck, who heard him speak for his country with no uncertain voice at the Congress of Berlin, went so far as to say: "Disraeli *is* England." Yet peacock and primrose still symbolise a dual nature, which only the genius of imagination—so well exemplified in the novels—fused into the statesman who created that peculiarly English compromise, a great political party which was at once progressive and conservative.

* * *

At Hughenden Manor (now the property of the National Trust) we can still recapture something of the grace of living that Disraeli loved.

In the library the richly mellow colours of the carpet and curtains which he and his wife chose are an admirable contrast to the sober and solid leather bindings of the books which line the walls. There is the great desk which he used, a chair covered with Mary Anne's embroidery, a model of her foot in white marble. Over the fine Adam fireplace Sir Francis Grant's portrait of the young Disraeli looks down upon the gracious and dignified setting of his later years; the poetic expression and the arrangement of the dark curls may be a little studied, but there is genuine charm and intellectual promise in the face.

The library and drawing-room were transposed by the Coningsby Disraelis, who succeeded Lord Beaconsfield, but each has its distinctive atmosphere still. The drawing-room has attractive period features, in the arches which divide it, the mouldings and rounded doors, and the thick flock wallpaper of deep Wedgwood blue. The settees, embroidered chairs and footstools are such as were to be found in every Victorian country-house. An idealised portrait of Mary Anne Disraeli has the place of honour here. From the windows we look out on to the terrace, which seems to mourn its vanished peacocks, and over a vista of lawn and groups of fine trees to the distant tower of a church.

Upstairs is the small study where Disraeli wrote in seclusion and which he called his workshop, preserved very much as it was at the time of his death. Here Queen Victoria shut herself up for two hours when she made her pilgrimage to Hughenden a few days after the funeral, retracing in her carriage the exact route, even including a detour from the direct road to pay a call, which Disraeli took when he returned there after his last visit to Osborne. It is to be hoped that during her vigil she did not open the volume of *Leaves from the Journal of Our Life in the Highlands* which she inscribed and presented to her fellow author ("We authors, Ma'am," he had said to her), and find that the pages were uncut! But perhaps he had another copy.

In the chief bedroom there still stands the great four-poster bed with its patchwork quilt in gay diamonds of silk made by Mary Anne's loving hands—some modern vandal has cut out a diamond—with the wardrobe painted white and gold, and a surprising basin and ewer, the handle a naked nymph, presented by Queen Victoria.

All over the house the portraits on the walls recall Disraeli's world. The handsome, mocking face of George Smythe gives life to the hall. D'Orsay's fine presence brings to mind again Disraeli's description of him as "the inimitable D'Orsay, the most accomplished and the most engaging character that has figured in this century, who, with the form and universal genius of an Alcibiades, combined a brilliant wit and a heart of quick affection". Lady Blessington, at the zenith of her soft and shining beauty, is represented twice, once beside her rival hostess, that great collector of the Rank and the Literature, Miss Monckton, afterwards Lady Cork, Disraeli's Lady Bellair. Lady Jersey, his

EPILOGUE

Lady St. Julians and Zenobia, is in the same room, and also Lady Chesterfield and Lady Bradford. Byron, of course, has his place, and even Tita his corner—he was painted for Isaac D'Israeli by Maclise—and if his moustachios do not quite "touch the earth", his beard is a noble embellishment.

There are statesmen and men of affairs: the handsome Palmerston, the Duke of Wellington, Lord George Bentinck, the second Lord Lonsdale, whom Disraeli drew so inimitably as Lord Eskdale. Lord John Manners gives an impression of serious grace, Edward Bulwer Lytton of somewhat sentimental romanticism. Amongst the many family portraits is a fascinating one of Isaac D'Israeli at the age of eleven, in which the large lustrous eyes are enchanting. Other portraits of him are alert and benign, rather than picturesque; there is none of him in old age, with the long white hair and black velvet cap his son described.

These are but a few of the great range of portraits which brings together so many personalities of the nineteenth century. They are, however, enough to show that here at Hughenden we can find the perfect illustrations for the novels in the perfect setting.